# Faith Cure

# Faith Cure

## Divine Healing in the Holiness and Pentecostal Movements

NANCY A. HARDESTY

HENDRICKSON
PUBLISHERS

Hendrickson Publishers, Inc.
P. O. Box 3473
Peabody, Massachusetts 01961-3473

ISBN 1-56563-714-3

All Scripture quotations, unless otherwise indicated, are taken from the King James Version of the Bible.

Printed in the United States of America

*First Printing — October 2003*


**Library of Congress Cataloging-in-Publication Data**


Hardesty, Nancy A.
    Faith cure : divine healing in the holiness and Pentecostal movements / Nancy A. Hardesty.
        p. cm.
    Includes bibliographical references and index.
    ISBN 1-56563-714-3 (pbk. : alk. paper)
    1. Spiritual healing. 2. Holiness churches—United States—History—19th century. 3. Pentecostalism—History. I. Title.
    BT732.5.H358 2003
    234'.131'08828994—dc22
                                        2003015558

# Contents

# Acknowledgments

I would like to acknowledge a number of people who have helped me along the way. Donald W. Dayton introduced me to this subject and passed on a lot of original books he found. Martin E. Marty supervised my dissertation and continued to encourage me by asking, "When are you going to write another book?" Charles Lippy opened the door at Clemson University and gave me a place to share my passions with students. He has mentored me and become a most trusted confidant and friend. Stanley Ingersol, archivist of the Church of the Nazarene and authority on Mary Lee Cagle, shared resources and encouragement with me.

A small grant from the Philosophy and Religion Department at Clemson University enabled me to visit the hometowns of Ethan Otis Allen and Sarah Freeman Mix in search of clues to their lives. Thanks to Gail Kruppa of the Torrington Historical Society for her assistance. The university also granted me a sabbatical in the fall of 2000, during which I was able to immerse myself in research. The interlibrary loan office at Clemson's Cooper Library became my lifeline to the rest of the world. Conversations with Rosemary Gooden about her introduction to the reprint edition of *Faith Cures, and Answers to Prayer*, by Mrs. Edward Mix,[1] kept me motivated to finish my work. My friend Vicki Byers keeps me on track with her listening ear and sage advice. To all of these friends and many unnamed, I give thanks.

My partner, Linda K. Davis, has supported me with steadfast love, abundant encouragement, and fervent prayer, for which I am most grateful.

Nancy A. Hardesty

## Note

1. Mrs. Edward Mix, *Faith Cures, and Answers to Prayer* (Springfield, Mass.: Press of Springfield Printing Co., 1882; repr., with critical introduction by Rosemary D. Gooden; Syracuse, N.Y.: Syracuse University Press, 2002).

Is any sick among you?
let him call for the elders of the church;
and let them pray over him,
anointing him with oil in the name of the Lord:
And the prayer of faith shall save the sick,
and the Lord shall raise him up;
and if he have committed sins, they shall be forgiven him.

James 5:14–15

# Introduction

This is a book about faith heal*ing*—not about faith heal*ers*.

As the Holiness movements developed in the second half of the nineteenth century and the Pentecostal movement branched off in the early twentieth century, divine healing based on the model in James 5:14–15 was a central belief and practice. The growth of these movements, their leaders, and their practice of healing will be outlined in chapters 2, 3, 4, 8, and 9.

## Distinctions

When I write of "Holiness movements" I mean Wesleyan Holiness as it was developed in Methodist circles by Phoebe Palmer, Oberlin perfectionism as it was developed at Oberlin College by President Asa Mahan and theology professor Charles G. Finney, and Keswick or Reformed Holiness as it was formulated in England by Americans William Boardman and Mary Boardman and Hannah Whitall Smith and Robert Pearsall Smith. All stressed some form of sanctification, or the development of a holy life subsequent to salvation. The preaching of Holiness resulted in the formation of such denominations as the Free Methodist Church, the Wesleyan Church (Wesleyan Methodist and the Pilgrim Holiness churches), the Church of God (Anderson, Indiana), the Christian and Missionary Alliance (C&MA), the Church of God (Holiness), the Church of the Nazarene, and the Salvation Army.

Pentecostalism blossomed in 1906 through the ministry of African-American Holiness preacher William Seymour in Los Angeles, often referred to as the Azusa Street revival. It was based on Charles Parham's assertion in 1900 that speaking in tongues is definitive evidence that one has been baptized by the Holy Spirit. Some Holiness groups accepted this notion and became Pentecostal: the Pentecostal Holiness Church, Church of God in Christ, Fire-Baptized Holiness Church of God, and Church of God (Cleveland, Tennessee). New denominations also emerged: the Assemblies of God, Church of God Prophecy, Pentecostal

Assemblies of the World, and United Pentecostal Assemblies. Charismatics, who also practice divine healing, emerged in the 1960s among members of older denominations, including Episcopalians, Roman Catholics, Lutherans, Methodists, Baptists, and Presbyterians. Today many charismatics and Pentecostals worship in huge independent congregations..

Because the mass media seldom have time for fine theological distinctions, Holiness and Pentecostal churches are often lumped together in the public mind with fundamentalists or evangelicals (see ch. 10). And sometimes these groups wish to be so grouped. But fundamentalism is a distinct theological movement that developed in the 1910s and 1920s, defending the authority of the Bible and the supernatural elements of the New Testament: the virgin birth of Jesus, his miracles, and his bodily resurrection. It was adamant, however, about rejecting modern miracles, especially divine healing and speaking in tongues. Fundamentalists argued that miracles were confined to biblical times and served only to authenticate God's prophets, Jesus Christ, and the apostles. The Southern Baptist Convention has officially adopted a more fundamentalist theology in recent decades. Evangelicalism is a less separatist and more socially aware version of fundamentalism associated with evangelist Billy Graham and *Christianity Today*. When *Time* proclaimed 1980 the "Year of the Evangelical," the term became fashionable and more socially acceptable, so many Holiness and Pentecostal people who have often been stigmatized as rural and working class were eager to be included.

# Medicine

People in the nineteenth and early twentieth centuries were no less concerned about their health than are people in our day. And they had reason to be concerned. Of the 3.7 million young men called up by the draft in World War I, more than half a million were rejected as unfit, and nearly half of those accepted were diagnosed as having some physical problem. A study of ten thousand workers of the period found *not one* in perfect health. Half of them had major health problems.[1]

But a favorite diagnosis of the period was neurasthenia, a term popularized by physician George M. Beard. An 1869 article in the *Boston Medical and Surgical Journal* on "Neurasthenia, or Nervous Exhaustion" led to an 1880 book titled *A Practical Treatise on Nervous Exhaustion* and then in 1881, *American Nervousness: Its Causes and Consequences*. "Brain-workers" were particularly prone to this malady. In businessmen it was brought on by overwork, but laborers seemed to develop it from an excess of alcohol, tobacco, or sex. For women, the etiology was biological—having a womb made women weaker and more prone to emotional upset. Preferred treatment was the rest cure. Ocean voyages and European trips seemed to work best. Holiness people went to camp meetings. This epidemic seemed to peak around 1900.[2]

Throughout the nineteenth century alternative treatments abounded inside and outside the medical community. Various medical ideologies had their devotees. In addition to the physicians known as regulars, there were the homeopaths, the eclectics, the botanics, and eventually osteopaths and chiropractors. There were no standards for medical education; many of the schools were proprietary. Joseph Lister (1827–1912) was trying to convince people that antiseptic practices in sickrooms and operating theaters would save lives. Crawford Long (1815–1878) was still experimenting with ether for anesthesia. At the turn of the twentieth century William and Charles Mayo began to operate regularly on patients suffering from appendicitis, gall bladder attacks, and ulcers. When William Mayo submitted an article about 105 gall bladder operations he had done, the medical journal rejected it because the editors were sure nobody had ever performed that many surgeries. In 1904 they finally printed his article. By then he had done one thousand surgeries.[3]

The smallpox vaccination was highly controversial. All childhood and adult diseases ran their course. Tuberculosis was epidemic, and physicians were only beginning to get a clue about how it developed, how it spread, and how it might be successfully treated. Influenza epidemics swept the nation and the world periodically. Quinine was the wonder drug of the day; digitalis was experimental. The regulars' favorite medicines were calomel (a mercury compound) and morphine. The benefits of aspirin were just being discovered. The alternative was patent medicines, which consisted of few, if any, active ingredients drowned in alcohol. Even many doctors agreed with Holiness and Pentecostal people when they dispensed with all medicines (see ch. 6).

Many Christian revivalists and reformers in the early part of the century adopted the Graham diet, developed by Sylvester Graham (1794–1851), son and grandson of preachers and trained as a minister. He promoted fresh air, frequent bathing, sensible dress, sexual restraint, plenty of water, vegetables, and whole grains—best embodied in the Graham cracker. Graham believed that the alimentary canal is the key to good health. His ideas influenced the work of Seventh-day Adventist physician John Harvey Kellogg (1852–1943). After graduating from the University of Michigan and Bellevue Hospital Medical College (M.D., 1875), Kellogg became superintendent of the Battle Creek (Michigan) Sanitarium. An advocate of a vegetarian diet, he invented corn flakes. (Graham's and Kellogg's influence is less clear on another Seventh-day Adventist enterprise, Little Debbie Snack Cakes.) Other cures were quite popular: water cure, rest cure, mesmerism, magnetism.

In addition to programs for nutrition and a healthy lifestyle, there were alternative theological programs. The most widespread was and is Mary Baker Eddy's

Christian Science. The people I am writing about vehemently opposed Christian Science on theological grounds and sought to distinguish themselves from it at every turn. However, both groups saw themselves as based in the Bible, following the practice of Jesus, and accomplishing the miraculous. Both saw themselves as exercising faith. The main point of difference is that Christian Science sees disease as rooted in incorrect thinking while Holiness people tend to see it as a physically real affliction, most often caused by sin or Satan. A variety of other groups shared Christian Science's viewpoint with regard to healing: Unity School of Christianity, Religious Science, and New Thought. They are sometimes collectively referred to as Mind Cure (in distinction to Faith Cure).

Liturgical groups such as Roman Catholic, Lutheran, and Episcopal churches sometimes practiced the laying on of hands and/or anointing for healing within ritual contexts. As will be seen, a number of Episcopalians played decisive roles in the Holiness divine healing movement. Other Episcopalians were experimenting with combining the ancient liturgical practices with conventional medicine and the newly emerging discipline of psychology. Most notable were Elwood Worcester, Samuel McComb, and Isador H. Coriat, who founded the Emmanuel Movement.[4]

## History

This is a work of history. As I explore the practices and beliefs of those in the early Holiness and Pentecostal movements, I have tried to convey their experience faithfully and accurately. I have no medical expertise, so I simply report what my sources said about their medical difficulties and about their healings. Some reported that they were instantaneously and completely healed. Others claimed healing at a given point and then said they gradually regained health and strength. Some relapsed and again prayed successfully for healing. Those who did not receive healing did not publish testimonies. "Healing" usually refers to the alleviation of specific symptoms; it does not convey immortality. All of these people eventually died, but they were grateful for the respite from pain and suffering that their healing gave them.

My interest in the topic of divine healing has been long-term. As a child I attended, was baptized in, and joined a country Methodist church in northwestern Ohio. At age ten I moved with my family to Lima, Ohio, where we affiliated with a Christian and Missionary Alliance congregation. Both of my parents' families had been members of a certain Methodist church before they were born (both parents were younger children in large families). But in the 1910s, a group of people withdrew from that Methodist church and formed a C&MA tabernacle, located, by the time I arrived, a block and a half away. My maternal grandmother, who had joined the breakaway group early on, lived half a block from the church. My grandmother, my mother, and my aunts always said, "Miss Marvin was our first pastor"—Isabel Marvin. By the time I was "converted," rebaptized by immersion, and joined the C&MA in the 1950s it was fairly well enmeshed in fundamentalism and male domination, but it had not abandoned the practice of having the elders lay hands on the sick and pray for healing. When I became an Episcopalian while a student at Wheaton College in Wheaton, Illinois, I appreciated the fact that many Episcopal churches did the same.

During my graduate work at the University of Chicago Divinity School, my mentor and dear friend was Donald W. Dayton. As I researched the women of Oberlin and the first woman's rights movement, I discovered Phoebe Palmer, and Holiness,[5] and divine healing. But I assumed that Don would cover all that needed to be said about the topic in his dissertation, which came to be titled *The Theological Roots of Pentecostalism*.[6] Still, with Don's generous help, I collected books on the subject anyway. Occasionally I would give papers at scholarly conferences on aspects of the topic.[7]

Along the way, I also discovered Paul G. Chappell's 1983 dissertation at Drew University titled "The Divine Healing Movement in America." Even though Chappell summarized the work in the *Dictionary of Pentecostal and Charismatic Movements*,[8] I assumed that he, too, would publish a book on the subject, but one has not appeared. Thus I have now undertaken to write my own. Several other scholars are now also exploring aspects of divine healing within the Christian tradition, so perhaps this important topic will at last receive some of the public attention it merits.

For many years I labored under the misperception (at least I now think it is) that there was a defining moment when the Holiness emphasis on encouraging the sick person to pray the prayer of faith shifted and tilted toward what I thought was the Pentecostal notion that healing is a divine gift given only to certain people, "healers," and is thence dispensed through the laying on of hands. What I finally understood is that Pentecostals and charismatics by and large still practice divine healing within local congregations and prayer meetings much the same way Holiness people did and do. But media attention has been focused primarily on those individuals who make their living as healing evangelists. Their emergence is a late development and a risky one (see ch. 9), partially chronicled by David Edwin Harrell Jr., in *All Things Are Possible*.[9]

In the twentieth century, as the modern medical establishment became more organized and discovered effective drugs, therapies, and technologies, many of these religious groups became far more cautious in their proclamation of divine healing. For other theological reasons, many drifted toward fundamentalism, which preferred to relegate healing miracles to the first century.

However, as I began to be aware of the growing interest in alternative medicine and the mind-body connection researched by such leaders as Herbert Benson at Harvard Medical School, Harold G. Koenig at Duke Medical School, the late David Larson at the National Institutes of Health, and Larry Dossey, former chief of staff at Humana Medical City in Dallas, I think that Holiness and Pentecostal people have a tradition that needs to be brought to the table (see ch. 11).

# Notes

1. Paul Starr, *The Social Transformation of American Medicine* (New York: Basic Books, 1982), 193.

2. F. G. Gosling, *Before Freud: Neurasthenia and the American Medical Community 1870–1910* (Urbana: University of Illinois Press, 1988), 26, 11, x–xi, 38, 12.

3. Starr, *The Social Transformation of American Medicine,* 157.

4. Elwood Worcester, Samuel McComb, and Isador H. Coriat, *Religion and Medicine: The Moral Control of Nervous Disorders* (New York: Moffat, Yard & Co., 1908); Elwood Worcester and Samuel McComb, *The Christian Religion as a Healing Power: A Defense and Exposition of the Emmanuel Movement* (New York: Moffat, Yard & Co., 1909); Elwood Worcester, *Life's Adventure: The Story of a Varied Career* (New York: Charles Scribner's Sons, 1932). Worcester was a graduate of Columbia University and General Seminary in New York. He received his Ph.D. from the University of Leipzig, where he studied with Gustav Theodor Flechner, who was influential in the thought of William James as well. Ordained an Episcopal priest, Worcester served churches in Philadelphia and the Emmanuel Church in Boston. McComb had master's and doctor of divinity degrees. He was Worcester's assistant at Emmanuel for ten years. Coriat was a physician. See also Raymond J. Cunningham, "The Emmanuel Movement: A Variety of American Religious Experience," *American Quarterly* 14 (Spring 1962): 48–63.

5. Nancy A. Hardesty, *Women Called to Witness: Evangelical Feminism in the Nineteenth Century* (Nashville: Abingdon, 1984; 2d ed., Knoxville: University of Tennessee Press, 1999). The dissertation was printed as *"Your Daughters Shall Prophesy": Revivalism and Feminism in the Age of Finney* (New York: Carlson, 1991).

6. Donald W. Dayton, *The Theological Roots of Pentecostalism* (Grand Rapids, Mich.: Francis Asbury Press, Zondervan, 1987).

7. "Faith Healing in the Holiness/Pentecostal Movement," American Academy of Religion, Southeast regional meetings, Atlanta, Georgia, March 18–20, 1994; "Holiness and the Rhetoric of Healing: Two Case Studies," Berkshire Conference on the History of Women, University of North Carolina, Chapel Hill, North Carolina, June 7–9, 1996; "Transatlantic Roots of the Holiness-Pentecostal Healing Movement," American Society of Church History, Seattle, Washington, January 9–11, 1998; "Faith and Healing," Perspectives '98 Lecture Series, University of Tennessee at Chattanooga, January 21, 1998.

8. Paul G. Chappell, "The Divine Healing Movement in America" (Ph.D. diss., Drew University, 1983); "Healing Movements," in *Dictionary of Pentecostal and Charismatic Movements* (ed. Stanley M. Burgess and Gary B. McGee; Grand Rapids, Mich.: Regency Reference Library, Zondervan, 1988), 353–74. Hereafter this volume will be referred to as *Dictionary*. Some years ago I read Chappell's dissertation and the summary in the *Dictionary*. However, in writing this work I have rarely referred to Chappell's work. Rather, I have attempted to draw my own narrative and conclusions from the original sources.

9. David Edwin Harrell Jr., *All Things Are Possible: The Healing and Charismatic Revivals in Modern America* (Bloomington: Indiana University Press, 1975).

# 1

# Beginnings

One icy, wintry day in late 1876 in Buffalo, New York, teenager Carrie Judd was on her way to normal school, her arms loaded with heavy books. Her foot slipped, her spine twisted, and she fell on the snow-covered stone sidewalk. She managed to struggle to her feet, gather her books, and enter the school, but classmates said she looked extremely pale all day. Several weeks later one of her closest school friends came down with typhoid fever and then died. Carrie's grief was overwhelming.

On January 6, 1877, Carrie contracted spinal fever. The fever was frighteningly high; her head was bursting with pain that no treatment could alleviate. The pain finally subsided, but the illness lasted weeks into months. The diagnosis was hyperaesthesia. Physicians offered little relief and no hope. She was forced to abandon her education and her hopes for a career as a school teacher. She became a complete invalid, unable to turn over in her bed without assistance, thrown into painful spasms by the slightest light or noise. She required constant care but could not tolerate even the shortest visit from friends or family members. Months turned into years. She grew weaker and could not eat solid food. In January 1879 her beloved grandmother, who also lived in the household, passed away. The family's resources—emotional, physical, and financial—were taxed to the limit.[1] Carrie wrote poems, and the family published her *Lilies from the Vale of Thought* to raise money.

One day her father, Orvan, was reading the newspaper and noticed a brief story about Mrs. Edward Mix, an African-American woman living in Wolcottville, Connecticut, now Torrington. Two years previously, in 1877, Mrs. Mix had been healed of tuberculosis in answer to the prayers of Ethan Otis Allen of Springfield, Massachusetts. Carrie's father shared the story with Carrie and her mother, Emily. Mrs. Judd wanted to send a letter immediately to Mrs. Mix, but Carrie was cautious. Finally she asked one of her sisters to write.[2]

On Tuesday, February 25, 1879, the answer came, written the day before:

Miss Carrie Judd:

I received a line from your sister Eva stating your case, your disease and your faith. I can encourage you, by the Word of God, that "according to your faith" so be it unto you; and besides you have the promise, "The prayer of faith shall save the sick, and the Lord shall raise him up." Whether the person is present or absent, if it is a "prayer of faith" it is all the same, and God has promised to raise up the sick ones, and if they have committed sins to forgive them. Now this promise is to you, as if you were the only person living. Now if you can claim that promise, I have not the least doubt but what you will be healed. You will first have to lay aside all medicine of every description. Use no remedies of any kind for anything. Lay aside trusting in the "arm of flesh," and lean wholly upon God and His promises. When you receive this letter I want you to begin to pray for faith, and Wednesday afternoon the female prayer-meeting is at our house. We will make you a subject of prayer, between the hours of three and four. I want you to pray for yourself, and pray believing and then *act faith*. It makes no difference how you feel, but get right out of bed and begin to walk by faith. Strength will come, disease will depart and you will be made whole. We read in the Gospel, "Thy faith hath made thee whole." Write soon.

Yours in faith,
Mrs. Edward Mix[3]

With understandable trepidation, Carrie discontinued all medication. She prayed for an increase of faith. When the appointed time came, members of her family prayed in another room. Carrie was alone with her nurse. At first she felt totally weak and overcome with doubt, but then she was filled with peace and childlike faith. For the first time in two years, she turned over in the bed, raised herself to a sitting position, and said, "Clara, I will get up now."[4] Supported by her nurse, she stood up and walked eight feet to a chair. Her pulse, color, and circulation began to improve immediately. Her appetite returned; her muscles strengthened. Within a month she walked downstairs. By April she could go outside and visit neighbors.[5]

Mrs. Mix, in her writings, notes that the weather was bad that particular Wednesday. No one came for the prayer meeting.[6] But she and her husband prayed for Carrie, and it was enough.

## Ethan Otis Allen

This account is central to the divine healing movement of the late nineteenth century. Carrie Judd (later Montgomery, 1858–1946) would play pivotal roles in many developments until her death. Mrs. Mix's ministry, begun only slightly more than a year earlier with her own healing, would end prematurely. Ethan Otis Allen (1813–1902) stands in the shadows.

A grandson of the famed Revolutionary War hero, Ethan Otis Allen was a native of Springfield, Massachusetts. Born August 25, 1813, in Belchertown, Massachusetts, he was apparently one of six children of Joel and Lydia Allen.[7] On March 22, 1837, in Springfield he married Kezia Davis, daughter of Joel and Kezia Phelps

Davis. She, too, had been born in Springfield, on April 7, 1813. The family's home place seems to have been a farm on South Wilbraham Road, on the eastern edge of present-day Springfield. An 1864–1865 *Springfield City Directory* lists brothers Henry and Joel as well as nephew Joel A. as living there. A Loren G. in the household may have been Ethan and Kezia's son Loring Davis, born January 6, 1838. The *Springfield City Directory* for 1896 says that Ethan "removed to California." Why a man of eighty-three would leave the city of his birth and his home of a lifetime to travel across the continent is intriguing, though it may have been an extension of his ministry. He died in California in 1902.

According to Allen's book *Faith Healing*,[8] he began proclaiming the notion of faith healing in 1846 after he was prayed for by his Methodist class leader and healed of consumption. For the next fifty years he proclaimed the notion all around New England and prayed for the healing of others with favorable results. Allen published *Faith Healing: or, What I Have Witnessed of the Fulfillment of James V: 14, 15, 16* in Philadelphia in 1881. He was also the subject of an undated biography by William T. MacArthur titled *Ethan O. Allen,* also published in Philadelphia. As the movement developed, Allen labored humbly in the camp meetings, conventions, and faith homes led by others.

## Mrs. Edward Mix

In Holiness periodicals there is scant mention of Ethan Allen but more references to Mrs. Edward Mix (1832–1884). She has been referred to by some secondary authors as Elizabeth Mix, but her real name was Sarah Anne Freeman Mix. She was the daughter of Diadatris (she called him Datus[9]) and Lois Freeman. Though she was healed of consumption through the prayers of Ethan Otis Allen in December 1877, she succumbed to the same disease on April 14, 1884, at age fifty-one.[10]

Sarah Freeman was born May 5, 1832, in Torrington, Litchfield County, Connecticut. Her mother was a Baptist from Newfield, Connecticut. After her father's death from consumption, the family moved to New Haven. Sarah found salvation during a February revival at the Bethel African Methodist Episcopal Church. For a short time after her mother's death, also of consumption, she returned to Wolcottville, then a predominately African-American village adjacent to Torrington. She later moved back to New Haven and finally to New York City in search of work as a domestic.[11] There she had her first bout with consumption. A physician told her she had less than two weeks to live and advised her to leave the city, so she returned to her sister Whitney's home in Goshen, Connecticut.

"The Spring following I was married," she wrote. The date was March 9, 1856, according to Rosemary Gooden.[12] She married Edward Mix (1834–after 1901) one of three Mix brothers—Chauncey, Edward, and Willard—described as

"all bright, well educated men." Although Torrington historian Charles H. Johnson says that Edward "was quite an exhorter in the Seventh Day Advent meetings
that were held on Sunday nights in the old town hall,"[13] the Mixes were more
likely members of the Advent Christian Church. The Mixes lived at 8 Pearl Street,
the same street on which two Advent Christian parsonages were located. The Advent Christians met in the old town hall, which was formerly a Methodist church,
before building their own church. The current Advent Christian Church in Torrington traces its ancestry only to an organizational meeting on April 26, 1886,
that included seven white individuals, one a prominent physician. But their history admits that the group was meeting earlier in the town hall.[14]

    "We had little ones," who "sickened and died," Sarah said tersely.[15] She and
Edward gave birth to seven children in rapid succession between October 1856
and January 1870. By August 1873 all were dead; none lived to become teen-
agers.[16] Cause of death was listed as consumption for three of them, and congestion of lungs for two more. Obviously consumption, or tuberculosis, and other
pulmonary problems were rampant in the Mix family, as well as in the rest of the
African-American community in Wolcottville. Courthouse records show that
numerous other relatives perished from the same maladies. As Mrs. Mix said, "I
was born of a consumptive family."[17] Concerning her children, she noted that "all
died with lung disease." Poignantly, she commented, "so we laid them away one
by one, those we loved in other years, till alone and brokenhearted we have nothing left but tears."[18]

    Weakened no doubt by this series of pregnancies and subsequent grief over
the deaths of all her children, Sarah Freeman Mix in 1877 began exhibiting again
the symptoms of consumption.[19] In her autobiography she said that "on the 19th
December, 1877, I was healed by faith and prayer and the laying on of hands by
Bro. Ethan O. Allen, of Springfield, Mass., one who has the gift of healing."[20] She
did not indicate how she learned of Allen's work, but she did say that Allen came
to Wolcottville because she urged a "brother Whitney" to call him to pray for his
wife, who was very sick. On December 19, 1877, Allen came, accompanied by a
"brother and sister Loomis," and prayed for Mrs. Whitney. As Mrs. Mix joined in
the prayer for Mrs. Whitney, Allen heard something that caused him to turn his
attention to Mrs. Mix. He asked if she enjoyed good health. She answered no, and
he prayed for her healing. As she described it,

> at that moment I believed I was healed, the room was filled with the glory of God, so
> much so that sister Loomis fell to the floor as one dead, and I was so overwhelmed with
> the power of God, I felt that everything like disease was removed; I felt light as a feather.
> . . . I leaped for joy into the other room, shouting victory in the name of Jesus.[21]

    While Allen, the Mixes, and Montgomery all emphasized the importance of
helping the sick person pray the prayer of faith, Mix did speak of Allen as having

the gift of healing. She said that on the occasion of her healing, he told her that he was "impressed" that she had the "gift of healing" as well.[22] She noted that "God in His goodness and mercy has blessed me [and] others, with this blessed boon, the gift of faith, and the healing by the laying on of hands and the prayer of faith."[23] She began by healing herself of several ailments, once laying her hands on her throat when she had diphtheria, and then started praying with her neighbors as they asked for her help. As people were cured, her fame spread.

Apparently prior to her healing Mix had already heard God's call to some form of service. At the time she was working as a dressmaker. One morning she said she heard the voice of God saying, "Go, work today in my vineyard." She wrote, "I began to plead with the Lord that I was unworthy; that I was illiterate; that I had no talent; but the same words followed me. I told Him my health was poor and memory very short, that I was insufficient in every way. Still the same persistent, urgent call."[24] For three years after her healing she enjoyed excellent health and was very active in a healing ministry to others.

Then, according to her obituary in *Victory Through Faith*, a paper she and her husband published, she "caught a severe cold, and symptoms of consumption appeared once more, and after being afflicted four years, she fell a victim to that dread disease." She died on Monday, April 14, 1884.[25] According to her obituary, written by Frank Burbank, who probably was her pastor,

> At her home, in the social meeting, in the homes of others, and in the pulpit, she exhibited those traits which are the adornments of the followers of Christ. During the last four years, notwithstanding her bodily affliction, she traveled thousands of miles, visited hundreds of homes, prayed with a multitude of sick folks, and saw many restored to health, preached in various pulpits, conducted praying and inquiry meetings.[26]

While Mr. and Mrs. Mix are often mentioned together and seem to have worked as a team, other references indicate that Mrs. Mix was the primary force in their ministry. The *Winsted and Torrington Directory* for 1883–1884 lists Edward Mix as a farmer but Mrs. Sarah A. Mix as a "faithcure physician." Even a powerful critic of faith healing, Methodist minister and editor of the *Christian Advocate*, J. M. Buckley, conceded that Mrs. Mix achieved "great fame" and respectability. Even physicians sent patients to her for prayer.[27]

## Carrie Judd

After her healing, Judd soon became part of the emerging divine healing movement. She gave her first testimony to healing at a Holiness meeting at a nearby Methodist church. She started her own Thursday evening faith meeting in her family's home. The story of her healing appeared in the local press, and the story was reprinted in many places, including *The Christian Herald* in England. Mr. and Mrs. Mix came to visit, and the two women went together to the homes of a number of people who were ill in Buffalo, praying for their recovery.[28] In 1880 she published *The Prayer of Faith,* containing her testimony, a letter of corroboration from her pastor, "rector of St. Mary's Church-on-the-Hill (Episcopal)," and eleven chapters outlining a biblical and theological understanding of healing. Her father had been Presbyterian, but her mother was Episcopalian. Carrie would keep the small book—possibly the first treatise on the subject published in the United States[29]—in print throughout her long lifetime. She would have a significant effect not only on the divine healing movement but also on Holiness and early Pentecostalism.

## Charles Cullis

At the end of her testimony, Judd also said, "I wish to add that Dr. Charles Cullis, of Boston, Mass., whose faith-works and faith-cures are so widely known, kindly added his prayers for my complete recovery."[30] Judd does not explain how she became acquainted with the work of fellow Episcopalian and physician Charles Cullis (1833–1892), although apparently her family received several religious periodicals. After her healing, Judd corresponded with Cullis and visited his work in Boston. For a while she entertained the idea of joining his staff.[31] Cullis was a devout and conscientious doctor, troubled by the fact that he had no effective treatment for many of his patients.

Born in Boston, on March 7, 1833, Cullis was a frail child. Baptized and reared as an Episcopalian, he quit Sunday school as soon as he was old enough. He was not strong enough to attend school, and an attempt to work in the mercantile world as a teenager proved too much for his health. But during a period of enforced rest, he read medicine and was able to graduate from the University of Vermont at age twenty-four. He initially entered practice with his brother-in-law, but after the sudden death of his wife, he vowed to devote all his income beyond basic expenses to charity and religion.[32] He may have been sanctified in 1862 after a visit to Phoebe Palmer's Tuesday Meeting for the Promotion of Holiness in New York City.[33]

Frustrated by the tuberculosis pandemic for which he had no effective treatment, Cullis dedicated a home for Indigent and Incurable Consumptives on Beacon Hill on September 27, 1864. In 1865, 1867, and 1869 he built three more homes. In April 1869 he dedicated a house for their caregivers, whom he referred to as deaconesses after the German model at Kaiserswerth. Children's homes provided care for children whose mothers were being treated and for orphans. In 1876 he opened a "spinal home" because one of his patients, Miss Josephine

Basford, who had been cared for at home for sixteen years by her sister, had nowhere to go when the sister died. In 1878 he completed a home for cancer patients.[34]

Initially all Cullis could offer, especially to those with consumption, was palliative care. His homes were essentially hospices. But as a committed Christian who had experienced entire sanctification, he became increasingly convinced of the truth and efficacy of James 5:14–15: "Is any sick among you? Let him call for the elders of the church; and let them pray over him, anointing him with oil in the name of the Lord: And the prayer of faith shall save the sick, and the Lord shall raise him up."

He wanted to do more for his patients. He writes in *Faith Cures:*

> For several years my mind had been exercised before God as to whether it was not his will that the work of faith in which he had placed me, should extend to the cure of disease, as well as the alleviation of the miseries of the afflicted. I often read the instructions and promise contained in the fourteenth and fifteenth verses of the fifth chapter of the epistle of James.

> They seemed so very plain, that I often asked of my own heart, why, if I can rely on God's word, "whatsoever ye shall ask in my name, that will I do," and every day verify its truth in the supply of the daily needs of the various work committed to my care,—why can not I also trust him to fulfil his promises as to the healing of the body: *"The prayer of faith shall save the sick, and the Lord shall raise him up"?* I could not see why with such explicit and unmistakable promises, I should limit the present exercise of God's power. I began to inquire of earnest Christians whether they knew of any instances of answer to prayer for the healing of the body. Soon afterwards the "Life of Dorothea Trudel" fell into my hands, which strengthened my convictions, and the inquiry arose, "if God can perform such wonders in Mannedorf, why not in Boston?"

> At this time I had under my professional care a Christian lady, with a tumor which confined her almost continuously to her bed in severe suffering. All remedies were unavailing, and the only human hope was the knife: but feeling in my heart the power of the promise, I one morning sat down by her bedside, and taking up the Bible, I read aloud God's promise to his believing children; *"and the prayer of faith shall save the sick, and the Lord shall raise him up; and if he have committed sins, they shall be forgiven him."*

> I then asked her if she would trust the Lord to remove this tumor and restore her to health, and to her missionary work. She replied, "I have no particular faith about it, but am willing to trust the Lord for it."

> I then knelt and anointed her with oil in the name of the Lord, asking him to fulfil his own word. Soon after I left, she got up and walked three miles. From that time the tumor rapidly lessened, until all trace of it at length disappeared.[35]

This breakthrough with Lucy Drake came in January 1870. Cullis announced his new practice to his constituency in his annual report issued September 30, 1873.[36]

Lucy Drake (1844–?) continued in good health and became part of Cullis's missionary outreach as well as the healing ministry. She gave her testimony at conventions held by William E. Boardman, and she opened her own faith home in Brooklyn. She later married a Mr. Osborne.

News of Cullis's work spread in a variety of ways. He began publishing a paper called *Times of Refreshing* on April 24, 1869. Initially it talked about salvation, sanctification, and mission work. The same year Cullis established the Willard Street Tract Repository (eventually shortened to the Willard Tract Repository) to publish tracts, pamphlets, and books. One of the books he reprinted was William E. Boardman's *The Higher Christian Life,* first published in 1858. Cullis and Boardman became friends, and Boardman wrote *Faith Work under Dr. Cullis* in 1874, and later *The Great Physician* (1881; U.K. title, *The Lord That Healeth Thee*).

Charles and his second wife, Lucretia Bramhall Reed Cullis, and William and Mary Boardman became friends. On May 20, 1873, they sailed for Europe together to visit some of the people and institutions that were also engaging in divine healing.

## Notes

1. Carrie Judd Montgomery, *"Under His Wings": The Story of My Life* (Oakland, Calif.: Office of Triumphs of Faith, 1936), 48–53; Carrie Judd, *The Prayer of Faith* (Buffalo, N.Y.: H. H. Otis, 1880, 1882), 9–11.
2. Montgomery, *"Under His Wings,"* 54–55.
3. Judd, *The Prayer of Faith,* 14–15.
4. Montgomery, *"Under His Wings,"* 56.
5. Judd, *The Prayer of Faith,* 15–18.
6. Mrs. Edward Mix, *Faith Cures and Answers to Prayer* (Springfield, Mass.: Press of Springfield Printing Co., 1882), 39; repr. with critical introduction by Rosemary D. Gooden (Syracuse, N.Y.: Syracuse University Press, 2002), 39 (hereafter Gooden).
7. Other children include Mary (b. March 25, 1807, in East Windsor), Betsey (b., n.d., in Springfield), Joel (b. December 11, 1810, in Springfield), Henry (b. February 9, 1816, in Springfield), and Horace Norman (b. December 9, 1818).
8. Paul G. Chappell, "The Divine Healing Movement in America" (Ph.D. diss., Drew University, 1983), citing Ethan Otis Allen, *Faith Healing: or, What I Have Witnessed of the Fulfillment of James V:14, 15, 16* (Philadelphia: n.p., 1881).
9. Mrs. Edward Mix, *The Life of Mrs. Edward Mix, Written by Herself in 1880* (Torrington, Conn.: Press of Register Printing Co., 1884), 5; Gooden, 201.
10. Vital statistics, vol. 3, p. 528, Torrington, Connecticut, courthouse. See also her obituary in the *Torrington Register,* April 19, 1884.
11. Mix, *The Life of Mrs. Edward Mix,* 5, 7, 9, 12; See Gooden, 201–7.
12. Mix, *Faith Cures,* 9; Gooden, critical introduction to *Faith Cures,* xlviii.
13. Charles H. Johnson, *Memories of Wolcottville* (Torrington, Conn.: Torrington Historical Society, 1947), 49, 50.
14. *Seventy-fifth Anniversary, 1886–1961, Advent Christian Church, Torrington,* unpaginated program.
15. Mix, *The Life of Mrs. Edward Mix,* 13; Gooden, 207.

16. Information found in the vital records of the Torrington City Hall. Helen J. was born October 1, 1856 (v. 2, p. 31b). She lived to age six, dying of consumption on December 9, 1862 (2:49b). Gaylord D. C. was born August 30, 1858 (2:38b). He lived only two years before succumbing to consumption on September 25, 1860 (2:42b). Theresa D. was born October 8, 1861 (2:48b). She lived the longest, dying of consumption at age twelve on August 16, 1873 (3:482). Helena Esther lived only eighteen months, from February 29, 1864 (2:55b) to August 21, 1866 (3:458). Elijah, born August 4, 1866 (3:2), also died on August 21, 1866, having lived less than a month (3:458). Emma was born September 1, 1868 (3:12); she died May 5, 1870 (3:468). Her younger brother Edward had already died January 20, 1870 (3:468); he was an infant whose birth had not yet been recorded. Cause of death for Emma and Edward is listed as "congestion of lungs."

17. Mix, *Faith Cures,* 8; Gooden, 8. This book was originally published in Springfield, Allen's hometown, rather than in Torrington, Connecticut, the Mixes' home.

18. Ibid., 9.

19. Ibid.

20. Mix, *The Life of Mrs. Edward Mix,* 17; Gooden, 210.

21. Mix, *Faith Cures,* 11; Gooden, 11.

22. Ibid., 10, 11; Gooden, 10, 11.

23. Mix, *The Life of Mrs. Edward Mix,* 17; Gooden, 210.

24. Ibid., 14; Gooden, 208.

25. "She Is Not Dead, But Asleep," *Victory Through Faith* 2 (May 1884): 38. Her funeral was held at the town hall, the sermon preached by the Reverend Frank H. Burbank, who also wrote the obituary. The city directory for that year lists Burbank as a resident but does not list a pastor for the Advent Christian Church; however, I assume that he was their supply pastor that year. Although city cemetery records do not indicate a marked grave for Sarah Mix, the obituary indicates that the funeral procession walked "to the cemetery nearby." A major cemetery lies behind the Torrington Historical Society and the current Torrington City Hall, built on the site of the old town hall. My intuition says that she is buried there.

26. Ibid., 38.

27. J. M. Buckley, "Faith Healing and Kindred Phenomena," *The Century* 32 (June 1886), 222. The article and a subsequent one are generally very critical of the entire faith healing movement.

28. Montgomery, *"Under His Wings,"* 60.

29. Ibid., 65.

30. Judd, *The Prayer of Faith* (1917 edition), 20.

31. Montgomery, *"Under His Wings,"* 64.

32. W. H. Daniels, ed., *"Have Faith in God": Dr. Cullis and His Work: Twenty Years of Blessing in Answer to Prayer* (Boston: Willard Tract Repository, 1885), 3–5.

33. Harold E. Raser, *Phoebe Palmer: Her Life and Thought,* Studies in Women and Religion 22 (Lewiston, N.Y.: Edwin Mellen, 1987), 87, 90, quoting from Cullis's testimony in George Hughes, *The Beloved Physician, Dr. Walter C. Palmer, M.D., and His Sun-Lit Journey to the Cellestial City* (New York: Palmer and Hughes, 1884), 132. Hughes also wrote *Fragrant Memories of the Tuesday Meeting and Guide to Holiness* (New York: Palmer and Hughes, 1886). But see S. Olin Garrison, *Forty Witnesses* (1888; repr., Freeport, Pa.: Fountain Press, 1955), 174–75. Cullis himself does not mention Palmer.

34. Daniels, *"Have Faith in God,"* on consumptives, 13, 21, 55, 57, 72; on children's, 55, 201; spinal home, 204–6; cancer, 141.

35. A. J. Gordon, *The Ministry of Healing, or Miracles of Cure in All Ages* (Boston: Willard Tract Repository, 1882; repr., Harrisburg, Pa.: Christian Publications, n.d.), 171–72. Quoted from Charles Cullis, *Faith Cures* (Boston: Willard Tract Repository, 1879).

36. Daniels, *"Have Faith In God,"* 339.

# 2

## Transatlantic Roots

In 1864 Boston physician Charles Cullis had opened a home for Indigent and Incurable Consumptives. Over the next few years he established a variety of charitable institutions. Inspired by the example of George Müller and his orphanage in Bristol, England, Cullis operated all his enterprises on the faith principle, the belief that God would supply, through prayer, all the work's financial needs.

Although Cullis's faith was often tested, it worked—perhaps aided by good publicity. His biographer W. H. Daniels noted that in the fourth year Cullis received, among other gifts, $25 from Paris, $150 from Berlin, and $500 from a woman in Argentina who had seen a story about the work in a Boston newspaper.[1] An 1878 report mentions contributions from Australia, New Zealand, and South Africa.[2]

### The Boardmans

Cullis also found good friends in Presbyterian pastor William Boardman (1810–1886) and his wife, Mary Morse Adams Boardman (1818–1904). William was a graduate of Lane Seminary in Cincinnati. A regular at Phoebe Palmer's Tuesday meeting, William Boardman outlined his more Reformed view of holiness in *The Higher Christian Life* (1858), published on both sides of the Atlantic.[3] The Boardmans had become Holiness evangelists in the United States and England. Once converted to the notion of faith healing, the Boardmans became its staunch advocates and publicists.

In 1873 the Boardmans visited Cullis's work in Boston on their way back to the Continent. When they set sail for London on May 20, 1873, Lucretia Cullis saw to it that she and her husband were on board for some much-needed relaxation. But the trip turned out to be a busman's holiday. Before their September 16 return, the Cullises managed to visit Müller's orphanage in Bristol; the Kaiserswerth, Germany, deaconess training institute; and Dorothea Trudel's faith-cure homes at Mannedorf, Switzerland.[4] In 1872 Cullis's Willard Tract Repository had published the first American edition of Trudel's *Prayer of Faith*.[5]

In 1874 and 1875 William and Mary Boardman, along with Robert Pearsall Smith (1827–1899) and Hannah Whitall Smith (1832–1911), were instrumental in creating Keswick Holiness. By the end of 1875 the Boardmans had permanently relocated to Great Britain. The Smiths relocated there in 1888. Thus the transatlantic connections were established.

In 1874 Boardman began to publicize Cullis's work in *Faith Work under Dr. Cullis*. In his influential 1881 book, published as *The Lord That Healeth Thee* in England and as *The Great Physician* in the United States (published by the Willard Tract Repository), Boardman said he became convinced of the possibility of faith healing early in life but then forgot about it. About 1850 he was reminded again when "Father Aikin of Platteville, Wisconsin," near the Boardmans' Potosi parish, was told by doctors that he had incurable "ossification of the arteries." He asked Boardman to hold a meeting and preach Holiness. Two weeks later Boardman returned to find Aikin sawing wood. When asked about his amazing recovery, he told Boardman: "I thought when I believed for my soul, I might believe also for the body."[6] Boardman said he was also convinced by the "simply stated" stories of Trudel and Johann Christoph Blumhardt.[7]

## Müller's Faith Work

George Müller (1805–1898) was the inspiration for many in the Holiness and Pentecostal movements. In 1835 he opened his orphanage in Bristol, England. Born in Prussia, Müller studied at Pietist schools in Halle. He was impressed there by the orphanage work of Hermann Francke (1663–1727). He was also impressed in Bristol by the premillennial dispensationalism taught by Irish cleric John Nelson Darby (1800–1882) and became an early member of Darby's Plymouth Brethren.

Müller's notions about living by faith came from Johannes Evangelista Gossner (1773–1858). Müller believed the biblical promise that "God shall supply all your need" (Philippians 4:19), and so he prayed for God to supply the financial and material needs of his orphanage. And his prayers were answered—sometimes at the last minute, but all the children's needs were met. He testified to God's provision in *A Narrative of Some of the Lord's Dealings with George Müller, Written by Himself*, first published in 1837. It was later expanded into the *Autobiography of George Müller*, available on both sides of the Atlantic.[8] His work became the paradigm for many Holiness and Pentecostal good works.

## Dorothea Trudel

Swiss practitioner of healing, Dorothea Trudel (1813–1862) first came to wider attention through a small tract titled *Eine Mutter*, initially published

anonymously. Written in German, it was translated into English and widely circulated. Dorothea told the story of her mother's faith. Married to a cruel and
profligate husband who even sold the cow on whose milk and cheese the family
had depended during his frequent absences, her mother never complained. She
trusted Jesus to supply her family's material needs. And since they could not af-
ford a doctor, she was forced to depend on Christ as her physician as well. Although a plague killed many of their neighbors, she and her children were spared.
When four-year-old Dorothea contracted smallpox and went blind, her mother
prayed, and the child was made well.

Converted in 1835 at age twenty-two, Dorothea learned to make artificial
flowers in one of her nephew's businesses. Several of the other workers took sick,
went to doctors, and received treatment but continued to decline. Dorothea, re-
membering her mother's practice, went to God in prayer:

> I told him how willingly I would send for an elder, as is commanded in James V., but,
> as there was not one, I must go to my sick ones in the faith of the Canaanitish
> woman, and without trusting in any virtue in my hand, I would lay it upon them. I
> did so, and, by the Lord's blessing, all four recovered.[9]

The powerful result convinced her that she should follow God's leading in the
matter. Soon people flocked to her home for instruction, the laying on of hands,
and anointing with oil. Eventually she opened two homes in Mannedorf, Switzerland, to care for the sick and to teach and practice the laying on of hands.

Local authorities charged Trudel with practicing medicine without a license
in 1856 and again in 1861. She testified that she was not administering any drugs,
and people who came to her were also free to engage any physician of their
choice. Still she was fined 150 francs and told to dismiss everyone from her pre-
mises even though documented cures were presented, including cancers and fevers, epilepsy and mental illness. She appealed to canton authorities in Zurich,
and in November 1861 she was acquitted of all charges.

Another accusation made against Trudel was that she used mesmerism to effect cures. She wondered about this, so she tried an experiment. She asked God
*not* to heal a certain person through her efforts if mesmerism were involved and
to heal the person rapidly if it was by divine grace. She also had no contact with
the woman to touch her, anoint her, or even pray aloud with her. Instead she did
nothing but pray privately for the woman's healing. And the woman recovered in
a very short time.[10]

Trudel was not without pain. As a young adult she suffered an injury to her
spine. She says that she "became a crooked, dwarfed, withered being," even unrec-
ognizable to casual acquaintances who had not seen her for a year or so. Though
she was unable to stoop over, she could and did carry on her work.[11] But eventually, aware that she was dying, in 1862 she committed her work to the care of a

colleague, Samuel Zeller, the son of the founder of a well-known boys' home at Beuggen, near Basel. Zeller had initially come to Mannedorf seeking healing for his body. His sister also worked with him, managing what had become ten homes by 1882.

Trudel wrote of her work in a book with the English title *Prayer of Faith*. It was apparently first published in England. Cullis discovered it, found it compelling, and published it in 1872.[12] A. J. Gordon in *The Ministry of Healing* cited *Dorothea Trudel, or the Life of Faith* (London: Morgan & Scott, n.d.). It is not clear whether this is the same book or a later biography.

Trudel taught that

> there is a close connection between the spiritual condition of the patient and the cure. In a case of cancer of the lip, the cure was contemporary with the sufferer's conviction of sin; and one singular example was narrated, where the progress of the cure seemed to keep pace with the spiritual history, when it seemed retarded by want of frank repentance. There is a receptivity on the part of the patient, as well as boldness of faith on the part of the suppliant.[13]

She was clear that "nothing is done by us: all these marvels in bodies and souls are wrought by the strength of Christ's blood."[14] She also had a very tender ministry with those who were mentally ill and eventually set aside one house for them.

## Johann Christoph Blumhardt

Johann Christoph Blumhardt (1805–1880) was born into a devout family in Stuttgart, Germany. By twelve he had read the Bible through twice. After study in Tübingen, he became vicar at the Lutheran church in Duerrmenz. In 1830 he became a teacher of Hebrew at the Basel Missionhaus. He returned in 1837 to Wurtemberg to pastor a very divided congregation. After bringing a measure of peace there, he was sent on July 31, 1838, to became pastor in the small village of Mottlingen, near Wurtemberg, in the heart of the Black Forest. There he met and married Johanna Dorothea Kollner.

Known for his strong faith and consecration, his ministry of healing was thrust upon him, according to Gordon.[15] Once Blumhardt suffered an anxiety attack. He prayed, and the anxiety ceased. Another time he felt a strong urge to pray for his brother, a missionary to India. Later he learned that the brother had been in mortal danger at sea.

Blumhardt's first case was a young woman parishioner in Mottlingen, Katarina Dittus. She saw eerie things in her new house; neighbors heard strange noises. When she went to say grace at the table, she fell into unconsciousness. When Pastor Blumhardt would visit her, she would lapse into unconsciousness. At first he thought she was stubborn and spiritually unrepentant, but when a dead widow began appearing to her, he began to suspect black magic or demon possession. He urged her to pray, "Lord Jesus, help me," and for a time she was freed of her symptoms. But then the battle began. Scripture suggested fasting might help, so he did. He asked her to come to the church for prayer rather than going to her home. The symptoms spread to other members of her family. The spiritual battle lasted two years. Eventually the evil spirit departed, declaring "Jesus is the Victor!" Katarina was delivered, as were other members of the family.[16] The phrase became Blumhardt's motto.

Blumhardt was requested to make a full report of the matters to his ecclesiastical superiors, and the report was published. Others started to seek him out for spiritual counsel and healing. One man came, confessed all his sins, and asked Blumhardt for a formal absolution. Since Martin Luther had wanted to retain the sacrament of penance, Blumhardt offered absolution and prayed for the man, laying hands on his head. The man was radiantly transformed. Others came seeking absolution, received it, and found healing at the same time.[17] When he and his superiors began to hear reports that people understood the laying on of hands to be magical or to transmit some kind of power, he discontinued the act and told people to partake of Holy Communion. Some critics said this was a misuse of the sacrament, and church authorities tried to limit his work to his own parishioners, but people flocked to the church until it overflowed.

So in 1852 Blumhardt, his family, and the Dittus family moved to Bad Boll, near Goppingen, where he ministered until his death of pneumonia in 1880. The house could accommodate a hundred guests; the ballroom was converted to a chapel, and it became his parish. His motto continued to be *Jesus ist Sieger,* "Jesus is Victor." After his death, his sons Christoph and Gustav, also ordained Lutheran ministers, carried on the ministry.

Because of ecclesiastical pressures and his humility, Blumhardt never publicized any testimonies of those cured. Nor did he ever publicly lay hands on people. At Bad Boll he preached at regular services at 10 A.M. on Thursdays and Sundays and sometimes gave a Bible reading at the Sunday evening service. Those who visited could request a private conference with him. His friend Pastor Marcus Spittler told his story in *Pastor Blumhardt and His Work,* published in London by Morgan and Scott. Charles Cullis publicized his work by publishing R. Kelso Carter's biography, *Pastor Blumhardt: A Record of the Wonderful Spiritual and Physical Manifestations of God's Power in Healing Souls and Bodies.*[18]

Another Lutheran, Pastor Rein, was also known for his healing ministry. He began as what Gordon called a "formalist," reading prayers at the bedside of sick parishioners. Eventually he began to lay hands on people and then to anoint with oil. His work became familiar to Americans when a sketch of his life appeared in 1878 in *Israel's Watchman.*[19]

# Elizabeth Baxter

Another leading participant in the divine healing movement on the other side of the pond was a woman usually designated as Mrs. Michael Baxter because her husband was a well-known minister and editor of the influential *Christian Herald* magazine. One writer called him "one of the eminent expounders of prophesy in his day" and her "if not the chief creator of the paper, its ablest writer."[20] Her given name was Elizabeth, nee Foster (1837–1926). Though her father was a birthright Quaker, she was reared in the Church of England. Finding personal salvation in 1858, she began to minister to women in the workhouse and to hold cottage prayer meetings. The workhouse matron asked her to meet with a woman suffering from epilepsy. After Elizabeth presented the gospel, the woman was saved. As Elizabeth pondered her case, she thought, if Jesus can save, can he not heal? So the next week she prayed for the woman's healing, and the woman never had another seizure.[21]

Elizabeth became involved with Mildmay's Association of Women Workers, heading a deaconess house and designing their bonnet. Elizabeth met Michael Paget Baxter (d. 1910) at a Mildmay conference, the British equivalent of D. L. Moody's Northfield conferences. They married in August 1868. On their honeymoon, they preached at street meetings. For the next fourteen years, they blended their ministries, traveling and preaching throughout the British Isles, the Continent, and India. One year they lived in Glasgow to help with the Moody-Sankey meetings. For some time Michael had been publishing a monthly, *Signs of Our Times.* They made it a weekly, and Elizabeth kept the books and did proofreading. She later undertook her own preaching tours on the Continent. She was asked to conduct the women's meetings at the first Keswick conference, but she was in Switzerland. She did give Bible readings for women at subsequent Keswick meetings. Bible readings were what a woman was allowed to do—reading a passage verse by verse, giving comments as she went.

Elizabeth also preached in Germany, learning the language as she went. German Christians were not used to a woman's speaking in public. As she noted,

> that a woman should presume to teach, and especially to teach religion, was an unheard-of enormity. Woman's rights, as the phrase is ordinarily understood, have never appealed to me; but to limit the Holy One of Israel was, it seemed to me, grieving the Holy Ghost, while my call to be a soul-winner, as well as my call to Germany, had come so directly from the Lord, that it would have been disloyal to Him to go back upon it and hold my peace for fear of offending public opinion.[22]

Elizabeth Baxter credited William Boardman with bringing the teaching of faith healing to London when he and his wife, Mary, settled there and began holding meetings in their home in Green Lanes, North London. Sick people began to seek them out. She cited Boardman's book *The Lord That Healeth Thee* and his summary of Cullis's views in *Faith Work under Dr. Cullis*. Elizabeth eventually became familiar with Carrie Judd's *Prayer of Faith* as well and oversaw its publication in German and French through a Swiss publisher. The book was also published in Swedish and Dutch.[23] Mrs. Baxter published more than twenty books, many of them Bible studies. She also published nearly twenty "useful tracts," including such titles as "The Lord for the Body," "Does Sickness Sanctify?" "If It Be Thy Will," "God's Purpose in Sickness," and "The Great Physician."[24]

Baxter pointed to her experience on Christmas Day 1877, when God "brought new life into my own body."[25] She had been plagued by spinal pain for two years. A doctor had told her "it was useless for me to continue taking his medicine or coming to him; he could not cure me."[26] A woman friend counseled her to give herself up to Christ. Elizabeth reported, "After I was anointed I did not for some hours feel any different in my health; then I had a sharp pain in my side, as if something broke. Since then the pain has been much better. . . . I have lost all depression, pain in my head, and my nerves are stronger."[27]

## Otto Stockmayer

In Berne, Switzerland, Elizabeth Baxter met Otto Stockmayer (1838–1917), then pastor of the Free Church at St. Croix in the Jura. Eventually she put her son in school at Hauptweil, Thurgon (his new parish) with the Stockmayers' two sons. A preacher and practitioner of faith healing, Stockmayer published a tract titled *Krankheit und Evangelium: ein Wort un Kinder Gottes,* translated into English as *Sickness and the Gospel.*[28] It was he who convinced Baxter of the validity of faith healing.[29]

Baxter introduced Stockmayer and Boardman during an 1880 Holiness conference in London's West End.[30] The Cullises visited England a second time in the spring of 1881. In May 1882 Mrs. Baxter, along with Charlotte Murray, opened Bethshan, meaning "House of Rest" in Hebrew. The first location proving too small, the faith home moved to 10 Drayton Park, Holloway Road, Highbury, North London.[31] Elizabeth Sisson of New London, Connecticut, who had been a missionary to India for seven years, joined them.[32] Here divine healing was taught and practiced. The Boardmans were also heavily involved at Bethshan, and in American writings it is often referred to as William Boardman's home base. When the Boardmans were present, William Boardman presided at the healing services, and Mary Boardman held inquiry meetings for those seeking sanctification. Elizabeth Baxter also visited friends in the U.S.

The teaching circulated around the world through the publication of various papers. Phoebe Palmer's husband, Walter, and her sister Sarah, who became his second wife after her husband and Phoebe died, were still publishing *The Guide to Holiness,* which included stories about faith healing. Cullis began publishing *Times of Refreshing* in 1869. In 1881 Carrie Judd began *Triumphs of Faith.* In 1883 Edward and Sarah Mix published *Victory Through Faith.* In the early days of Bethshan, Mrs. Baxter published a monthly magazine called *Thy Healer.*[33]

## Conference on Divine Healing and True Holiness

The whole transatlantic movement gained status and cohesion with the International Conference on Divine Healing and True Holiness, held in the Agricultural Hall, London, from Monday, June 1, through Friday, June 5, 1885.[34] In his call for the meeting, William Boardman noted that "about half a century ago, the Lord began to revive the truth of His direct HEALING of the body through Faith. This was in Germany, principally through the revered Pastors Blumhardt and Rein, and in Switzerland, thought the no less revered Dorothea Trudel."[35] Trudel and Blumhardt were already dead; one American writer on the subject, Robert L. Stanton, died aboard ship.[36] Neither Zeller, Stockmayer, Cullis, nor Judd could attend. Boardman chaired most of the sessions.

The other major American leader present was the Reverend A. B. Simpson (1843–1919), a Canadian-American Presbyterian, who was in the process of creating the Christian and Missionary Alliance. A strong advocate of Holiness and faith healing, he spoke several times. Taking his text from John 3, Simpson spoke of regeneration as "the 'motherhood,' . . . of the Holy Ghost, giving us new life as we are born from above." Another sermon, titled "Himself," is still widely reprinted. Elizabeth Baxter printed it immediately in *Thy Healer,* and Simpson published it in his *Word, Work, and World* as well. In another speech he noted that "Mrs. Mix has only lately passed away. She was also greatly used of God." He then referred to "a dear old saint, Mr. Allen, who, as a quiet farmer, is doing a great work for God."[37]

From Haupweil came Stockmayer's assistant, Pastor Schrenk, who spoke at length. He had known Trudel. Madame Malherbe from France, an assistant to Pastor Stockmayer, told how she had been instantly healed during a ten-minute visit with him. Mrs. Baxter in her presentation defined entire sanctification as "the soul coming into right relation with God" and divine healing as "the body coming into right relation with God."[38] Participants included men and women from the United States, England, Scotland, Ireland, Germany, Switzerland, Spain, Italy, British Honduras, and Australia. More than six hundred leaders of the movement attended, with seventy coming from outside the British Isles. Some services had as many as two thousand people in the congregation. At the Wednesday afternoon service eight of the leaders, men and women, anointed about 250 people. From London the leaders fanned out to hold subsequent meetings on Holiness and healing in more than a dozen cities, including Liverpool, Manchester, Edinburgh, and Aberdeen. Some, however, did denounce the group as "neophytes" deluded by "irrational" and "unscriptural" doctrines. Headlines referred to them as "A New Cult."[39]

Simpson invited Elizabeth Baxter to visit the United States, which she did at a later point. She preached in Simpson's church in New York, in Mennonite congregations in Pennsylvania, and in Holiness churches in Detroit, Philadelphia, Baltimore, Nashville, Chicago, and Pittsburgh. She visited Cullis's work in Boston, and Mary Mossman in Philadelphia. She even paid a visit to Carrie Judd, by then living with her husband, George Montgomery (1851–1930), in Oakland, California. In 1894 she again visited the United States with Pastor Stockmayer as part of a round-the-world tour.

While American practitioners of faith healing Charles Cullis, Ethan Otis Allen, Sarah Mix, Carrie Judd, A. B. Simpson, and others widely publicized their own work, they were encouraged and challenged by their compatriots across the Atlantic. From Europeans they adopted the notion of faith work, depending on God to meet their material needs. Their faith was encouraged by European examples of divine healing, although their theology was shaped primarily by the American Holiness movement. They adopted and adapted the European model of faith homes where the sick could come for rest, instruction, and prayer. Travelers such as William and Mary Boardman, Charles and Lucretia Cullis, and Elizabeth Baxter tended the transatlantic lines of communication of what became a truly international movement.

# Notes

1. W. H. Daniels, ed., *"Have Faith in God": Dr. Cullis and His Work: Twenty Years of Blessing in Answer to Prayer* (Boston: Willard Tract Repository, 1885), 59.

2. Ibid., 140.

3. See [Mary] Boardman, *Life and Labors of the Rev. W. E. Boardman* (New York: D. Appleton and Company, 1887), 104. The biography's preface was written by the Reverend Mark Guy Pearse of Bristol, England. *The Higher Christian Life* was published in England by Miss Marsh at Nisbet & Co. A cheaper edition was published by Strachan & Co.

4. Ibid., 126.

5. Ibid., 196.

6. William E. Boardman, *The Great Physician (Jehovah Rophi)* (Boston: Willard Tract Repository, 1881), 7. Mrs. Boardman told another version of this story in *Life and Labors*, 61–63.

7. Ibid., 124.

8. Donald W. Dayton, *The Theological Roots of Pentecostalism* (Grand Rapids, Mich.: Francis Asbury Press, Zondervan, 1987), 121.

9. A. J. Gordon, *The Ministry of Healing, or Miracles of Cure in All Ages* (Boston: Willard Tract Repository, 1882; repr. Harrisburg, Pa.: Christian Publications, n.d.), 148.

10. Dorothea Trudel, *The Prayer of Faith,* introduction by Charles Cullis (3d ed.; Boston: Willard Tract Repository, 1872), 87.

11. Dorothea Trudel, *Answers to Prayer; or, Dorothea Trudel* (Boston: Henry Holt, n.d.), 67, 70.

12. Trudel, *The Prayer of Faith.* Charles Cullis is listed as author of the 184-page book, listed as the third edition, revised and enlarged. It is not clear whether this is the third English edition or American edition. To further confuse things, Cullis's biographer W. H. Daniels says that the first American edition of the Trudel book was published in 1874. The Online Computer Library Center (OCLC) also lists *Dorothea Trudel, or, The Prayer of Faith, with Some Particulars of the Remarkable Manner in Which Large Numbers of Sick Persons Were Healed in Answer to Special Prayer* (London: Morgan & Chase) with no publication date. The identification again of Cullis as author suggests that this may be a later reprint, but it contains only 124 pages.

13. Trudel, *Answers to Prayer; or, Dorothea Trudel,* 21.

14. Ibid., 86.

15. Gordon, *The Ministry of Healing,* 159.

16. William G. Bodamer Jr., "The Life and Work of Johann Christoph Blumhardt" (Th.D. diss., Princeton Theological Seminary, 1966), 19–26.

17. Ibid., 28–29.

18. R. Kelso Carter, *Pastor Blumhardt, A Record of the Wonderful Spiritual and Physical Manifestations of God's Power in Healing Souls and Bodies* (Boston: Willard Tract Repository, 1883). Blumhardt was also known through a biography published in German in 1880 by the Reverend Frederick Zundel, a Swiss pastor, and a derivative English *Life of Blumhardt,* by the Reverend W. Guest, published in London. Zundel's work was also available in French and Dutch. Carter consulted the Guest and Zundel books. Carter described services at Bad Boll (54–55), quoting from a report by famed British preacher Henry Drummond.

19. A. J. Gordon, *Ministry of Healing,* 165–66.

20. Nathaniel Wiseman, *Elizabeth Baxter (Wife of Michael Paget Baxter): Saint, Evangelist, Preacher, Teacher, and Expositor* (2d ed.; London: The Christian Herald Co., 1928), 7.

21. Ibid., 35.

22. Ibid., 69.

23. Carrie Judd Montgomery, *"Under His Wings": The Story of My Life* (Oakland, Calif.: Office of Triumphs of Faith, 1936), 67.

24. See the list of her publications in Wiseman, *Elizabeth Baxter, The Story of My Life,* 204.

25. Ibid., 84.

26. Ibid., 88.

27. Ibid., 88.

28. Otto Stockmayer, *Sickness and the Gospel* (London: Partridge & Co., n.d.). American editions were published by George McCalla, Arch Street, Philadelphia, and by Charles Cullis's Willard Tract Repository.

29. Wiseman, *Elizabeth Baxter,* 225. He also was instrumental in convincing Salvation Army leaders Arthur and Kate Booth-Clibborn (La Maréchale) of the truth of faith healing (see 224).

30. Boardman, *Life and Labors,* 224.

31. Wiseman, *Elizabeth Baxter,* 86–87. Mrs. Baxter also told the story of Bethshan's founding in Boardman's *Life and Labors,* 234.

32. Boardman, *Life and Labors,* 235.

33. Wiseman, *Elizabeth Baxter,* 182; as her ministry changed, she refocused the magazine. When she began her mission training school it became *Jungle Need,* and then *The Eleventh Hour,* reflecting her continuation of her husband's emphasis on

dispensational eschatology. It was discontinued in 1910, but she continued to write for the *Christian Herald.*

34. *Record of the International Conference on Divine Healing and True Holiness* (London: J. Snow & Co., 1885). Letters from Asa Mahan and Alexander Dowie are appended.

35. Ibid., iv.

36. See *Record,* v.

37. *Record,* 38, 64.

38. *Record,* 28.

39. Charles W. Nienkirchen, *A. B. Simpson and the Pentecostal Movement: A Study in Continuity, Crisis, and Change* (Peabody, Mass.: Hendrickson, 1992), 17.

# 3

# Holiness Roots

The divine healing movement in the United States is also rooted in the various Holiness movements of the nineteenth century, especially the theology and practice of John Wesley, Church of England minister, founder of Methodism, and father of Wesleyan Holiness.

Wesley (1703–1791) logged thousands of miles on horseback, preaching and establishing Methodist societies. He also did a fair amount of healing. At times he laid hands on the sick and prayed for them with good results. Since he spent much of his life on horseback, traveling from one place to another, he also prayed for his horse. For example, he recorded the following in his journal for March 17, 1746:

> When I left Smeaton my horse was so exceeding lame that I was afraid I must have lain by too. We could not discern what it was that was amiss, and yet he would scarce set his foot to the ground. By riding thus 7 miles I was thoroughly tired, and my head ached. . . . I then thought, Cannot God heal either man or beast, by any means, or without any? Immediately my weariness and headache ceased, and my horse's lameness in the same instant. Nor did he halt any more either that day or the next.[1]

Wesley's interest in health led to the publication of his *Primitive Physik,* a compilation of home remedies for a variety of ills. He was also interested in the possibilities of the use of newly discovered electricity to promote healing.

In the theological realm, Wesley preached not only salvation but also sanctification. He wrote and revised a *Plain Account of Christian Perfection.* The Reformers had stressed salvation, justification by faith. Martin Luther had decreed, however, that even after salvation, human beings were always *simul justus et peccator,* at the same time justified and sinner. Wesley, more widely read in Greek Orthodox Christianity, stressed that after salvation one should strive to be Christlike, to live a sanctified life, a life of practical holiness.

Within Wesley's lifetime there was great discussion of the topic among his ministerial colleagues and followers. Some, like George Whitefield (1714–1770), were more inclined toward Calvinism and less inclined to countenance sanctification.

Wesley tended to view sanctification as a lifelong process. The goal was "perfect love" as outlined in the summary of the Law, "Thou shalt love the Lord thy God with all thy heart, and with all thy soul, and with all thy mind. This is the first and great commandment. And the second is like unto it, Thou shalt love thy neighbor as thyself" (Matthew 22:37–39; see Deuteronomy 6:5; Mark 9:29–31; Luke 10:27). Wesley noted that this was not sinless perfection in the sense that one could still make errors in judgment due to lack of information, discernment, or wisdom. But one could increasingly focus one's spirit on love for God, and one could guide one's actions by love for self and neighbor. Wesley felt that one might achieve this perfect love but only in later life, near to death. Wesley never claimed to have achieved it.

Others, however, were not so reticent. Some in the circle around Wesley's designated successor John Fletcher (1729–1785) and his wife, Mary Bosanquet Fletcher (1739–1815), began to claim they had achieved perfect love or to impute it to others. Wesley took a wait-and-see attitude, but eventually he conceded that the attitude and actions of certain individuals did give evidence that they may have attained entire sanctification in the midst of life. Either way, sanctification was a process, something to be striven for. Many American Holiness people read not only John's theological works but also *The Life of Mary Bosanquet Fletcher*.

As Methodists in colonial America began to plant churches and build a denomination over vast areas, sanctification became a secondary issue. The *Plain Account* was printed in the United States and required reading for aspiring Methodist circuit riders, but holiness was not stressed[2] until the mid-nineteenth century. In the 1840s two sisters experienced sanctification and began a movement. On May 21, 1835, at 2:30 P.M., Sarah Worrall Lankford (1806–1896) experienced the assurance of entire sanctification. Her sister, Phoebe Worrall Palmer (1807–1874), attained the same on "the evening of July 26th, 1837, between the hours of eight and nine o'clock" when "the Lord gave me such a view of my utter pollution and helplessness, apart from the cleansing, energizing influences of the purifying blood of Jesus, and the quickening aids of the Holy Spirit, that I have ever since retained a vivid realization of the fact."[3]

The sisters and their husbands shared a New York townhouse. Sarah was married to architect Thomas A. Lankford. Phoebe was married to Walter C. Palmer (1804–1883), who was trained at the Rutgers Medical College of Physicians and Surgeons in New York City and practiced homeopathic medicine. (Another Worrall sister, Hannah, married Walter Palmer's brother, Miles, also a physician.) In August 1835, Sarah consolidated two prayer meetings she regularly attended at Allen Street and Mulberry Street Methodist churches by inviting them to meet at her home. The group came to be known as the Tuesday Meeting for the Promotion of Holiness and endured for more than sixty years.

Initially it was for women only. However, in December 1839 Phoebe L. Upham visited and asked to bring along her husband, Congregational theologian Thomas Upham (1799–1872), professor at Bowdoin College in Maine. For Thomas Upham, the experience was life-changing. He laid aside his writing projects in philosophy and began to research and write about Holiness. The result was *Principles of the Interior or Hidden Life* (1843), *The Life of Faith* (1845), and *A Treatise on Divine Union* (1852). He also introduced American readers to the lives of French Quietist mystics Madame Guyon (1648–1717) through *Life and Religious Opinions and Experience of Madame de La Mothe Guyon* (1847) and her confidant, priest François Fénelon (1651–1715).[4] Guyon's writings are still reprinted and widely read by American evangelicals.

Thereafter the Tuesday meeting drew participants from around the country and around the world. And many of them went home and started similar meetings. For example, in Boston Charles Cullis instituted his Tuesday Consecration Meeting. Carrie Judd held such a meeting on Thursday evenings.

The notion of conversion as a conscious process is a legacy of the Reformation. Traditionally since the fifth or sixth century, Christians have been those born into Christian families, baptized as infants, confirmed as young teens, and given last rites at death. One did not even think of oneself as an individual who had individual experiences. One was simply part of a family, a community, the Church. But Martin Luther had a life-changing experience while teaching the book of Romans, the realization that justification is by faith, a gift of God's grace. Followers of John Calvin argue that only some are elected to salvation. The English Puritans said that election is confirmed by a definite experience of one's total depravity and God's gift of forgiveness. The Anabaptist or Mennonite wing of the Reformation insisted that adults make a decision to be rebaptized and that only those believers who had made this commitment would be counted as members of a local church. The Reformation in general forced many people to choose between staying within the Church (with a capital C), the Roman Catholic Church, or becoming Protestants—and that meant choosing again among the ever-increasing number of Protestant sects.

New England Puritans initially limited church membership and colonial government to those who could "own the covenant" or testify to an experience confirming they were among the elect. This worked for the first generation, but by the time it got to their grandchildren, few of them were eligible for baptism as infants because their parents had not experienced owning the covenant and were thus not full-fledged church members. This led to a compromise called the halfway covenant. This allowed children to be baptized whose parents had been baptized. But many saw this as a serious sign of "declension." In 1734 Northampton, Massachusetts, pastor Jonathan Edwards (1703–1758) began to preach a series of sermons on justification by faith, illustrated with images of human souls as spiders dangling over the hearth fire ("Sinners in the Hands of an Angry God"). And revival was born. Edwards wrote *A Faithful Narrative of the Surprising Work of God in the Conversion of Many Hundred Souls in Northampton*. Historians have dubbed the event the First Great Awakening. John Wesley read the book and was moved. Whitefield made seven trips to the colonies to fuel the revival, preaching to vast crowds in the seaboard cities from Savannah to Boston. He visited Edwards in Northampton. But salvation was still something to wait for, something to seek, yet something that came in God's time.

The Second Great Awakening occurred in the late 1820s and 1830s when Presbyterian preacher Charles Grandison Finney (1792–1875) declared that salvation is not something to wait for but something to do, now! Having studied law, he said that he preached as a lawyer presenting his case to a jury. He urged people to make an immediate decision about their salvation. As a pastor in New York City, he wrote the how-to book *Lectures on Revivals of Religion* (1835). He also eventually dropped by the Tuesday meeting.

Phoebe Palmer was familiar with Finney's work. And she began to reshape the understanding of sanctification accordingly. In the first chapter of *The Way of Holiness* (1843) she said that a Presbyterian pastor asked her "whether there is not a *shorter way?*" After prayerful consideration, Palmer decided there was. Did Jesus not command, "Be ye holy" in Matthew 5:48 (KJV, author paraphrase)? Surely God would not demand something attainable only by a few after a lifetime of work. Palmer was sure that the fact that God commands it guarantees it is possible for anyone who follows God's Word. So the question was how? One must "consecrate all upon the altar of sacrifice to God."[5]

The first step is "laying one's all on the altar" in entire consecration. Hundreds of published testimonies to the experience follow a similar pattern. Easiest to place on the altar were material goods. For men, children usually came next, and one's wife was most difficult. For women, the husband was easier than the children. Sometimes it was difficult to dedicate one's public esteem or reputation. For women, this was sometimes followed by an especially challenging call to public ministry. But once the person managed to lay his or her all upon the altar, the rest was fairly automatic. Palmer deduced from Exodus 29:37, Matthew 23:19, and Romans 12:1–2 that Christ was the altar and the altar sanctified the gift. Therefore, one need only believe God's Word and claim one's holiness. One need not wait for feelings, though many did testify to the witness of the Holy Spirit that they were sanctified.

Thus the Wesleyan Holiness movement was built on the expectation that a person would have a datable conversion experience, followed by a definite experience of holiness, which many referred to as "baptism of the Holy Spirit." This flexibility in terminology goes back to Wesley's era.

# Reformed Holiness

Several other strands of Holiness teaching contributed to the divine healing movement as well. Finney, a professor of theology at Oberlin College, and the school's president, Asa Mahan (1799–1889), developed a strand usually referred to as Oberlin perfectionism.

Located in northern Ohio, Oberlin drew many students from what has been called the burned-over district in upstate New York, where numerous innovative and sometimes fanatical religious and social movements flourished in the early nineteenth century. One of these was the Oneida Community founded by John Humphrey Noyes (1811–1886), who had been converted in a Finney revival in 1831. His brand of Holiness was labeled antinomian perfectionism because he argued that true Christians could not sin. At Oneida, the community practiced a form of economic sharing called Bible communism and a form of sexual sharing called complex marriage. The Congregational Church denied Noyes ordination. (In 1880 the community became the corporation that still manufactures flatware.)

When copies of Noyes's magazine, the *Perfectionist,* and news of his teaching reached Oberlin, students began to raise questions for their teachers. During a meeting for "prayer, praise, and inquiry" in October 1836, a recent graduate asked Finney and Mahan, "When we look to Christ for sanctification, what degree of sanctification may we expect from him? May we look to him to be sanctified wholly, or not?" President Mahan, a Presbyterian minister, replied that they would give "prayerful and careful attention" to the issue and "in due time" the faculty would give the student body a "full and specific answer."[6]

The school term falling in the summer in those days, Finney and Mahan spent the winter of 1836–1837 in New York City, studying the issue. Finney pastored a church, and Mahan raised money for the school. Both read and pondered Wesley's *Plain Account,* and probably the work of John Fletcher. Mahan felt that he experienced a second work of grace in which Christ "filled and occupied the entire compass of his being."[7] He would later write *The Scriptural Doctrine of Christian Perfection* (1839) and *The Baptism of the Holy Spirit* (1870). Finney did not have the experience until 1843, but he began to preach on the topic immediately. Two of his sermons on the topic were published in *Letters to Professing Christians* (1837). He would later note in his *Memoirs* that "in looking at my revival labors," he was "led earnestly to inquire whether there was not something higher and more enduring than the Christian church was aware of, whether there were not promises, and means provided in the Gospel for the establishment of Christians in altogether a higher form of Christian life."[8]

All this merged into what came to be called Oberlin perfectionism. Finney and Mahan agreed that human beings do have a sinful, depraved nature as a result of the fall and do inevitably sin. But they rejected the traditional Calvinist belief in depravity of the will, thus preserving free will. Natural depravity is overcome by grace at conversion, through justification. People can will to be perfect. Again, Finney and Mahan did not teach sinless perfection but the possibility of moral perfection, perfect willing, the ability to make consistently good moral choices. One can choose perfect obedience to the law of God, and God will give the wisdom and power to make right choices. Finney continued to develop this position as time went on; Mahan was always closer to Wesleyan Holiness. Both Finney and Mahan witnessed divine healing in their ministries. Mahan's autobiography was published by Cullis's Willard Tract Repository in 1876. Titled *Out of Darkness into Light; or, The Hidden Life Made Manifest*, it contained a chapter offering numerous accounts of what Mahan called "prayer-cure." Mahan said that when he was a Presbyterian pastor in Cincinnati, which would have been in the early 1830s, he preached about healing during a severe cholera epidemic. Among the city's 40,000 residents, 2,500 died, but none of his parishioners succumbed.[9] Mahan also wrote an essay titled "Faith-Healing" in 1884 after his wife was healed.[10]

## Keswick Holiness

William Boardman was born in Smithfield, New York, and pursued a variety of unsuccessful business ventures before having a transforming faith experience. Working in the small mining town of Potosi, Wisconsin, at the time, he assumed leadership in a small Presbygational church (Presbyterians and Congregationalists were cooperating at the time in a Plan of Union). By 1843 he had enrolled in Lane Theological Seminary in Cincinnati. After graduation he was ordained as a Presbyterian. Boardman was quite familiar with the works of Finney and Mahan. When in New York, he also frequently visited Phoebe Palmer's Tuesday meeting. For a time he headed the Union Holiness Convention. After his experience of the second blessing, he published *The Higher Christian Life* in 1858, which established his name among Wesleyan Holiness people and spread the message into more Reformed circles.

Sometimes called Reformed Holiness by scholars, this strand was more often called the Higher Life, Deeper Life, or Victorious Life by devotees. It developed out of the work of Boardman in England, alongside Robert Pearsall Smith and Hannah Whitall Smith. The Smiths were birthright Philadelphia Quakers. Hannah's family owned the Whitall-Tatum glassworks, and Robert managed one of their factories in New Jersey. Both were seeking deeper spiritual lives. Hannah read and underlined her copy of Phoebe Palmer's *Way of Holiness*—I know because I have her signed copy. Robert claimed holiness at the Vineland, New Jersey, camp meeting in 1867. Hannah found the experience at a Methodist prayer meeting in her neighborhood. To further the cause, Robert started a periodical titled *The Christian's Pathway to Power*. Hannah, in the midst of raising a family, was a reluctant writer, as she later explained to her daughter:

> I did not want to write at all and only did it at Father's earnest entreaties. He had started a Paper, which I thought was a great mistake, and I declared I would not write a line for it. But he begged so hard that at last I said I would write one article and no more, if he would give up drinking wine at dinner. Then when that article was published, everybody clamored for another and Father begged, and I was good-natured and went on, but under a continued protest.[11]

Thus *The Christian's Secret of a Happy Life* came to be written. First published as a book in 1875, it can still be purchased in many Christian bookstores and even on book racks in pharmacies and supermarkets, at least in the South.

In the fall of 1873 William and Mary Boardman, along with Robert Pearsall Smith, arrived in London to hold meetings on the higher Christian life. Revivalist D. L. Moody, with musician Ira Sankey, was already spreading revival throughout the British Isles. Smith and the Boardmans followed with their second-blessing message. Robert soon urged Hannah and the children to join him. At Broadlands, the estate of William Cowper Temple and his wife, Georgina, Church of England evangelicals of the privileged classes gathered to hear Robert preach and Hannah give Bible readings. In 1874 Christians from throughout Europe assembled for the Oxford Union Meeting to hear the Smiths again. Continental Christians urged Robert to tour France, Germany, and Switzerland, which he did in the spring of 1875.

To celebrate his triumphant tour, English friends organized a meeting at Brighton for the first week in June. Hannah and the children rejoined Robert. Her book had just been published and was an instant bestseller. Interest was so keen that she gave her afternoon lectures twice each day to accommodate the crowds. Robert spoke each evening to enthusiastic throngs. The meetings closed as a spectacular success, but suddenly the Smiths were enveloped in a whirlwind of gossip and innuendo. Future meeting were canceled, and those who had so recently promoted their work now advised them to sail at once for home and issued ambiguous public statements.

Historians are still uncertain about exactly what happened. It seems that Robert may have been taking Paul's frequent injunction to "greet one another with a holy kiss" (Romans 16:16; 1 Corinthians 16:20; 1 Thessalonians 5:26) too literally. Or perhaps his American friendliness and informality were misinterpreted by his British hosts. One historian is fairly sure that Robert was sitting one day when a young woman came up and sat down on his lap; he put his arm around her as they talked; that was all.[12] Whatever happened, Robert clearly was not involved in marital infidelity. Some scholars have said it was not a matter of behavior but that his teaching was interpreted to be dangerously close to Noyes's antinomianism. Whatever the issue, it apparently shocked the eminent Victorians and opened the way for malicious gossip.

Back home in New Jersey, the Smiths were devastated. Hannah described her husband's anguish in a letter to a friend:

> his life is blasted.... A more sensitive, tender-hearted, generous man never lived, and this blow has sorely crushed him in every tender spot. It would have been so impossible for *him* to have treated anyone, even an enemy, as he has been treated by those who professed to be his dearest friends, that it has utterly crushed all power from his nature of trusting anyone, and he has shut himself up from everyone.

> ... he has been wounded past healing.... and I have not the faintest hope that he will ever recover from it.

> There *are* storms which uproot and overturn even the stateliest trees, and what wonder then if the weaker ones are utterly prostrated by them. *Such* a storm has swept over us, and has left only a few broken and withering branches.[13]

Hannah was right; Robert never did get over it. Despite attempts by American friends, especially Boardman and Cullis, to rehabilitate his ministry, he refused help and became increasingly bitter and morose. Hannah responded differently. She was able to live out the entire consecration she had articulated as *The Christian's Secret of a Happy Life*. Although she and Robert were not present for the first Keswick conference, held in 1875, their teachings on Holiness shaped the movement.

Keswick conferences became a tradition on both sides of the Atlantic. Their brand of consecration was spread not only in works of theology and devotion but also in the poems of Irish missionary Amy Carmichael (1867–1951), who heard the call at Keswick in the reading of a poem by Frances Ridley Havergal (1836–1879). Many of Havergal's poems have been set to music and have become favorites in evangelical hymnals, for example, "Take My Life and Let It Be Consecrated, Lord, to Thee."

The Boardmans took up permanent residence in England in December 1875. The Smiths did the same in 1888 to be near daughter Mary (1864–1945) and new granddaughter Rachel Conn Costelloe, better known in later life as feminist Ray Strachey (1887–1940).

All facets of the Holiness movement agreed that salvation deals with the guilt of sin. Keswick Holiness declared that sanctification releases one from the power of sin. Wesleyans taught that sanctification eradicates the sinful nature; Keswick taught that it suppresses sin. Palmer said one must lay one's all upon the altar; Smith counseled entire consecration. Palmer offered an immediate experience; Smith and Boardman talked more about a process. Wesleyans spoke of cleansing and purity of heart; Keswick advocates promised filling and power.

# Getting Organized

Initially Wesleyan Holiness was rooted in the northern Methodist Episcopal Church. The Lankfords and Palmers were members of local Methodist churches and friends with many laypeople and pastors. Palmer's Tuesday meeting was visited by leading educators, clergy, and bishops, many of them Methodist, from across the country. Phoebe and Walter Palmer held meetings throughout New England and into Canada. From 1859 to 1863 they held meetings all around the British Isles, chronicled in Phoebe's *Four Years in the Old World.* Much of the material first appeared as correspondence from abroad in Holiness periodicals. Upon their return, the Palmers purchased *The Guide to Holiness* (founded by Timothy Merritt [1775–1845] in 1839 as the *Guide to Christian Perfection).* Phoebe edited it until her death in 1874. Walter and Sarah, who married in 1876, continued it for many more years.

The Palmers spoke not only in churches but often at campgounds, favorite summer retreats for the increasingly urban population. Some camp meetings came to be especially identified with Holiness teaching, especially Old Orchard, Maine; Sing Sing, New York; and Ocean Grove, New Jersey. In 1867 a group of New York-area Methodist pastors formed the National Camp Meeting Association for the Promotion of Holiness. The group sponsored a series of national camp meetings. The first was at Vineland, New Jersey, in 1867, where Robert Pearsall Smith found sanctification. Subsequent meetings were at such places as Manheim, Pennsylvania (1868); Round Lake, New York (1869); Des Plaines, Illinois (1870); Urbana, Ohio (1871); Knoxville, Tennessee (1872); Cedar Rapids, Iowa (1873); near Lincoln, Nebraska (1876); Lawrence, Kansas (1879); and Augusta, Georgia (1885). After the first three years, there were multiple sites. The group continued to hold meetings through 1942, the last thirty-five years consistently at University Park (near Oskaloosa), Iowa.[14]

First president of the group, who served from 1867 to 1884, was the Reverend John S. Inskip (1816–1884), who with his wife, Martha Foster Inskip (1819–1891), were close friends with the Palmers and ardent advocates of Holiness. John edited his own paper, the *Christian Standard.* Martha's ministry in song complemented John's revival preaching.[15] Martha received the second blessing at the Sing Sing camp meeting in 1864. Her ardent testimony to their congregation embarrassed her husband. However, on Sunday, August 28, 1864, while preaching on Hebrews 12:1, John found his own blessing. "I am, O Lord, wholly and forever Thine," was John Inskip's commitment, written in large letters at the top of every page in his diary for eight years. At the time he was sanctified, he was a heavy smoker. The Palmers urged him to quit. With prayer, his addiction was broken within a few days.[16]

While setting up the grounds at the Urbana, Ohio, camp meeting in 1871,
John Inskip suffered a sunstroke that nearly killed him. He was forced to take two
months off for rest. By December he was able to attend a Holiness convention in
Boston, but while there he relapsed, and colleagues feared for his life. Someone
arranged for a private tea with Charles Cullis, who asked, "Why don't you ask
God to cure you?" Struck by the phrase "the Lord shall raise him up" in the reading of James 5, Inskip knelt in prayer as Cullis and others anointed and laid hands
on him. The next day he attended four services. He wrote Martha to say, "I am
fresh and well." Eight years later he wrote his testimony for Cullis, and Boardman
included it in *The Great Physician*.[17]

As Holiness gained new adherents, it began to come into conflict with local
ministers and denominational leaders who did not share this new emphasis. Obviously the movement gave new meaning to the phrase "holier than thou." The
"thous" turned resentful. The holy seemed cliquish, if not heretical. Indeed some
Holiness preachers began to teach that those who had not "gone on to Holiness"
had not really found salvation either. Holiness advocates also began to take on
two additional new emphases that further alienated their fellow Christians. The
first was divine healing, the subject of this study. The second was a new view of
the second coming.

This new view, formally known as dispensational premillennialism, was developed (i.e., invented) by John Nelson Darby, a graduate of Trinity College,
Dublin. He became a Church of England deacon in 1825. Although he was a successful parish priest in Ireland, he left the church in 1831 to affiliate with a separatist group in Britain that came to be known as Plymouth Brethren. From
the Vulgate or Latin translation of 1 Thessalonians 4:17, Darby posited an any-
moment "rapture" in which Jesus would return to the clouds above the earth. According to Darby, select Christians would be "caught up to meet him in the air,"
thus avoiding a Great Tribulation on earth, ruled by the Anti-Christ (this *pre*-
tribulation rapture escape was disputed even by some within the Brethren).
Eventually Jesus would return to earth (the Mount of Olives, to be exact), lead
triumphant armies at the battle of Armageddon, vanquish Satan, and reign for a
millennium.[18]

The majority of nineteenth-century American Christians, including the
evangelical groups who adopted Holiness, were postmillennial, believing that
their job was to prepare the earth for a millennium of peace and justice that
would precede Jesus' second coming. The dispensational aspect of Darby's message was that history could be divided into a series of epochs or dispensations, in
which God interacted differently with humanity. According to Darby, humanity
is currently in the sixth or church age; the millennium would be the seventh and
final dispensation. Many Holiness people considered their movement as evidence
they were living in the latter days, and early Pentecostals often spoke of healing

and speaking in tongues as "the latter rain," which Jeremiah 5:24 indicated would come just before the final harvest.

Between 1859 and 1874 Darby made seven tours of the United States and Canada, spreading his views. Most influential in adopting and propagating dispensationalism was revivalist D. L. Moody. The definitive dispensational reading of the Bible was codified in the notes of the 1909 Scofield Bible. Holiness and subsequent Pentecostal people generally adopted this view, as did fundamentalists, who disagreed with the former groups on almost everything else. Beyond their beliefs about sanctification, the notions of divine healing and a dispensational reading of the second coming began to drive wedges between Holiness people and their church communities.

As often happens with revivalist movements, Holiness people began to criticize their churches as dead and formalistic, their denominations as bureaucratic and unbiblical. They began to speak of becoming the New Testament church again, led by those baptized by the Holy Spirit, including only the holy ones, free of rules and restrictions and structure. The leaders of the National Camp Meeting Association, most of whom were Methodist ministers, urged people to stay within their local churches and work for change. But some were already or were soon to become Put-Outers, people more or less pushed out of their congregations. Others felt it was time to be Come-Outers and leave behind the dead wood.

In the 1870s, state Holiness associations began to spring up, parachurch communities of Holiness people that sponsored revival meetings in sympathetic churches and at camp meetings on property purchased by sympathetic laypeople. And some denominations already existed that stressed Wesleyan Holiness. The Wesleyan Methodist Church had been formed in 1843 in the struggle against slavery. The Free Methodist Church, formed in 1860, also favored freedom for slaves, free pews, and Holiness. Founder B. T. Roberts (1823–1893) wrote an editorial on "The Lord Our Healer" in 1862 for his periodical, *Earnest Christian and Golden Rule,* making a biblical argument for the practice.[19] William (1829–1912) and Catherine Booth (1829–1890) founded the Salvation Army in England in 1865. He was a former Methodist minister, and she defended Phoebe Palmer's right to speak publicly in a pamphlet titled *Female Ministry, or Woman's Right to Preach the Gospel* (1859).

The first to advocate leaving churches behind was Daniel S. Warner (1842–1925), initially licensed to preach by the Churches of God of North America (Winebrennerian), based in northern Ohio. In July 1877 he experienced sanctification. Subsequently brought to trial for his new teaching, Warner was ejected by the Winebrennerians on January 30, 1878. He continued to preach and gather followers into what eventually became the Church of God (Anderson, Indiana). Many of the women and men in the evangelistic team that traveled with Warner across the country preached healing as well.

By the 1880s, Holiness advocates were more numerous. According to Vinson Synan, by 1891 more than 354 "Tuesday Meetings" met in churches and homes across the country. In 1887 the National Holiness Association listed 206 "Holiness evangelists." By 1891 that number had swelled to 304. In 1888 four publishing houses produced Holiness literature. By 1892 the association listed 41 Holiness papers, most of them published by independent leaders. The association held three "General Holiness Assemblies"—in Jacksonville, Illinois, in 1880, and in Chicago in 1886 and 1901. Leadership was trying to keep members within their original denominations, but it was a losing battle. The movement was beginning to fragment.[20]

As time wore on, many people's experience of salvation and sanctification faded into their distant past. Their ardor waned, and they longed to be rekindled. People talked of multiple baptisms of the Holy Spirit and fillings and enduements with power. Some Holiness state associations such as those in Iowa and the Southwest became increasingly radical. For example, C. W. Sherman, a Free Methodist preacher and fan of A. B. Simpson, was the most ardent advocate of divine healing in the Southwest. Founder of the Church of God (Holiness) and editor of *The Vanguard,* his motto was "Radical in Holiness; Neutral in Nothing."[21]

One of the more radical Holiness leaders was Benjamin Hardin Irwin (1854–?), a practicing lawyer from Missouri sanctified in 1891. Although he was a Baptist by birth, he adopted Wesleyan Holiness. From 1892 through 1895 he was a traveling evangelist for the Wesleyan Methodist Church and the Iowa Holiness Association. He taught that "doctors should be denounced as imposters and their remedies as poisons." In John Fletcher's writings, he found references to a "baptism of burning love" and of being "baptized with fire." For Irwin this meant being blessed with "power from on high." He received this "third blessing" in 1895 in Enid, Oklahoma. Iowa Holiness leaders were not impressed and rejected his teaching in 1895. He began to organize Fire-Baptized Holiness Associations and publish *Live Coals of Fire.* For those who had already been saved and sanctified, he preached continued blessings through baptism with fire, dynamite, lyddite, and other explosives. At the conclusion of an 1897 camp meeting in Mound Valley, Kansas, which ended with a street meeting attended by three thousand people, Irwin reported thirty "radical sky blue conversions, fifty cases of sanctification, over fifty healings, and twenty-five or thirty cases of the baptism of fire."[22] Although most Holiness leaders dismissed his "third-blessing heresy"—one leader called Irwin's teaching "fanaticism" and suggested that what his followers really needed was "the baptism of common sense"—the South proved particularly receptive to his message. J. M. Pike's *Way of Faith* in Columbia, South Carolina, published articles by and about Irwin as well as ads for his pamphlet "Baptism of Fire." It also touted his tour of South Carolina and Georgia in 1895. The international Fire-Baptized Holiness Association was formed in Anderson, South Carolina, in August 1898. Irwin's success made it clear that many people were looking for something more.

# Notes

1. Nehemiah Curnock, ed., *The Journal of the Rev. John Wesley, A.M.* (London: Epworth Press, 1938), 3:236; see also 6:334 for September 5, 1781; and 6:412 for May 23, 1783.
2. John L. Peters, *Christian Perfection and American Methodism* (New York: Abingdon, 1956).
3. Phoebe Palmer, "Gracious Revivings," *Guide to Holiness* 33 (January 1858): 10, as quoted in Nancy A. Hardesty, *Women Called to Witness: Evangelical Feminism in the Nineteenth Century* (Nashville: Abingdon, 1984; 2d ed.; Knoxville: University of Tennessee Press, 1999), 38.
4. Timothy L. Smith, *Revivalism and Social Reform: American Protestantism on the Eve of the Civil War* (New York: Harper & Row, 1957), 105–6.
5. Phoebe Palmer, *The Way of Holiness* (2d ed., New York: Printed for the Author, 1854), 17.
6. Barbara Brown Zikmund, "Asa Mahan and Oberlin Perfectionism" (Ph.D. diss., Duke University, 1969), 113–14, and Asa Mahan, *Autobiography: Intellectual, Moral, and Spiritual* (London: T. Woolmer, 1882), 322–24.
7. Asa Mahan, *Out of Darkness into Light; or The Hidden Life Made Manifest* (Boston: Willard Tract Repository, 1876), 135, as quoted by Zikmund, "Asa Mahan," 122.
8. Charles G. Finney, *Memoirs of Rev. Charles G. Finney* (New York: A. S. Barnes, 1876), 340.
9. Mahan, *Out of Darkness into Light,* 248–53.
10. Donald W. Dayton, *The Theological Roots of Pentecostalism* (Grand Rapids, Mich.: Francis Asbury Press, Zondervan, 1987), 134, citing Asa Mahan, "Faith-Healing," *Earnest Christian* 48 (September 1884), 76.
11. Robert Parker, *The Transatlantic Smiths* (New York: Random House, 1959), 17.
12. Melvin E. Dieter, paper given at the World Methodist Historical Society meeting in Toronto, 1989.
13. Logan Pearsall Smith, *Philadelphia Quaker: The Letters of Hannah Whitall Smith* (New York: Harcourt, Brace & Company, 1950), 29–30. Published in England under the title *A Religious Rebel.*
14. For a list of sites and history of the organization see Kenneth O. Brown, *Inskip, McDonald, Fowler: "Wholly and Forever Thine." Early Leadership in the National Camp Meeting Association for the Promotion of Holiness* (Hazleton, Pa.: Holiness Archives, 1999), 268–71.
15. Ibid., 157–211; William McDonald and John E. Searles, *The Life of the Rev. John S. Inskip* (Boston: McDonald and Gill, 1885).
16. Kenneth O. Brown, " 'The World-Wide Evangelist'—The Life and Work of Martha Inskip," *Methodist History* (July 1983): 181–82; Brown, *Inskip, McDonald, Fowler,* 175–83.
17. Brown, *Inskip, McDonald, Fowler,* 189–91. See John S. Inskip, ltr. to Charles Cullis, May 27, 1879, in William E. Boardman, *The Great Physician* (Boston: Willard Tract Repository, 1881), 202–7.
18. This teaching has been further fictionalized in the incredibly popular Left Behind series of novels published in the 1990s and early 2000s by Timothy LaHaye and Jerry Jenkins.

19. Dayton, *The Theological Roots of Pentecostalism,* 133–34, citing B. T. Roberts, "The Lord Our Healer," *Earnest Christian and Golden Rule* 4 (July 1862), 1–7.

20. Vinson Synan, *The Holiness-Pentecostal Tradition: Charismatic Movements in the Twentieth Century* (Grand Rapids, Mich.: Eerdmans, 1971, 1997), 32, 35, 41–42.

21. Robert Stanley Ingersol, "Burden of Dissent: Mary Lee Cagle and the Southern Holiness Movement" (Ph.D. diss., Duke University, 1989), 86, 171.

22. Vinson Synan, *The Old-Time Power* (Rev. ed.; Franklin Springs, Ga.: Advocate Press, c. 1973, 1986), 94, 82–83, 87; H. V. Synan, "Irwin, Benjamin Hardin," *International Dictionary,* 804–5.

# 4

# The Flowering

The divine healing movement flourished in the United States in the last third of the nineteenth century, especially at camp meetings and conventions. Charles Cullis held his first "faith convention" in 1874 in Framingham, Massachusetts. From 1876 to 1883 he hosted weeklong meetings at the Methodists' Old Orchard, Maine, campgrounds. When in 1884 he was temporarily excluded from there by a change in management, he bought property in the White Mountains, at Intervale, New Hampshire, and that became the site of regular meetings for spiritual refreshment and healing until his death in 1892.[1] When he quit Old Orchard, the new management invited a popular New York pastor to offer a Holiness and healing convention.

## A. B. Simpson

Albert Benjamin Simpson was born December 15, 1843, on Prince Edward Island, Canada, to Scottish Covenanter Presbyterian parents, James and Jane Clark Simpson. An 1865 graduate of Knox College in Toronto, he had a very successful ministry at Knox Presbyterian Church in Hamilton, Ontario, before accepting a call to Chestnut Street Presbyterian Church in Louisville, Kentucky, in 1873. After reading William E. Boardman's *The Higher Christian Life* in 1874, he experienced a spiritual crisis that he felt was a baptism of the Holy Spirit.

In November 1879 Simpson accepted the call to Thirteenth Street Presbyterian Church in New York City. But when he came to believe that he could not baptize anyone too young to confess their own faith, he felt obliged to submit his resignation. Thus in November 1881 he struck out on his own. Only seven people came to his first service. However, by May 1882 he was able to move the group to the Grand Opera Hall, where they met for the next two years. In the spring of 1884 the congregation became the Twenty-Third Street Tabernacle.

Another tension for Simpson in remaining a Presbyterian was his growing belief in divine healing. In Louisville he had been impressed with the healing of a young man who had been for many years an actor and—his mother feared—a "stranger to the Lord." Suffering from a "most aggravated case of paralysis and softening of the brain," he had not eaten or spoken for days. The doctors had given him up. Simpson felt led not to pray for the young man's healing but only that he might recover long enough to assure his mother of his salvation. After the prayer, Simpson stood to leave and would have gone except that other friends arrived and the group stood chatting. After a while Simpson glanced back at the bed, and the man's eyes were open. The young man began to speak, recovered rapidly, and lived for years. The case was written up for a medical journal by one of his physicians.[2] In fact Simpson was nearly convinced of the doctrine of divine healing until a devout Christian physician talked him out of it, calling such views presumption.

Simpson himself was increasingly beset by various physical ailments. Eventually he carried a bottle of ammonia in his pocket at all times to revive himself when feeling faint when his heart fluttered. A prominent doctor in New York finally told him that he did not have the constitutional strength to survive for more than a couple more months.

Needing time to relax in the summer of 1881, Simpson took his family to the campground at Old Orchard Beach, Maine. The week, led by Dr. Charles Cullis, was devoted to the teaching of divine healing. Simpson went to only a couple of services, but on Friday afternoon he went out into the woods to pray. In the course of his prayers, he made three pledges to God. First, he declared, "I solemnly accept this truth as part of Thy Word." Second, "I take the Lord Jesus as my physical life, for all the needs of my body until all my life work is done." And third, "I solemnly promise *to use* this blessing for the glory of God and the good of others." He found that "every fibre of my soul was tingling with a sense of God's presence." And from that time his heart difficulties were gone. Before this time it had usually taken him until Wednesday to get over the pastoral work of Sundays, but in the first three years after he was healed, he preached more than a thousand sermons and sometimes held twenty meetings a week.[3]

When the camp meeting ended, Simpson was scheduled to be in New Hampshire. Friends asked him to join them in climbing a three-thousand-foot mountain. He at once panicked at the thought of the exertion and his fear of heights. Ascending a flight of stairs usually exhausted him. In Europe mountain vistas had terrified him. But then the thought came, "If you refuse to go, it is because you do not believe God has healed you." So he agreed to go in faith. At first he felt fear and weakness, but then he became conscious of a divine strength bearing him up. Concluding the story, he wrote, "Thank God, from that time I have had a new heart in this body, literally as well as spiritually, and Christ has been its glorious life."[4]

Not long after, his young daughter suddenly became very ill with diphtheria. She had a raging fever and her throat was coated white inside. Her mother insisted that he call a physician. Margaret Henry Simpson (1840–1924) was already feeling vulnerable since her husband had relinquished a steady salary even though they had a growing family. When he took up this idea of healing, her brother said, "Divorce him, Margaret. Bertie always seemed a little queer!"[5] But Simpson held the child, anointed her fevered brow, and claimed her healing in the name of the Lord Jesus. That night he lay beside the child and prayed, knowing that "if the sickness lasted until the following day, there would be a crisis in my family and I should be held responsible." In the morning the little girl was well. Simpson reported: "I shall never forget the look my wife gave me when she saw the ulcers gone and our child ready to get up and play."[6] Margaret eventually became a firm believer in healing. Margaret Simpson allowed him to open a healing home in their residence. Eventually it moved into a six-story building on Forty-Fourth Street.

Simpson's other passion was foreign missions. In October 1883 he founded a Missionary Training College, which eventually moved to Nyack, New York, up the Hudson River. At Old Orchard in 1887 he formed a Missionary Society and the Christian Alliance—not a church but an alliance of Christians who believed in the fourfold gospel: Jesus Christ as Savior, Sanctifier, Healer, and coming King. In 1897 the two groups were officially merged into the Christian and Missionary Alliance. A. B. Simpson was president; Margaret Simpson was financial secretary.

Simpson had some trepidation at first about teaching divine healing:

> I had a large amount of conservative respectability. I had high regard for my ecclesiastical reputation. I knew intuitively what it might cost to be wholly true in this matter. At the same time, I shrank unutterably from the thought of having to pray with anyone else for healing. I feared greatly that I should involve God's name in dishonor by claiming what might not come to pass.[7]

Simpson was clear that salvation must come first. And he preferred that a person seek and receive sanctification before asking for healing. This was always the order of emphasis in his preaching. He did so because his view of healing took a distinctive form. While most people came for the alleviation of a particular, acute problem—and often found it—Simpson saw healing more as a continuous state to be sought. Speaking of his own condition, he said, "Physically I do not think I am any more robust than ever. I am intensely conscious with every breath, that I am drawing my vitality from a directly supernatural source." He was clear that a person who experienced a particular healing could not assume he or she would be free of sickness in the future. He stressed that just as a person maintained a holy life by remaining entirely consecrated to God, so a person remained healthy by daily dependence on God's healing grace.[8]

To promote healing, Simpson instituted in May 1882 the Friday meeting. Initially it met at the Grand Opera Hall and resulted in "very many marvelous cases of healing in answer to prayer."[9] A reporter in 1886 found fifteen hundred people gathered at the Gospel Tabernacle. Another newspaper article noted that people had been cured of consumption, cancer, blindness, and paralysis after attending the Friday meeting. Much of Simpson's thinking about healing was presented in his *Friday Meeting Talks,* later distilled in *The Gospel of Healing* and *The Lord for the Body.* Simpson continued the meetings until his death and suggested that all C&MA branches hold Friday meetings for healing too.[10]

In 1882 Simpson began the publication *Word, Work, and World.* At the conference in London in 1885 he estimated there were forty to fifty Holiness papers being published in the States. There was Charles Cullis's *Times of Refreshing;* Carrie Judd's *Triumphs of Faith;* George McCalla's *Words of Faith* from Philadelphia; the Mixes' *Victory Through Faith;* the Palmers' *Guide to Holiness;* and many more. Books on the subject were pouring from the presses.

Simpson also was constantly on guard against the temptations of success. He noted, "It is very solemn ground and can never be made a professional business or a public parade. Its mightiest victories will always be silent and out of sight, and its power will keep pace with our humility and holiness. . . . We hope the wonder-seeking spirit will not be allowed to take the place of practical godliness and humble works for the salvation of men."[11] When he was preaching on the subject of healing, he would generally let others do the anointing, so that people would not assume that healing came through a particular act or a particular person. He insisted, though, that those doing the anointing felt called by God to such a ministry. He was also known to refuse anointing to persons who had not yet experienced salvation and sanctification.

## Camp Meetings and Conventions

In September 1884 Simpson held a "Convention for Christian Life, Divine Healing, and Evangelistic and Missionary Work" at the New York Gospel Tabernacle. In 1885 the meeting was moved to October and became a tradition. That year members of the Old Orchard Camp Meeting Association, Methodists all, visited and asked him to do a similar convention in Maine the next summer, August 3–10, 1886. The theme was "Christian Life, Work, and Divine Healing."

Simpson's 1887 Old Orchard convention was galvanized on opening day by the healing of a twenty-year-old local resident, Ina H. Moses. She had been severely injured in a sledding accident in 1884 and unable to walk without crutches. At the 1886 convention she had been converted and was trusting God for healing. Still much in pain, she came to the Friday afternoon healing service. By Simpson's account,

Suddenly the power of God fell upon her and she sprang to her feet, crying out, "I am healed! Jesus has healed me."

Throwing away her crutches, she began to walk to the platform, and, ascending the steps, she stood before the vast assembly with a face shining like the sun. The audience rose spontaneously to their feet, some shouting, many of them weeping and others singing the Doxology. It was a moment that will live like a sunburst in a tempest as long as memory lasts.[12]

Simpson gathered an ecumenical group of speakers for these conventions. The first convention, in 1884, included H. Goatton Guiness of London, Methodist John Cookman, and Episcopalian Henry Wilson. The 1885 New York convention included, among others, three Episcopal priests: Wilson, Kenneth Mackenzie, and W. S. Ranisford; two Methodist ministers, Cookman and Stephen Merritt; and the young Carrie Judd. Judd had come to New York City to meet Simpson and learned that he had just republished her tract "Faith's Reckonings" in his paper. He became "like a father" to her, assisted at her wedding, and dedicated her baby daughter.[13]

Such meetings, often referred to as a faith-cure convention, became the mode for spreading the word for the next two decades. Simpson and his colleagues also took the show on the road—to Philadelphia, Pittsburgh, Buffalo (1885), Chicago (1889), Detroit, Kansas City (1895), Atlanta (1899), Toronto (1891), and Los Angeles (1895). Four days to a week in duration, a convention began with morning prayer and Bible study. Speakers were interspersed with testimonies. After lunch, there was a featured address followed by meetings focused on specific topics such as holiness, the work of the Holy Spirit, biblical perfection, and foreign missions. Evening evangelistic meetings were followed by an altar service for those seeking salvation. At least one day toward the end of the week was devoted to healing. The impact was multiplied by the reports Simpson published in his various periodicals.[14]

For example, John Salmon (1831–1918), an ex-sailor who became a leader in the Canadian C&MA, first met Simpson when he traveled to Buffalo for a convention hosted by Carrie Judd on October 26–30, 1885. Having read Judd's book, Salmon was anointed during the convention and miraculously healed of a terminal kidney disease. A childhood Presbyterian, he had trained for the Methodist ministry and was pastoring a church in Toronto. After his healing, he helped to anoint others at the convention. In 1887 he became a founding vice president of the Alliance, a post he held for twenty-five years.[15]

Carrie Judd met George S. Montgomery at one of these conventions at the campgrounds in Western Springs, Illinois. Brought up a Scottish Presbyterian, he had been healed of diabetes and consecrated himself to God's service. He came from California for the meeting. He came back East again for the meeting at Linwood Park, Ohio, where Carrie was on the program. They began to correspond, and he arranged for her and Elizabeth Sisson to speak in California. During their week of meetings he proposed. They were married May 14, 1890, and lived in San Francisco for a few months before taking up residence on a large tract of property Montgomery owned in Oakland. Their daughter, Faith, was born in 1891. They took her back East to be dedicated by Simpson at the Gospel Tabernacle on Easter 1892.[16]

## Daniel S. Warner

In the Midwest Daniel Sidney Warner was also leading a touring road show. He first mentioned healing in his *Gospel Trumpet* in a report of a September 1878 Holiness camp meeting at the fairgrounds in Marion, Ohio, noting that a number of people were healed during the meeting. Commenting on a December 1880 Holiness convention at Jacksonville, Illinois, he said, "A notable miracle at that convention was the healing of Sarah Gillillen, of cancer." In another camp meeting held near Bangor, Michigan, in June 1883, Emma Miller of Battle Creek, who had been an invalid for three years and was blind most of that time, was healed completely. She never lost her good eyesight again. Her healing was the talk of a generation because she later became the wife of A. B. Palmer, a well-known minister.[17]

One who traveled with Warner's party was Iowan Mary Cole (1853–after 1914). As a child she was sickly, stammered, and had "spinal trouble." At fifteen she became a helpless invalid for months at a time. Converted in 1871, she was led into sanctification by her brother Jeremiah. She felt called to preach in 1875, but she resisted for seven years, spending the time at home as "a hopeless invalid" whom doctors could not cure, reading books by John Wesley, John Fletcher, Hester Ann Rogers, and Phoebe Palmer. In 1880 Jeremiah found healing through prayer for his dyspepsia and urged her to try it. She suggested that perhaps God "is leaving me afflicted to keep me humble." Jeremiah read her the biblical promises again. Finally she became willing "for God's glory alone," and she was healed of all her afflictions. She and her family praised God so loudly the neighbors said, "Mary Cole is having a whole camp meeting by herself!" In 1882 she joined Jeremiah in his evangelistic endeavors. Because she was fearless in the face of a mob, some said she was Jesse James in drag. She was twice egged, once with frozen eggs.[18]

J. W. Byers (1859–1944) and Jennie M. Shirk Byers (1861–? ) were also associates of Warner, who ordained them both. After traveling as itinerant evangelists in Illinois for two years, they felt called to the West Coast. So with their three children, they set out in late 1890 for San Diego, traveling north through Los Angeles and on into Oregon and Washington. Committed to divine healing, the Byerses operated a healing home from 1896 to 1899 in Oakland, California. For a time they published *Tidings of Healing*, and J. W. wrote *Grace of Healing*.[19]

## African-American Holiness Churches

Holiness teachings and divine healing were also popular in African-American churches. Within Simpson's C&MA a number of black churches flourished in the 1890s. The Pittsburgh branch, as Alliance groups were termed in those days, was led in 1893 by William P. Robinson, an African Methodist Episcopal minister born in slavery. Several evangelists traveled in the area, including E. M. Collette from the A.M.E.; Edward M. Burgess, and Charles S. Morris. In 1899 some of the strongest branches in Ohio and Pennsylvania were black. By 1903 they were gathering for conventions in Pittsburgh, Cleveland, Columbus, and Mansfield. By 1919 there were African-American C&MA congregations in New York, Virginia, North Carolina, and Louisiana as well, plus four missions for West Indians in New York and Brooklyn. Groups were also gathered in Michigan and Washington, D.C. In the 1920s the musical highlight of many conventions, black and white, was the Cleveland Coloured Gospel Quintette.[20]

The A.M.E. Church's *Christian Recorder* carried numerous articles reporting Holiness meetings within A.M.E. congregations in Missouri, Pennsylvania, and New Jersey. Women Holiness preachers were mentioned in North and South Carolina. In fact, the first original book published by the A.M.E. Church contained an essay by James E. Taylor urging members to seek sanctification. A.M.E. minister B. Abraham Grant preached on Holiness at the Ocean Grove camp meeting in the late 1890s.[21]

Charles Price Jones (1865/66–1949), founder of the Church of Christ (Holiness), was born near Rome, Georgia. After his mother's death in 1882, he left home at seventeen for Chattanooga, Memphis, and Arkansas, where in 1884 he was converted and began preaching. Licensed in 1887, he was ordained a Baptist preacher in October 1888 while a student at Arkansas Baptist College in Little Rock. He experienced sanctification in Selma, Alabama, in 1894, under the ministry of Joanna Patterson Moore, a white woman ministering in the black community. Jones testified, "As a Baptist I had doctrinal assurance; I wanted spiritual assurance, heart peace, rest of soul, the joy of salvation."[22]

In 1895 Jones became pastor of Mt. Helm Baptist Church in Jackson, Mississippi. The church hosted in 1897 one of the first Holiness conventions among African Americans. People came from across the Deep South, North Carolina to Louisiana. According to Jones's account, the work of the convention involved "healing of the sick, blessing of the afflicted, preaching to the poor." Charles Mason said it was "a wonderful meeting of power and outpouring of the spirit of the Lord in which many were converted, sanctified, and healed by the power of faith."[23]

When the 1898 General Missionary Baptist Convention of Mississippi adopted a resolution condemning the emerging Holiness movement and Mt. Helm in particular, Jones withdrew from the Jackson Association, saying that he was "not a Baptist." Mt. Helm declared itself no longer Baptist but "Church of Christ." This led to a legal battle. Eventually the General Missionary Baptist Church revoked the credentials of Jones, Charles Mason, and two other pastors and barred their followers from the convention. One of the charges made against Jones by dissident members of Mt. Helm was that seven or eight people died because they followed Jones's teachings concerning healing and abstained from medications. When local Baptist clergy reviewed Jones's teachings, they declared he departed from the Baptist faith on six counts, including faith healing and instantaneous sanctification. Jones's successor at Mt. Helm charged in court that Jones ceased to be Baptist when "he accepted the doctrines of faith cure, divine healing, and sinless perfection."[24] Patrick M. Thompson, in his 1898 *History of Negro Baptists in Mississippi*, says that at Mt. Helm,

many of the members have entered into a new covenant and are striving with God's help to be "perfect even as He is perfect." The motto of those living the higher Christian life is: "Christ all in all."

There are still others who have renounced earthly physicians and have put not only the keeping of their souls, by faith, into Christ's care, but their bodies and those of their families.[25]

Jones published a hymn titled "All on Jesus" that was written after he had spent a night in fevered pain. After a friend anointed him and prayed, he was healed. The chorus says,

Yes, it's all on Jesus,
Ev'ry whit on Jesus,
All on Jesus, And I am free;
He bore my sins and sickness in His body
on the shameful cross of Calvary.[26]

Jones's colleague was Charles Harrison Mason (1866–1961), who later adopted Pentecostalism and led the Church of God in Christ. He was born near Bartlett, Tennessee, to former slaves Jerry and Eliza Mason. His mother was a woman of great faith with the gift of prayer. He experienced conversion in November 1879 after the family had relocated to Plumersville, Arkansas. However, he almost died in a yellow fever epidemic that swept the area over the next year and claimed his father's life. The first Sunday in September 1880, though, as Charles lay sick in bed, the glory of God came down upon him. He got up and walked to the door with totally renewed strength. He and his mother walked to the Mt. Olive Baptist Church, where he was baptized as an act of thanksgiving. Two years later he was licensed to preach. In 1893 he was sanctified after reading *An Autobiography: The Story of the Lord's Dealings with Mrs. Amanda Smith, The Colored Evangelist.* Smith (1839–1915) was a regular on the Holiness camp meeting circuit, singing and preaching.[27] Sanctification for Mason meant separation from sin and power for ministry. He met Jones in 1895.[28] From 1896 to 1899 they worked as a team, spreading Holiness teachings at Mt. Helm and elsewhere through conventions and publications. Their work split Baptist and Methodist churches in the area, giving rise to what is now called "the sanctified church." Eventually both were expelled from the National Baptist Convention.

In North Carolina black Holiness advocates formed the United Holy Church. Among the leaders were Charles Craig (d. 1928) and Emma Collins Craig (1872–1966). Emma was born in Roxboro to emancipated slaves. She married Craig in 1892. Expelled from the A.M.E. Church because of their Holiness views, they and others founded a Gospel Tabernacle in Durham. In their home on October 13, 1894, a group of independent Holy churches came together to form the United Holy Church. The group incorporated in 1918. They also proclaimed a fourfold gospel of salvation, baptism with the Holy Spirit (in the Wesleyan sense), divine healing, and the second coming of Jesus. The group's tenth Article of Faith declared, "We believe in Divine healing of the body through the precious atonement of Jesus, by which sickness and disease are destroyed."[29] Most members came from Methodist backgrounds, but several leaders had previously been part of the C&MA. Julia A. Delk was an active minister and president of the church's Missionary Department.

## Joanna Patterson Moore

Joanna Patterson Moore (1832–?) was a white woman who worked among blacks in the South from the early 1870s as a missionary sponsored by the American Baptist Home Missionary Society. Born in Clarion County, Pennsylvania, she was sent to an Episcopal boarding school by her Irish father. Her mother was Presbyterian. But Joanna in 1852 found personal salvation and was baptized as a Baptist. She found sanctification at a Methodist camp meeting in Illinois and again in a Quaker meeting in Iowa. She taught school for fifteen years. The family moved west to Illinois in 1858. Within five years her father died, her three younger siblings succumbed to measles and whooping cough, the family home burned, and her blind sister died.

During the Civil War, while a student at the Rockford (Illinois) Seminary, Moore heard speakers talk about the plight of slaves in the South. In November

1863 she landed on Island #10 in the Mississippi River where a group of blacks were encamped. The group was later moved to Helena, Arkansas, by Indiana Quakers who came to establish an orphanage and an industrial school. For five years she worked with them. For the next decade she went back and forth between the South and the Chicago area to care for her aging mother. In the fall of 1873 she sought help from students at Leland University in New Orleans to go door to door reading the Bible, helping people, and starting Sunday schools. From 1876 to 1881 she made a bit of money by selling and giving away Bibles for the American Bible Society. She developed what she called a Fireside School Plan to encourage mothers and fathers to read the Bible and other good literature to and with their children. She enlisted pastors to encourage parents through recognition in church. She started Bible bands in various black schools and colleges and training schools for wives and mothers. She taught them not to give newborns a whiskey toddy or drink it themselves as a postpartum remedy, as many physicians suggested. She distributed leaflets on such topics as "Rules of Politeness for Home and Church." She worked with Spellman College students in Atlanta and ministered for a time in Nashville. In 1885 she began a paper called *Hope,* mostly to offer Bible lessons for each day to be used by parents in the Fireside Schools program. She published it until 1901, when she turned it over to the National Baptist Publishing House.

In the early 1880s Moore discovered a tumor growing on her throat, which physicians in Chicago feared was cancer. They suggested surgery. Having heard about divine healing, she began to pray. An emergency caused the surgeon to delay her operation for a day. When he looked at the growth the next day, he said, "I think the character of the sore is somewhat changed and we will wait a few days." She went back to God in more fervent prayer, and the tumor gradually disappeared. She declared, "Ever since, Jesus has been my doctor for soul and body."[30] It was she who introduced the teaching to Charles Price Jones and Charles Harrison Mason.

## Healing in the South

Divine healing took hold more slowly in the South, in part because in north Georgia, the hotbed of Holiness, leaders were confronted by reporters for the *Atlanta Constitution* when Lawrenceville pastor Michael Turner committed suicide. (He had a history of depression, and his suicide note mentioned marital infidelity.) In an interview Methodist minister William Asbury Dodge (1844–1904) mentioned that "God will answer prayer for any lawful object . . . , even to curing the sick." And he said he knew people who had been cured. Miss Kate Strickland of Forsyth County had been healed of consumption. Mrs. Wimpey, who for twenty-two years had been "unable to raise her foot or extend her arm," regained "the strength of her youth."[31] He might have mentioned his wife, who broke her hip in a fall from an electric street car in Rome, Georgia. Physicians told her she would never walk again. She noted, "I told Mr. Dodge to pray for me, for I knew the Lord would answer his prayer. I felt I would walk again. He prayed earnestly to God to lay his hand on the broken bone and heal it. In prayer he said, 'Lord, I know you can, and I believe you will.'" She spent an uncomfortable seven weeks in a metal cast, but she walked freely after that.[32] Reporters took up the stories, and Methodist leaders became even more alarmed about Holiness "fanaticism."

Another early advocate of faith healing in the South was Free Methodist minister C. W. Sherman, who published *The Vanguard* and eventually founded the Church of God (Holiness). His paper as well as *The Way of Faith*, edited from the 1890s to 1931 from Columbia, South Carolina, by J. M. Pike (1840–1932), carried theological defenses and personal testimonies on the subject.

## Alexander Dowie

Many of those in the Holiness and healing movements interacted in one way or another with one of the most famous advocates of healing in the period: John Alexander Dowie (1847–1907). When Dowie arrived in the United States in 1888, he was forty-one and unknown, but an established healer in Australia. Born in Edinburgh, Scotland, he was sickly but precocious. By age six he had read the Bible through and signed the temperance pledge to abstain always from alcohol, opium, and tobacco. When he was thirteen, the family emigrated to Australia. Around age twenty-one he felt a call to ministry. After studying with a tutor for a time, he returned to Edinburgh to study at the university. As a student he served as a chaplain at the Edinburgh infirmary and observed the work of famed surgeon John Simpson, but he said he developed a strong antipathy for surgery and the medical arts.

Returning to Australia, Dowie served several Congregational churches. In 1874 a terrible plague swept Western Australia. Within a couple of weeks he buried forty parishioners, and thirty more were ill. As he prayed and studied Scripture, he concluded from Acts 10:38 (in which Peter said that Jesus "went about doing good, and healing all that were oppressed of the devil") that Satan is the cause of illness and Christ is still a healer. Shortly thereafter he was called to the sickbed of a young woman named Mary. When the doctor suggested, "Are not God's ways mysterious?" he reacted with anger, and the doctor left. Mary's mother then requested that he pray, and afterward the child drifted into a peaceful sleep. He then prayed for two of her siblings, and they too began to mend.

Thus began his healing ministry. Not another member of the congregation died in the epidemic.

In 1876 Dowie married his cousin Jean. In 1877 he severed ties with the Congregational Church and became an independent evangelist. In 1883 he organized the Free Christian Church and in 1884 built the Melbourne Tabernacle. Each February in the church he held a healing convention. One of the first healed in the new church was Mrs. Lucy Parker, who had been under physicians' care for more than two years because cancer was destroying her left eye. When Dowie laid hands on her and prayed, the cancer burst, discharge flowed down her face, the swelling went down, and she could see perfectly.

In Australia and New Zealand, Dowie formed the International Divine Healing Association. He received an invitation from William Boardman to the International Conference on Divine Healing and True Holiness in London but was unable to attend. In his response, however, he expressed plans to visit the United States and London soon. In March 1888 he sailed with his family for San Francisco, where he immediately began a healing ministry that garnered wide press coverage. After a tour up the coast as far as Victoria, British Columbia, he crossed to Chicago and decided to settle there.

He opened a tabernacle near the gate of the World's Fair, which opened on May 7, 1893. He began publishing *Leaves of Healing*. In 1895 he was arrested for practicing medicine without a license. When questioned, he replied, "I do not heal anyone. I do it for the purpose of obeying God, who uses me in the healings." Under oath, he testified, "I preach the gospel of salvation through faith in Jesus Christ, and with it the gospel of Divine healing. I also preach true holiness through faith in Jesus Christ. . . . Divine healing does not come first in my ministry."[33] In the fall of 1899 he retaliated with a three-month holy war on "Doctors, Drugs, and Devils." The College of Physicians instigated a riot in front of his tabernacle. Students from Rush Medical College heeded a notice printed by the *Chicago Tribune* advertising a protest and showed up at his church with stink bombs they had concocted. Several attempts were made on his life.[34]

Court proceedings did include affidavits from a number of well-connected people affirming their miraculous cures. Amanda Hicks, first cousin of President Abraham Lincoln and president of Clinton (Kentucky) College, was carried four hundred miles by ambulance, from Clinton to one of Dowie's healing homes in Chicago. She had been taking large doses of morphine prescribed for her pain. Dowie first insisted she be weaned off the morphine. When that was done, Dowie and his wife laid hands on her in prayer, and "in a moment the terrible agony of months departed, and later in the evening she rose and walked freely." Her story had been printed in the *Clinton Democrat*. The reporter noted that when she returned on the train, she walked the mile from the depot to the college, and "her carriage was as erect as ever in the days before her illness."[35]

Sadie Cody was a niece of Buffalo Bill, whose Wild West show was right across the street from Dowie's Tabernacle. (Dowie's followers complained that whoops from the show disrupted their services, even on Sundays.) Sadie, twenty-five, had fallen ill while visiting the World's Fair and become totally helpless. For a year she was attended by four physicians, including her uncle. Eventually she was put in a full body cast to protect her back. But while she was in the hospital, a copy of Dowie's *Leaves of Healing* fell on her bed. It took four men to carry her cot from her home in Rensselaer, Indiana, to the train. Parents and friends accompanied her. A police ambulance took her from the Chicago train station to Dowie's healing home. Dowie prayed for her. She felt struggle within and momentarily went to sleep. But when she awoke there was no pain. Abcess and tumor were gone; her legs were now of equal length, her spine was strong.[36]

Eventually Dowie organized the Christian Catholic Church and built a community called Zion, Illinois, on Lake Michigan, north of Chicago. Many Holiness people from across the country visited Zion; some took up residence. But Dowie had gone too far. In June 1901 he declared himself "Elijah the Restorer." Later it was "the Messenger of the Covenant" and the "Prophet foretold by Moses," titles others applied to Jesus.[37] Some said he was mentally ill; others said he was merely greedy; some blamed his younger wife, who had a taste for fine gowns from Paris. In Los Angeles in 1904, the press taunted him, saying that if he was Elijah, he should pray for rain to end the city's eight-month drought. So one night he did pray in the service, and when the service was over it poured rain. However, he suffered a stroke in September 1905 and died March 9, 1907.[38]

Dowie's work and the publicity it garnered brought divine healing to the public's attention. Although he did not interact much with other leaders of the movement, many local church leaders read his paper and visited Zion. His work, however, provides a cautionary tale for those who would adopt the title "healer" when there is only One who is Lord and Healer.

## Opposition

In the 1890s Holiness teaching ran into strong opposition in some quarters, particularly in the South. In December 1890 five presiding elders in the North Georgia Conference of the Methodist Episcopal Church, South, were demoted to "city missionary." All were Holiness advocates. By 1890 there were state Holiness associations in South Carolina, Georgia, Tennessee, Alabama, and Texas. So in 1894 the southern Methodist bishops moved to oust all Holiness pastors.

The teaching of divine healing also ran into strong opposition from some within the Holiness movement. In the 1880s, William McDonald (1820–1901), Inskip's successor as president of the National Camp Meeting Association, was critical of Simpson and R. Kelso Carter in the pages of the *Christian Witness,* which he edited for twenty-five years. In the April 15, 1886, issue McDonald disagreed point by point in a review of Carter's *Atonement for Sin and Sickness.* Carter founded *The Kingdom* in order to respond and promote Holiness and healing. McDonald even negatively reviewed Simpson's and Carter's hymn books. He gloated when several years later Carter went to a Pennsylvania sanitarium to recover from malaria. *Modern Faith Healing* (1892) was the summation of his opposition.[39]

Charles J. Fowler (1845–1919) succeeded McDonald in 1894. In his 1897 President's Report, he warned against "extreme advent-*ism*" and "extreme healing-*ism.*" In response, the National Association passed "Resolutions on Unity of Teaching," forbidding the preaching of divine healing and the premillennial second coming of Christ at national Holiness camp meetings. Both topics were considered divisive, secondary, and particularly offensive to mainline clergy. Most of the association's leaders were Methodist Episcopal Church ministers and hoped to stay that way.[40]

# Notes

1. Raymond J. Cunningham, "Ministry of Healing: The Origins of the Psychotherapeutic Role of the American Churches" (Ph.D. diss., Johns Hopkins University, 1965), 11; William Boyd Bedford Jr., "'A Larger Christian Life': A. B. Simpson and the Early Years of the Christian and Missionary Alliance" (Ph.D. diss., University of Virginia, 1992), 257; W. H. Daniels, ed., *"Have Faith in God": Dr. Cullis and His Work: Twenty Years of Blessing in Answer to Prayer* (Boston: Willard Tract Repository, 1885), 175.

2. A. B. Simpson, *The Gospel of Healing* (1885; repr., Camp Hill, Pa.: Christian Publications, 1994), 123–24.

3. A. E. Thompson, *A. B. Simpson: His Life and Work* (rev. ed.; Camp Hill, Pa.: Christian Publications, 1960), 75–76; Simpson, *The Gospel of Healing,* 121.

4. Simpson, *The Gospel of Healing,* 129–30.

5. William Boyd Bedford Jr., "'A Larger Christian Life,'" 318, quoting Katherine A. Brennen, "Mrs. A. B. Simpson: The Wife or Love Stands" (n.p.: n.p., n.d.), 10–11. Brennen was the Simpsons' granddaughter.

6. Simpson, *The Gospel of Healing,* 136–37.

7. Ibid., 135.

8. Thompson, *A. B. Simpson,* 79.

9. *Word, Work, and World* 3 (1883), 37.

10. Bedford, "'A Larger Christian Life,'" 271–72.

11. Thompson, *A. B. Simpson,* 140.

12. Robert L. Niklaus, John S. Sawin, and Samuel J. Stoesz, eds., *All for Jesus: God at Work in The Christian and Missionary Alliance over One Hundred Years* (Camp Hill, Pa.: Christian Publications, 1986), 74.

13. Carrie Judd Montgomery, *"Under His Wings": The Story of My Life* (Oakland, Calif.: Office of Triumphs of Faith, 1936), 98–99, 143. She was present in Old Orchard when he first called together friends and asked them to pray about founding the Christian Alliance. She became its first recording secretary (100).

14. Bedford, " 'A Larger Christian Life,' " 273, notes lengthy reports on healing in particular at meetings in Toronto (1891), Old Orchard (1891, 1894, 1899, 1903, 1904, 1906), New York City (1891, 1906), Kansas City (1895), Los Angeles (1895), Ohio (1906), Colorado (1906), and on the Pacific Coast (1906).

15. Charles W. Nienkirchen, *A. B. Simpson and the Pentecostal Movement: A Study in Continuity, Crisis, and Change* (Peabody, Mass.: Hendrickson, 1992), 122. See Salmon's "Testimony" in *Christian and Missionary Alliance Weekly* 24 (March 24, 1900), 185. See also Niklaus, Sawin, and Stoese, *All for Jesus*, 63–64.

16. Montgomery, *"Under His Wings,"* 127–29, 132, 142, 143, 146.

17. Charles Ewing Brown, *When the Trumpet Sounded: A History of the Church of God Reformation Movement* (Anderson, Ind.: Warner Press, 1951), 74–75, 105, 111.

18. Mary Cole, *Trials and Triumphs of Faith* (Anderson, Ind.: Gospel Trumpet, 1914), 66, 71–75; Brown, *When the Trumpet Sounded*, 140–41.

19. Brown, *When the Trumpet Sounded*, 153–55.

20. Bedford, " 'A Larger Christian Life,' " 147.

21. David Douglas Daniels III, "The Cultural Renewal of Slave Religion: Charles Price Jones and the Emergence of the Holiness Movement in Mississippi" (Ph.D. diss., Union Theological Seminary, 1992), 4.

22. Otho B. Cobbins, ed., *History of Church of Christ (Holiness) U.S.A., 1895–1965* (New York: Vantage, 1966), 21–23; Daniels, "The Cultural Renewal of Slave Religion," 28–30.

23. Daniels, "The Cultural Renewal of Slave Religion," 248–49.

24. Ibid., 34, 52–53, 36, 46–47, 55.

25. Patrick M. Thompson, *The History of Negro Baptists in Mississippi* (Jackson, Miss.: R. W. Bailey Printing Co., 1898), 35.

26. Daniels, "The Cultural Renewal of Slave Religion," 196.

27. Amanda Berry Smith, *An Autobiography: The Story of The Lord's Dealings with Mrs. Amanda Smith the Colored Evangelist* (Chicago: Meyer & Brother, 1893). For a critical biography see Adrienne M. Israel, *Amanda Berry Smith: From Washerwoman to Evangelist*, Studies in Evangelicalism 16 (Lanham, Md.; Scarecrow, 1998).

28. Daniels, "The Cultural Renewal of Slave Religion," 92–93.

29. William Clair Turner Jr., "The United Holy Church of America: A Study in Black Holiness-Pentecostalism" (Ph.D. diss., Duke University, 1984), 41–43, 50, 68, 115, 138. See also Chester W. Gregory, *The History of the United Holy Church of America, Inc., 1886–1986* (Baltimore: Gateway Press, 1986).

30. Joanna Patterson Moore, *"In Christ's Stead": Autobiographical Sketches* (Chicago: Women's Baptist Home Mission Society, 1902), 229–30.

31. Briane K. Turley, *A Wheel Within a Wheel: Southern Methodism and the Georgia Holiness Association* (Macon, Ga.: Mercer University Press, 1999), 104–5, 130.

32. Mrs. J. William Garbutt, comp., *Rev. W. A. Dodge As We Knew Him* (Atlanta: The Franklin Printing and Publishing Company, 1906), 76.

33. Gordon Lindsay, *The Life of John Alexander Dowie* (Dallas: The Voice of Healing Publishing, 1951), 115–16.

34. Ibid., 161–62.

35. Ibid., 140–43.

36. Ibid., 137–40.

37. Ibid., 189.

38. Ibid., 239, 255.

39. Kenneth O. Brown, *Inskip, McDonald, Fowler: "Wholly and Forever Thine." Early Leadership in the National Camp Meeting Association for the Promotion of Holiness* (Hazelton, Pa.: Holiness Archives, 1999), 225, 228.

40. Ibid., 109–10, 250–51.

# 5

# Healing Homes

After her healing Carrie Judd vowed to God that she would testify to her healing whenever and wherever there was an opening. As her story appeared in papers across the United States and in England, the letters began to pour into her Buffalo home—letters from those who had also been healed and letters from those who needed to be. Members of her family helped her answer the inquiries. With her mother's urging she wrote *The Prayer of Faith*, the first book in the United States to contain a biblical defense of the doctrine of faith healing rather than just testimonies to it. With Elizabeth Baxter's help, the little book was published across the Continent. More letters poured in. Judd began publishing a periodical titled *Triumphs of Faith*.

This normally shy and reserved Episcopalian attended a gathering of Holiness people in the Asbury Methodist Church parlor in Buffalo and decided to host Thursday afternoon faith meetings in her home. During her illness, the family had avoided using the parlor under her bedroom to give her peace and quiet. Now they dedicated the unused room as Faith Sanctuary.[1]

As these meetings continued and healings occurred in them, more visitors came and others wrote to ask, "May I come to you for a little time, and see this life of faith lived out?" Initially the Judd family welcomed such visitors and gave them the use of Carrie's old sickroom. As more requests came, a small but cozy room on the third floor was set aside and christened the Prophet's Room after the one offered to Elisha in 2 Kings 4:10. Finally the requests were too much even for the commodious Judd home and its generous family, so they rented another house in the neighborhood, furnished it, and called it Faith Rest Cottage.[2] It opened April 6, 1882, as a guest house for those who came from out of town to attend the faith meetings and seek healing. The rent was paid out of thank offerings left by visitors and with contributions sent by readers of *Triumphs of Faith*. For example, once when the rent was due and Carrie had no funds, a letter containing $50 arrived from a woman in Georgia. The woman had never given before and did not do so afterward, but her one-time gift paid the rent.

Carrie and her family maintained Faith Rest Cottage for the next decade, closing it in 1892 only after she had married and moved to the West Coast. There she built a three-story healing home called Home of Peace in 1893. It was in Beulah Heights, the community she and George Montgomery established on a tract of land he owned five miles from downtown Oakland. They engaged the Reverend and Mrs. J. P. Ludlow, retired missionaries from Japan, to supervise it. The Montgomerys held a healing meeting every Monday for more than twenty-five years. About 2 P.M. the staff met to pray for healing requests that had come by mail. At 2:30 a public meeting was held. Scriptures were read, and those who wished received prayer and the laying on of hands. In *Triumphs of Faith* during the 1890s Montgomery publicized numerous faith homes across the United States and in Europe.[3]

Healing homes were an aspect of the movement that has received little study. Virtually all the leaders of the movement opened such homes and encouraged others to do so as well. Some, such as Judd's Faith Rest Cottage, A. B. Simpson's Berachah, Mrs. Baxter's Bethshan, and Alexander Dowie's healing homes in Chicago were well-known and oft-visited by those who wrote for religious periodicals.

Many were established by single women such as Mary Shoemaker (c. 1846–1916) in Springfield, Massachusetts, who got little notice, even though she was "well known for her benevolent work," according to her obituary. Apparently at least an acquaintance of Ethan Otis Allen, she built an addition onto her home, which she dedicated to religious service, calling it Shiloh Chapel. City directories from 1897 onward referred to it as a faith home. At her death, her $90,000 estate was divided among several religious institutions, including several Presbyterian agencies. The house she left to the Christian and Missionary Alliance.

Ethan Allen also encouraged Miss Sara M. C. Musgrove (1839–1933) to found her Fourfold Gospel Mission in Troy, New York. Healed under Allen's ministry, she, too, became active in the Christian and Missionary Alliance. She pastored this mission and healing home for forty-one years.[4]

Charles Cullis, of course, began in 1864 by establishing a home for Indigent and Incurable Consumptives long before he believed in divine healing. As he explored the doctrine, he realized that he was following in the tradition of Dorothea Trudel and Johann Cristoph Blumhardt. He consciously followed the model of George Müller's orphanage. His own ministry expanded in several ways, including homes for others with specific conditions, orphanages for those children left behind, housing for staff, a publishing house, and Beacon Hill Chapel in which to hold religious services, including a Tuesday 11 A.M. healing service. On May 23, 1882, he opened a building specifically called House of Healing and dedicated to this work.[5]

Estimates vary on how many such homes there were around this country and the world. R. Kelso Carter said there were at least thirty in the United States and many in Europe when he wrote in 1887.[6] Elizabeth Baxter in the record of the 1885 International Conference on Divine Healing and True Holiness listed a number in various countries.[7] Some homes operated for only a few years; some operated over longer periods; and some, such as Elizabeth V. Baker's Elim in Rochester, New York, evolved into all sorts of related enterprises. In trying to compile a list in my research, I also found it difficult to document exactly which homes were operated in connection with healing. Those in the Holiness movement used the term "faith home" to refer to institutions that met all sorts of needs.

They were called faith homes because the proprietors had faith that God would supply all their expenses, as God had done for George Müller's orphanage in Bristol, England. Even those begun to accommodate seekers of healing often became temporary retreats for burned-out Christian workers. Carrie Judd Montgomery was not the only one to open a home that welcomed foreign missionaries returning home on leave. Joanna Patterson Moore toward the end of her life opened several homes in Louisiana to care for elderly black women—precursors to today's nursing homes.[8] Mother Lee's mission was to build homes for "wayward girls" in an age when a young woman who had sexual relations outside of marriage was expelled from her family and her community and often came to the big city with prostitution as her only employment opportunity.[9] So "faith home" can refer to a variety of ministries.

## Hospitals

One should also remember that in this era hospitals were closer to charity institutions than medical establishments. A government survey in 1872 found only 178 in the whole country; there were more asylums for the insane.[10] Only the truly isolated went there—seamen away from home, soldiers, travelers, accident victims, the homeless, the desperately ill urban indigent, and often the insane. There were open wards where disease was more often spread than contained. (A 2002 study found that infections picked up in hospitals are still the fourth leading cause of death in the United States.[11]) The medical equipment and advanced technology we take for granted had not yet been dreamed of. Indeed before the 1880s medical practice and hospitals had little to do with each other. The majority of doctors never set foot inside one. The vast majority of sick people were cared for at home by family or hired help.

The first three nurses' training programs began in 1873—at Bellevue in New York City, Massachusetts General in Boston, and Connecticut Hospital in New Haven. It was not until the 1890s, when work shifted away from the home and families became smaller and less able to care for the sick, that hospitals began to be built. By 1910 there were four thousand; by 1920, six thousand.[12] Hotels were just starting to be built in the major cities. But there was a longer tradition of people traveling to health spas for the water cure, mineral baths, the ideal Graham diet, and so on. A visit to a healing home fit into this earlier pattern.

## Mary Mossman

Mary H. Mossman (c. 1826–after 1909) opened her healing home in June 1881 in Ocean Grove, New Jersey, one of the favorite summer haunts of New York Holiness advocates. An "Evangelical" church member (probably a member of the Evangelical church that united with the Brethren to become the Evangelical United Brethren), she had felt for some time that in her life, "the claims of God were not met." Sharing her questions with pastors garnered no satisfactory answers. When her mother, whom she had nursed, passed on, she felt that the only useful thing she had been doing in life had come to an end. She began reading: Hermann Francke, François Fénelon, Madame Guyon, Thomas Upham, Asa Mahan, Charles Grandison Finney, Augustine, and Hannah Whitall Smith.

In the spring of 1868, Mossman began to go from place to place giving Bible readings, taking a biblical passage and commenting on it verse by verse, an acceptable female alternative to preaching. She renounced tea and coffee as well as other stimulants. She adopted a simple style of dress as "a quiet and delightful testimony to the half-consecrated that I had left their ranks" (Amanda Smith and other Holiness women speakers often adopted a form of Quaker dress, which Hannah Whitall Smith always retained). Mossman's biggest struggle was giving up feathered hats.[13]

Finally in 1872, Mossman and a friend felt powerfully led to attend a Holiness convention in New York State. Although she got food poisoning and had an awful week there, eventually she entered into entire consecration and adopted an even more rigorous lifestyle. But after five months, God said, "Enough!" and she relaxed a bit. She became acquainted with the work of Charles Cullis and A. B. Simpson.

As a young woman, Mossman said, she was "very feeble, oftentimes confined to my room and bed." Elsewhere she said she "had always been considered frail and had much to do with physicians." In 1859 she was seriously ill. Studying her Bible, she came to James 5:15, "The prayer of faith shall save the sick." She responded, "Yes, Jesus; Jesus is enough," and turned her body over to God. "Soon after, a simple remedy was suggested to me by the still small voice. I had never heard of it before, but accepting it, at once felt the power of disease was broken, and from that hour began to mend. From that time Jesus only has been my physician." On another occasion she had hemorrhaging in the lungs and was coughing up blood. God asked if she were willing to follow where God led, and she con-sented. Then one day in March, God told her to dress and go out into the winds to see a friend. Reluctantly she walked to the friend's house, laid down for an hour, and walked back. The next day, the weather being even more inclement, she received the same instructions. She walked to the friend's house, sat and talked, walked back, and realized she still had enough energy to read and sew. She was healed. [14]

Yet another time, in the spring, a growth, an "excrescence," appeared on her finger, diagnosed as cancer. Friends urged her to get it removed, but she replied that her finger and its growth were God's. Then God directed her to rent a tent for the season at a campground where her testimony about healing had previously been rejected, promising her, "I am with you in blessing. I am with you in heal-ing." Forgetting her finger, Mossman assumed it meant that God would give her strength or clear her lungs. So she went. And the first day, when she washed her hands, the finger was fine. And then she found out why she was really sent to Ocean Grove that year: to meet the Reverend Smith H. Platt.[15]

## Smith H. Platt

Platt, a Methodist minister, published his testimony in 1875 and titled it *My Twenty-fifth Year Jubilee; or Cure by Faith after Twenty-five Years of Lameness*. Platt was then pastor of DeKalb Avenue Methodist Episcopal Church in Brooklyn. Platt's troubles began in March 1850, shortly before he took his first pastorate. A horse kicked him in the left knee. Floating cartilage and chronic inflammation compelled him to walk with a crutch and cane for the next five years. He was able to dispense with the crutch but still could not stand or kneel or walk any distance for the next six years because of the knee's tendency to swell and cause great pain. In the winter of 1866 he fell on the same knee, reinjuring it. In July 1872, walking in the dark, he struck his right knee against the sharp corner of a wooden box and ruptured a ligament. Then he could move about only very painfully with two canes. He had never been able to preach standing up. In the winter of 1874 he de-veloped sciatic pain as well.[16]

Platt had long believed in miraculous healing, having published "The Gift of Power" in 1856, but he had not claimed it for himself. In December 1872 he even visited Dr. Cullis in Boston. Cullis recounted a number of miraculous stories and finally asked if Platt had faith to be healed. Platt stammered something about not wanting to presume on the will of God. Cullis challenged him to put himself en-tirely in God's hands and then offered a short prayer, "during which a singular sensation, something like the thrills from an electro-galvanic battery, passed *downward*, with a diffusing kind of motion, through both knees." When they arose, Platt stood firmly, walked easily down a flight of stairs, and returned to his hotel without using his cane. But the next day the pain and swelling returned, and he concluded that the Lord had healed him to honor Cullis's faith but that it was not God's will for him to remain well.

In July 1875 Platt went to Ocean Grove for a vacation. Sunday, July 18, his knees were worse than usual, and he could not even drag himself over to the nearby tabernacle for services. So he took up some reading, including a tract titled "Were They Miracles?" which contained stories of healing. The first had been sent to the *Advance* by Oberlin College president Finney. It concerned Mrs. Jane C. Miller, wife of a Congregational minister, who had suffered for forty years from chronic rheumatism. After her prayer circle read the story of Dorothea Trudel, they prayed for her, and suddenly she was able to walk without assistance and had "more than my youthful vigor." The next story was about an eight-year-old girl lame with sciatic rheumatism. Her siblings, after reading a story about a healing in a church paper, challenged their mother to pray with them for their older sister. And she was healed. The third was of a woman who had been an invalid for many years. At fifteen she had fallen and hurt her left knee. Six years later she reinjured it; then due to the weakness in her knees, she fell on an icy walk and broke her tailbone. Several years later she fell down a stairs. By 1873 she was almost suicidal, but one night the thought came to her, "Why not cast it all on Jesus?" And then God led her through a series of surrenders. Finally, God asked, "Would you be willing to be raised up and work for the Lord?" She replied, "Thy will be done." God's presence filled the room; she sprang from the bed and walked across the room, pain-free.[17]

On Wednesday night Platt heard black Holiness evangelist Amanda Smith preach in the tabernacle on "what things soever ye desire, when ye pray, believe that ye receive them, and ye shall have them" (Mark 11:24). Platt was beginning to get the message. The next Sunday, July 25, he preached in the tabernacle on "[Who] giveth us the victory through our Lord Jesus Christ" (1 Corinthians 15:57). About 6 P.M. that evening two ladies whom Platt had never met appeared at his door. They introduced themselves as Miss Mossman and Mrs. Beach and announced that the Lord had sent them.

Even before taking a seat, Mossman declared, "You may think it very singular, but the Lord has sent me here to tell you that you may be cured of your lameness if you will only believe." He waffled. He recounted his struggle and his excuses. She told him another story about a woman whose broken ankle was healed by prayer. He double-checked to see if she really felt she was sent to him by God. Finally he let her pray. "And kneeling, she rested one hand upon each knee, just as she would upon a chair, with no pressure and no motion of any kind, and in a short prayer of not even two minutes, she asked 'For the healing of these knees.'"[18]

Platt did not set much store by the laying on of hands, and later wrote,

> I was conscious of no change whatever, either mental, spiritual or physical, until
> about a minute after she had resumed her seat, when a sensation, unlike anything
> ever before or since experienced by me, began about four inches below each knee and
> slowly swept upward with a sort of enveloping, condensing and toning-up feeling,
> seeming to permeate every fibre of tissue about the joints, and then faded out at
> about the same distance above the knees. I mentioned this sensation.

"Oh, yes, you are cured," was her confident reply, "Only hold on and don't lose it."[19]

Each person in the movement had a personal style. Mary Mossman seems to
have had a very clear sense of God's voice directing her. In her autobiography,
*Steppings in God; or the Hidden Life Made Manifest,* she recounts other similar
stories of her activities. It became clear to her that she was to share her spiritual
life with others and that she was to do that through a home. "When and where
this home was to be I knew not. I owned a small vacant lot at a sea-side watering-
place [Ocean Grove], but there were apparently insurmountable obstacles to going
there, and I could only wait the will of God." Several years later she was at Ocean
Grove, staying with friends, and the woman of the house was healed through her
prayers. They urged her to build a house; God gave her a picture of it, and she
drew it for the builders. She built until her money ran out, then quit. But news
had gotten around, and gifts poured in. The house was finished and furnished.
"In June 1881, with rooms well filled and appropriate services, the house was formally dedicated to God."[20]

And its influence radiated outward. A report in Simpson's *Word, Work and
World* noted that the Reverend T. C. Easton, pastor of First Reformed Church in
New Brunswick, New Jersey, suffered severe pain for thirty-six years after he injured his right foot as a boy in Scotland. Both Scottish and American doctors said
the foot should be amputated. In 1876 he met Platt. He visited Simpson's Tabernacle. In 1883 he went to Ocean Grove and the home on Embury Avenue for a
Bible study given by Mossman. There he made a full surrender of himself on August 23, 1883. The pain departed.[21]

Mossman had a decidedly mystical bent. She described the work of her home:

> This work touches soul, body and spirit. . . . Souls have been saved, wanderers re-
> claimed, and many, very many have entered into spiritual liberty. Many Christian
> workers have gone forth better fitted for the work before them. Physical healing is
> claimed and sought as one of the benefits of the atonement. Yet the especial teaching
> of the house is union with God.[22]

She gave some insight into the workings of the house:

> The Lord alone determines who is to be received as guests. Requests for admission
> are laid before Him, and if it is shown that it is His order to receive them, they are
> welcomed and cared for as His guests. A board bill is never presented; each one is free

to give to, or withold from giving to, the work as the Lord may direct. God has markedly protected us from imposters. . . . The work has been well sustained.[23]

## Bethshan

One of the most famous healing homes was Bethshan, a faith home in London associated on this side of the Atlantic with William and Mary Boardman and on the other side of the Atlantic with Elizabeth Baxter, Charlotte Murray, and Elizabeth Sisson (1843–1934), an American from Connecticut who arrived in London via time as a Congregational missionary in India. Sisson had received sanctification under Boardman's preaching, so when she became very ill in India, she came to London to find healing. The home's work was publicized in its magazine *Thy Healer,* giving testimonies of those healed and reprinting talks given by the Boardmans, Murray, and Baxter. Baxter said that Murray purchased the house at 10 Drayton Park, Hollaway Road, Highbury, London. It opened in 1882. Later the original house was renovated and then a new hall built. Baxter outlined its mission:

> to afford facilities for those who have been led of God to seek the Lord as their Healer in spirit, soul and body, that they, remaining for a short time, may attend the Meetings of Holiness and Healing, and withdrawn from their ordinary surroundings, may have time and opportunity for communion with God. . . . Bethshan is no hospital, but rather a nursery for faith.[24]

Within the house, seven meetings a week were held. Baxter conducted a Bible class every Sunday afternoon as well as meetings on Wednesdays for testimonies to healing, followed by a time of anointing. Conferences and special meetings were also held there. Although her biographer declared that "Mrs. Baxter was the centre of everything,"[25] the Boardmans were very involved until William's death in January 1886 and Mary's in 1904.

In 1886 the group purchased the house next to Bethshan and founded another home, this one a Training Home for Missionaries. It was not to be a college, but it did offer a course of study steeped in the Bible. Courses included "Bible History, Bible Interpretation and Illustration, Bible Doctrines, Church History, Missionary History, Heathen Religions, Geography (especially Mission Geography), Arithmatic, Grammar, Elocution, Languages (when required), Music (vocal and instrumental)." Students conducted "open-air preaching, house-to-house visitation, visiting in hospitals, lodging-houses, etc." and also learned such practical skills as "housework, baking, cooking as well as soldering, tailoring, boot-making, carpentering, dressmaking, etc."[26]

One of the most influential guests of Bethshan was Capetown, South Africa, Dutch Reformed pastor and writer Andrew Murray (1828–1917), a popular

Keswick speaker. He came with a throat disorder that threatened to end his preaching career. He emerged after three weeks, healed. He continued to preach almost to his dying day at age eighty-eight. His book *Divine Healing* (1900) was very much influenced by William Boardman. He said,

> When I arrived [at Bethshan] my mind was chiefly set on the healing; faith was a secondary consideration, which was to be employed simply as a means of healing. But I soon discovered that God's first purpose was to develop faith and that healing was a secondary question. God's purpose with us, as with Abraham, is, first of all, to make us true believers. Disease and cure, to His mind, derive their importance from the fact that they can awaken in us a stronger faith.

He quoted Boardman as saying that faith healing "has a much higher aim than the mere deliverance of the body from certain maladies; it points out the road of holiness and full consecration which God would have us follow."[27]

## Berachah

The practice of opening healing homes received a major impetus when on Wednesday, May 16, 1883, a group gathered at A. B. Simpson's home at 331 West 34th Street in New York City to dedicate it as a Home for Faith and Physical Healing. In his initial announcement of the opening, Simpson wrote: "Any sufferer who is really willing to exercise *and act* faith for healing will be received for a limited time for instruction and mutual waiting upon God for temporal and spiritual healing." Services were to be held daily from noon until 1 P.M. and from 5 to 6 P.M., plus every Wednesday at 8 P.M.[28] For the general public, healing services were held at Simpson's Tabernacle every Friday.

A year later E. G. Selchow (d. 1915; yes, Trivial Pursuit and Scrabble fans, he was the founder of Selchow and Righter), who had been miraculously healed under Simpson's ministry, donated a building at 328 West 23d Street, which was formally dedicated on May 5, 1884, as Berachah Home, "the House of Blessing." Over the next two and a half years, approximately seven hundred guests stayed in the home. The home later moved to 61st Street and Park Avenue, and then in March 1890 to a six-story building at 258–260 West 44th Street, adjoining Simpson's Gospel Tabernacle. This facility, which could accommodate a hundred guests at a time, was often full and overflowing. In 1897 the facility moved finally to a house on the hillside in Nyack, New York, on the campus of the C&MA Bible institute.

Berachah was initially led by Ellen A. Griffin and Sarah A. Lindenberger. Griffin, active in city missions, had been healed. After Griffin's death in 1887, Lindenberger, a member of a wealthy Louisville family, carried on the work until the home finally closed around 1917 and the building became a college dormitory.[29]

Berachah operated in conjunction with Simpson's famous Friday meetings for healing. The meetings were usually led by a minister—Simpson, Cookman, Henry Wilson, Kenneth Mackenzie—but a number of women also participated, including Mrs. Simpson's sister Mrs. E. J. McDonald, Margaret B. Home, Minnie T. Draper (1858–1921), Emma M. Whittemore, and many others. Whittemore, for example, had been healed of a serious spinal injury under Simpson's ministry in 1884. She later gained fame for her Door of Hope homes for reforming prostitutes.[30] Medical doctors also took part.

Simpson's example encouraged other Alliance people to open homes across the country. For example, Frederic H. Senft, a future president of the C&MA, with his wife operated the Hebron Home in Philadelphia.[31] Other homes included the Bethany Home in Toronto, operated by the Reverend John Salmon and Mrs. Fletcher; Sara M. C. Musgrove's home in Troy, New York; Mrs. J. P. Kellogg's in Utica, New York; Dora Dudley's in Grand Rapids, Michigan; Mrs. S. G. Beck's Kemuel House in Philadelphia; and a home in Pittsburgh, led by the Reverend E. D. Whiteside and William Henry Conley.[32] Other homes affiliated with the Alliance were located in Atlanta, Chicago, Cleveland, Los Angeles, and Santa Barbara.[33] Around 1900, David Wesley Myland operated a healing home in Cleveland for about three years. called El-Shaddai and affiliated with his C&MA church. Later, as a Pentecostal, he operated a home by the same name around 1932 in Van Wert, Ohio.[34]

Visitors to the homes received biblical and theological instruction about divine healing. They were encouraged to read testimonies and other devotional literature. They were prayed for and with. They were anointed with oil and received the laying on of hands. But increasingly the homes also functioned as places where stressed-out Christian workers could rest and recuperate. By World War I most homes were closed, in part because the generation that established them was passing away.

## Beulah

Dora Griffin Dudley learned about healing in the way so many did, through a friend who told her about Carrie Judd's healing, her home, and her meetings and gave her a copy of Judd's *Prayer of Faith.* Dora's mother had died of "scrofulous consumption" (tuberculosis of the lymph nodes in the throat) when Dora was an infant, and from earliest childhood Dora seemed to be filled with disease. Every two to three weeks as a young adult she would suffer an asthma attack. The least ray of light would give her a migraine, and eventually she began to lose her sight. Initially she laid aside Judd's book because her eyes were too bad to read. She was confined to her bed in a dark room. But she did begin to seek healing by giving up all medications and trying to surrender her heart to God. She thought about going to see Miss Judd or Dr. Cullis, but decided that since God was everywhere, she did not need to make a trip. She did write to request prayer from Cullis and Captain Carter (R. Kelso Carter, who wrote on the subject). She asked her Congregational pastor to pray for her, but he knew little of faith healing. She said, "I took the ground that I was healed by faith, and I was; but some days I seemed and felt worse, even for months after. But I held firmly to the promises, repeating them often to myself."[35]

For nearly eighteen years Dudley had been unable to go out into the light without dark glasses, but she felt called by Christ to lay them aside. So she went out without them. It was painful at first, but that got better. Then one day, out of habit, she put them on again and went out. This time she developed such a headache that she had to return home immediately. Another time camping with friends by a river, everyone put on sunglasses. Again an immediate headache reminded her of her promise, and she removed them and felt better. After that, "I have never used them since." Interestingly, Dudley experienced what she described as a healing rest. After some exertion, she would lie down, pray, and immediately go into a deep sleep "unlike my other sleep" and that felt like "a thrill passing through my whole being." Her eyes would grow heavy and impossible to hold open. After a short nap, she would awake, totally refreshed.[36]

Dudley dated her healing as July 16, 1885, but the next winter she was "tested most of the time with a cough and severe hoarseness." Still she kept up a steady stream of meetings, four to six a week, talking constantly about her new life of faith.

As word of her experience of healing and her work with others spread, she, like Judd, received letters from people who wished to come and stay a few days. She had no place for them but began to pray about it. She consulted Scripture by opening the Bible at random, and the messages were encouraging. The Lord gave her a name for it: Beulah (from Isaiah 62:4). She made inquiries around town and found a house at 85 Baxter Street. She bought it on faith for $2,750 at 7 percent; payments were $15 a month. She moved in on January 13, 1887. The dedication took place February 10, 1887. Carrie Judd was the speaker and guest of honor.[37]

Dudley advertised Beulah Home as follows:

Faith prayer meetings and Bible readings are held at "Beulah" every Thursday at 2:30 p.m. Requests can be sent at any time and will be presented for prayer at once; also at the first meeting after receipt. In correspondence, please enclose stamps. All letters will be answered as soon as possible.

"Beulah" is a quiet home, with "Jesus in the midst," where the weary, sick, tired, unsaved ones may come for a time and learn more perfectly the way of faith.

Guests will please communicate with me before coming and state whether they are able to wait upon themselves. If they are not, it will be necessary for them to bring an attendant.

Those who may desire me to go out of town to hold meetings or visit the sick, will please send money for expenses.[38]

The mention of stamps and expense money are the pleas of a woman who lived by faith rather close to the edge. Dora had previously made her living by selling hair products and cosmetics. She continued to do so for a while, but then one day she was counseling a woman who had kept a house of ill repute for twenty years and had now become a Christian. Dudley's first advice to her was to wash off her makeup. Then Dora came home to find a sizable order for her face preparations. She could have sold her supply and then gotten out of the business. And she did have debts. But instead, she wrote a letter declining to fill the order and giving her reasons. Holiness women did not cut or curl their hair. Nor did they use cosmetics to enhance their inner beauty. From that day on, people began to give her money to support her ministry.[39]

Dudley's ministry included prayer meetings, Bible readings, visits to the sick in their homes, consultation with people from out of town, and correspondence. It was not uncommon for her to be called to sit all night at the bedside of a sick person. Dudley is the only person I have read who spoke of asking God for "the gifts of faith, healing, and miracles." She said that later she realized that healing and miracles are two different gifts, but she did not elaborate. And she had a distinct sense that God answered her prayers, even before she was sure that she herself had been healed entirely. The confirmation of her gifts and her healing was that about a month after her consecration and healing in July 1885, she felt led to visit an elderly woman with a broken arm, Mrs. J. A. Shepley. Since Dudley had no nickel for carfare, she walked the ten blocks and up some stairs. The woman had fallen down the stairs and broken her wrist. Improperly set and put in a cast by a doctor, it had become infected and the flesh had rotted away, leaving two deep cavities at wrist and elbow. Dudley read to her Judd's testimony from *Prayer of Faith* and Psalm 103. Then she prayed, after which the woman took her arm out of its sling, took off the bandages, and declared her headache gone as well. The next day Mrs. Shepley did her laundry and went to a religious meeting.[40]

## Alexander Dowie's Healing Homes

Dowie opened Healing Home #1 in Chicago in 1894. He operated several healing homes in Chicago before moving to Zion City. His homes served those attracted to his ministry through the meetings in his tabernacle near the World's Fair and those who read of his work in *Leaves of Healing*. They served as boarding houses where people could find food and lodging at a nominal charge, receive spiritual encouragement, and be conveniently located near his religious services.

Of all the homes, Dowie's seem to have met the most opposition from local authorities. The *Chicago Dispatch* headlined a story about one home "Dr. Dowie's Lunatic Asylum." Apparently neighbors were disturbed by the emotionalism of the services. Dowie was charged numerous times with practicing medicine without a license. He replied that "no medical treatment of any kind was offered." The city tried to pass a Hospital Ordinance and apply it to his homes. He acknowledged that "services of praise and prayer and teaching of the word of God are held at least twice daily in the large assembly rooms when I gather the guests of three homes and pray with them in accordance with the directions of our Lord Jesus Christ in St. Mark." But, he declared, "nothing more is done in these Houses than may be done by every Christian minister in the homes of his people, or even by Christian people in their own homes without the presence of a minister." He argued that his homes could not be classified as hospitals because "divine healing has no association with doctors and drugs, or surgeons and their knives."[41] The Hospital Ordinance was eventually declared unconstitutional.

## Elim

Another well-known healing home was that of Elizabeth V. Baker (c. 1849–1915). She opened Elim Faith Home on April 1, 1895, in Rochester, New York. Elizabeth was the eldest daughter of Methodist minister James Duncan. Her sisters joined her in the ministry: Mary E. Work, Nellie A. Fell, Susan A. Duncan, and Harriet "Hattie" M. Duncan. The healing home came first, followed by Elim Publishing House, Elim Tabernacle, and then Rochester Bible Training School.

To escape an unhappy home, she married W. A. Dawson at age twenty, but she soon divorced him because he was abusive.[42] She came to full consecration and sanctification after attending a temperance meeting. In 1881 she heard an evangelist talk about being healed, and the idea intrigued her. As she prayed about it, she felt Jesus' presence enter the room. Christ asked, "Will you trust me as your Physician for the rest of your life?" She was "half invalid" at the time with no energy, so she replied, "Lord, if You will show me how to trust, I will." Again came a question, "Will you trust me for every dollar and cent that you will need for the rest of your life?" She had just read George Müller's *Life of Trust,* so she understood the question and replied, "O! I cannot do it" but finally agreed. Then Jesus asked, "Will you go into pulpits and preach for Me?" Since she had "a great aversion to women in the pulpit," she replied, "O, I cannot, I cannot" but finally "I am willing to be brought." A year or so later a very severe throat condition threatened her health. Her second husband, C. W. Baker, the son of a Methodist minister, was a physician. He consulted with specialists, who offered her no hope. But after being anointed by C. W. Winchester, pastor of Asbury Methodist Church, she could swallow immediately.[43]

As Baker began to speak of her experience and her convictions, the sick began to come to her for prayer, and many were healed. But that caused trouble: "My husband objected to my praying with the sick, I think his professional pride was hurt. While he knew I had been perfectly healed and was a well woman, yet he wanted it to end there." Her husband also objected to her leading public meetings: "The dear man got directly in God's way for me and God had to take the matter in hand Himself." Her husband got tuberculosis and could not practice, so he decided to become a traveling drug representative. Eventually he took up medical practice again in Chicago, but she stayed in Rochester.[44]

In late 1894 Baker felt called to open a mission, so she did. She assumed the emphasis would be a message of salvation, but the first night her sister Hattie was severely burned and then healed, so she testified to that. The meetings were so successful they soon had to rent larger space. They took up no collections but had offering boxes near the door. Healings continued, and on April 1, 1895, she felt led to open Elim Faith Home. Eventually she stepped out in faith and purchased a $35,000 building. Hebron Home was housed in three floors above the mission, serving as a dormitory for homeless and derelict men. One winter from November to April the staff served approximately 5,500 free Sunday breakfasts to unemployed men and provided about 1,500 overnight lodgings for them. After Elizabeth traveled to India in 1898 (stopping at Bethshan to visit Elizabeth Baxter along the way), Elim became a resting place for visiting missionaries as well. In 1902 the sisters launched the paper *Trust*, devoted to "themes of interest to all earnest Christians, namely; Salvation, the Holy Spirit, Divine Healing, the Premillennial Coming of our Lord, and Foreign Missions."[45] Rochester Bible Training School opened in October 1906.

Initially Elim held two conventions each year, in June and August; eventually they added a week in January "for the deepening of spiritual life." According to Baker,

> On each of these occasions many of the sick are healed, weak Christians strengthened, the strong encouraged by a larger outlook on truth, while many for the first time enter a truly consecrated life. The themes presented are: the Premillennial Coming of our Lord; Consecration, leading to a life in the Holy Spirit; healing for the body through the atonement of Christ (not Christian Science, so called), and Foreign Mission work.[46]

The faith healing homes described here are only the tip of the iceberg. Some operated for a year or so, some for much longer. They filled an important role in furthering the movement, and they provided opportunities for ministry to many obviously talented and faith-filled women.

# Notes

1. Carrie Judd Montgomery, *"Under His Wings": The Story of My Life* (Oakland, Calif.: Office of Triumphs of Faith, 1936), 68, 78.

2. Ibid., 83–84.

3. Ibid., 136, 149–50, 198–99. See also Daniel F. Albrecht, "Carrie Judd Montgomery: Pioneering Contributor to Three Religious Movements," *Pneuma* 8 (fall 1986), 105–9, 114.

4. Paul G. Chappell, "The Divine Healing Movement in America" (Ph.D. diss., Drew University, 1983), 99.

5. W. H. Daniels, ed., *"Have Faith in God": Dr. Cullis and His Work, Twenty Years of Blessing in Answer to Prayer* (Boston: Willard Tract Repository, 1885), 349–50.

6. R. Kelso Carter, "Divine Healing," *The Century* 34 (March 1887), 780.

7. *Record of the International Conference on Divine Healing and True Holiness* (London: J. Snow & Co., 1885), 56, 155, 158–59.

8. Joanna Patterson Moore, *"In Christ's Stead": Autobiographical Sketches* (Chicago: Women's Baptist Home Mission Society, 1902), 73.

9. Mother [Martha A.] Lee, *Mother Lee's Experience in Fifteen Years' Rescue Work with Thrilling Incidents of Her Life* (Omaha, Neb.: n.p., 1906).

10. Paul Starr, *The Social Transformation of American Medicine* (New York: Basic Books, 1982), 72–73.

11. The study was compiled by investigative reporters at the *Chicago Tribune*. Michael J. Berens (*Chicago Tribune*), "Hospitals Suffer Infection Epidemic," *The Greenville News*, July 21, 2002, 1A, 6A.

12. Starr, *The Social Transformation of American Medicine*, 169, 144, 146, 151, 72–73. The material about nursing programs comes from Ruth Abram, ed., *"Send Us a Lady Physician": Women Doctors in America, 1835–1920* (New York: Norton, 1985), 123.

13. M[ary] M[ossman], *Steppings in God; or The Hidden Life Made Manifest* (6th and rev. ed. with appendix, New York: Eaton & Mains, 1909), 10, 15, 21–51, 94. She originally published her story in a tract titled "Life in God." She then expanded it into a slim volume in 1885, of which this is a further expansion and revision.

14. Ibid., 71, 161, 106–7, 114–16.

15. Ibid., 126–27.

16. S. H. Platt, *My Twenty-fifth Year Jubilee; or, Cure by Faith after Twenty-Five Years of Lameness* (Brooklyn, N.Y.: S. Harrison, 1875), 3–6.

17. Ibid., 13–28.

18. Ibid., 34–38.

19. Ibid., 40.

20. Mossman, *Steppings in God*, 140–42.

21. "Physical Redemption," *Word, Work and World* 3 (September 1883), 131.

22. Mossman, *Steppings in God*, 142–43.

23. Ibid., 143.

24. Nathaniel Wiseman, *Elizabeth Baxter (Wife of Michael Paget Baxter): Saint, Evangelist, Preacher, Teacher, and Expositor* (2d ed.; London: The Christian Herald Company, 1928), 86–87.

25. Ibid., 91.

26. Ibid., 93–94.

27. Quoted in Ibid., 250. See Andrew Murray, *Divine Healing: A Series of Addresses and a Personal Testimony* (New York: Christian Alliance Publishing Co., 1900). My copy belonged to my grandmother.

28. "Pastor's Home for Faith and Physical Healing," *Word, Work and World* 3 (June 1883), 82.

29. A. E. Thompson, *A. B. Simpson: His Life and Work* (Camp Hill, Pa.: Christian Publications, 1960), 141–43. See also William Boyd Bedford Jr., "'A Larger Christian Life': A. B. Simpson and the Early Years of the Christian and Missionary Alliance" (Ph.D. diss., University of Virginia, 1992), 268–70. See Sarah A. Lindenberger, *Streams from the Valley of Berachah* (New York: Christian Alliance Publishing Company, n.d.).

30. Charles W. Nienkirchen, *A. B. Simpson and the Pentecostal Movement: A Study in Continuity, Crisis, and Change* (Peabody, Mass.: Hendrickson, 1992), 38.

31. Bedford, "'A Larger Christian Life,'" 270, 277, based on the denomination's *Annual Report* for 1897–98, 1902, and 1903–1904.

32. The list in this sentence is from Thompson, *A. B. Simpson*, 144.

33. Bedford, "'A Larger Christian Life,'" 270, citing *Annual Report* for 1897–1898, 11; 1902–1903, 61, and 1903–1904, 10.

34. David Wesley Myland, *The Latter Rain Covenant and Pentecostal Power, with Testimony of Healings and Baptism* (2d ed.; Chicago: Evangel Publishing House, 1910), 164; J. Kevin Butcher, "The Holiness and Pentecostal Labors of David Wesley Myland: 1890–1918" (master's thesis, Dallas Theological Seminary, 1983), 60–61, 136, 143.

35. Dora G[riffin] Dudley, *Beulah: or Some of the Fruits of One Consecrated Life* (rev. and enlarged ed.; Grand Rapids, Mich.: published by the author, 1896; originally published 1887 or 1888 as "Two and One-half Years of Consecrated Life"), 17–23; quote, 21. Until about 1887 or so, Dora was Mrs. Griffin, but then John H. Dudley visited Beulah, stayed, made himself useful, and asked her to marry him. They seem to have had great love for each other and ministered well together. But he apparently suffered from grave mental illness. He once left for a week without contacting her. Eventually he lived on the shores of Lake Michigan and she commuted between him and Elim. He died at Beulah around 1896 at age sixty-two. See 118–26.

36. Ibid., 27–28, 26, 29.

37. Ibid., 76–84.

38. Ibid., 90–91.

39. Ibid., 55.

40. Ibid., 36–41.

41. Gordon Lindsay, *The Life of John Alexander Dowie* (Dallas: The Voice of Healing Publishing 1951), 106, 112, 107–8, 121. Lindsay was the editor of *The Voice of Healing*, which publicized and promoted the healing revival chronicled by David Edwin Harrell Jr., in *All Things Are Possible: The Healing and Charismatic Revival in Modern America* (Bloomington: Indiana University Press, 1975). Lindsay's parents were members of the Zion City community.

42. G. B. McGee, "Baker, Elizabeth V., *Dictionary*, 37; Elizabeth V. Baker, and co-workers, *Chronicles of a Faith Life* (1915; repr. New York: Garland 1984), 16. It is surprising how many of the women and men in this study were divorced at some stage in their lives. Maria B. Woodworth-Etter, Aimee Semple McPherson, and J. H. King come to mind.

43. Baker, *Chronicles of a Faith Life*, date from 233; narrative, 20–21; healing, 234, 237–38.

44. Ibid., 26–27, 34–35.

45. Ibid., 118.

46. Ibid., 129–30.

# 6

# No Doctors, No Drugs

One of the more controversial aspects of the divine healing movement in the nineteenth century was its insistence that the sick person discontinue the use of all medications and remedies. Once people had adopted the teaching of healing, they usually declared Jesus Christ as their Physician and saw no need for human doctors. Instead they relied solely on biblical means, as outlined most clearly in James 5: anointing with oil, the laying on of hands, and the prayer of faith.

Several people cite as warrant Karl Andreas's book, *Healing of Sickness by Scriptural Means*,[1] which forbade the use of medicines and physicians. Jesus was enough. For example, Carrie Judd Montgomery boasted that although her husband, George, was suffering in 1914 from double pneumonia and malaria picked up on a trip to Mexico, "we had no physician but the Lord Jesus Christ, for my dear husband had known Him as his Physician for about twenty-five years."[2]

John Alexander Dowie put it most colorfully in the 1890s when he declared a "holy war" against "Doctors, Drugs, and Devils." He said that the most dread disease in the world was "bacillis lunaticus medicus."[3]

However, it is clear in the vast majority of healing testimonies that most of these people had at least initially given the medical professionals of their day ample opportunity to effect a cure or even offer some relief, without success. Some examples from Mrs. Edward Mix's *Faith Cures* should suffice. Vidella V. Cornell of New Haven, Connecticut, reported that she was "under the treatment of a doctor who had been recommended to me by some friends; after taking some of his medicine I grew worse, and I rapidly grew worse the more he tried to relieve me." He came twice a day to make sure she was taking his prescribed medicine: "a teaspoonful of French brandy every half hour with ice." Mary E. Mack of Hinsdale, Massachusetts, consulted the best doctor in Pittsfield. He "used over fifty blisters" to treat her inflamed kidneys, put leeches on her head, and then began to inject morphine into her "limbs . . . five or six times in twenty-four hours. . . . The doctor said it would kill me to leave it off," but she did. Indeed, the longest testimony in Mix's *Faith Cures* is from a physician, Charles Wesley

Buvinger of Pittsburgh, Pennsylvania, who had suffered many years from asthma. He said he tried "every known remedy to effect a cure, but without success."[4]

R. Kelso Carter, in *Divine Healing, or the Atonement for Sin and Sickness* (1888), said "there is not a single command or intimation in the whole Bible which directs the use of medicine." Indeed "the only human physicians mentioned in the Bible, are those who embalmed a dead body [Jacob's in Egypt in Genesis 50:2], those who killed King Asa, those of whom the poor woman suffered many things [Mark 5:26], and Luke, who changed his profession for the ministry."[5] The story of Asa was found in 2 Chronicles 16. By and large a godly king and blessed by God, Asa became "diseased in his feet, until his disease was exceeding great: yet in his disease he sought not to the LORD, but to the physicians" (v. 12) and "Asa slept with his fathers, and died" (v. 13). Carter and others also argued that Moses had been schooled in the advanced medical lore of the Egyptians but rejected it (citing Clement of Alexandria and Herodotus as sources).[6]

Carter also quoted from the physicians of his day on the reliability of their means. According to Philadelphia's famed Benjamin Rush, "We have multiplied disease." Dr. Frank said, "Thousands are slaughtered in the sick room." Dr. Evans of Edinburgh, Scotland, purportedly declared, "The medical practice of the present day is neither philosophical nor common sense."[7]

## Nineteenth-Century Physicians

Yet the words "physician" and "doctor" seem to have carried a certain mystique for some time. People in the nineteenth century—as well as those in the twenty-first—seem to make the assumption that anyone given those titles since Hippocrates (c. 460–c. 377 B.C.E.) and Galen (129–c. 199 C.E.) has had access to the same body of esoteric knowledge. Especially today, in looking back at these believers in divine healing, it is dangerously easy to assume they were rejecting all the childhood vaccines, antibiotics, and diagnostic and surgical technologies that we have access to today. And we are prone to overlook the fact that medicine even today has its share of failures and mysteries.

Nineteenth-century medicine was deeply divided and largely ineffective. Indeed until the late nineteenth century "domestic medicine," centered in the household, was most common.[8] Only in the twentieth century did medicine become a profession, with specialists.

For example, Joanna Patterson Moore, born in 1832 in Pennsylvania, said of her parents, "Father was a kind of a doctor, extracted teeth and gave medicine. Mother was very kind to the sick and poor and knew how to nurse and take care of them."[9] John Wesley's intent in publishing his *Primitive Physik* (London, 1747; Philadelphia, 1764) was to make available the best home herbal remedies and recipes for concocting them. And he was critical of doctors, suggesting that they filled their writings with Latin jargon to confuse ordinary people and elevate their own status. Another classic popular in nineteenth-century American homes was William Buchan's *Domestic Medicine; or, a Treatise on the Prevention and Cure of Diseases, by Regimen and Simple Medicines* (Edinburgh, 1769; Philadelphia, 1771). Reprinted in New Haven in 1816, it was retitled *Every Man His Own Doctor*, which appealed to the ideals of Jacksonian democracy that elevated the common person and resisted elitism and claims of esoteric knowledge. Buchan somewhat agreed about the jargon and vowed to write in plain English. While not questioning the value of treatment by a physician, he said, "everything valuable in the practical part of medicine is within reach of common sense" and "ordinary abilities."[10] Not to be outdone, American John C. Gunn published *Domestic Medicine, or Poor Man's Friend* (Knoxville, 1830), which replaced Buchan in many households by midcentury and went through a hundred editions by 1870. All three stressed simplicity, common sense, and readily available herbal ingredients, often combined with piety. For example, Gunn declared that God had "stored our mountains, fields and meadows, with simples for healing our diseases."[11]

Physicians themselves followed a variety of paths. The regulars practiced what is often termed heroic medicine. They were fond of bleeding, blistering, and purging. Their leader was Philadelphia's Benjamin Rush (1745–1813), who believed that "there is but one disease in the world . . . marked excitement induced by capillary tension." His tool of choice was the lancet.[12] Since doctors were for the most part clueless about the causes of disease, they treated the symptoms. So if a person was flushed or fevered, one could bleed that person until he or she was pale and cool (i.e., in shock). Various poultices were applied to the body to produce blistering, and emetics were given to induce vomiting.

In reaction, medicine became sharply sectarian, with almost as many divisions as Protestantism and sometimes paralleling them. For example, Paul Starr notes that Millerites of the 1830s usually leaned toward Thomsonian medicine and Swedenborgians favored homeopathy.[13] In addition to the Thomsonians and the homeopaths, there were the botanics and the eclectics.

A New Englander without formal education, Samuel Thomson (d. 1843) began practicing botanic medicine around 1800. In 1813 he patented his system and in 1822 published a *New Guide to Health*. By 1839 he claimed to have sold 100,000 rights to his system. An individual or a family would purchase the system and were then given the recipes but sworn to secrecy. According to Thomson, cold was the cause of disease; heat the cure. His principal medication was a violent emetic called Indian tobacco or lobelia. His critics labeled him a "puke doctor." He also recommended red pepper and hot or steam baths to increase body heat. After 1840 various Thomson disciples published their own versions of his system.

The botanics, sometimes called "empirics," were herbalists. They and Thomson were particularly critical of regulars who tended to use mineral compounds, especially mercury. They also appealed to American chauvinism by asking, "Must we go to Europe to import mineral poisons" when an abundance of herbs are readily available in North America?[14]

Homeopathy, with its more elaborate philosophical base developed by German Samuel Hahnemann (1755–1843), appealed to German immigrants and to the urban upper classes, who considered Thomsonians backwoods. Advocates included Daniel Webster, John D. Rockefeller, Julia Ward Howe, Louisa May Alcott, Henry Wadsworth Longfellow, and William Lloyd Garrison. Homeopathy was based on several principles: (1) the law of similars, that like cures like; (2) minute doses are sufficient; and (3) nearly all diseases are a result of a suppressed itch or "psora." It was seen as more scientific and, because homeopaths listened to their patients, more compassionate. The minute doses were a welcome alternative to the excesses of the regulars. And their pleasant-tasting remedies generally produced no uncomfortable side effects. Phoebe Palmer's husband, Walter, and his brother Miles were trained in homeopathy. When homeopaths prospered in the 1840s and 1850s, regulars fought back and tried to have them excluded from the profession. Homeopaths, too, sold domestic kits, wooden boxes with a set of infinitesimal medicines and guides for their use—large boxes for the home, small pocket cases for travel. There were even foreign-language versions for recent immigrants.[15]

Wooster Beach (1794–1868), trained as a botanical practitioner, developed the eclectic school, which claimed to take the best from all the other schools.

Feuds between physicians were blatant, bitter, often personal, and sometimes armed. Medical colleges, most often proprietary and very short on rigor, were particularly fertile ground for sectarian warfare. This did nothing to bolster public confidence. In the late nineteenth century new sects joined the fray: osteopathy and chiropractic, both based on the premise that if the spine is adjusted, all will be well. Andrew Still (1828–1917) developed osteopathy. Chiropractic was discovered in 1895 by magnetic healer Daniel David Palmer (1845–1913), of Davenport, Iowa. His son, Bartlett J. Palmer (d. 1961), founded Palmer School of Chiropractic in 1906.

And the disagreements between doctors were not strictly philosophical. Sometimes they were personal and violent. According to scholar Paul Starr, "Philadelphia, the center of early American medicine, was a maelstrom of professional ill will." Within medical schools there were "open and acrimonious" personal feuds between professors (a not uncommon occurrence in academia). One medical school in Cincinnati was divided into two factions, one of which locked out the other. "Knives, pistols, chisels, bludgeons, blunderbusses" were part of the fray, according to the school's historian. The dispute was resolved when one side bought a six-pound cannon. Similar "fraternal hatred" between medical schools was not uncommon. The night that President Abraham Lincoln was shot, the Surgeon General of the U.S. helped to treat Secretary of State William Seward, who was also wounded. He was strongly denounced by some because he worked with Seward's personal physician, a homeopath. Since Seward survived, the American Medical Society muted its usual censure.[16]

## Doctors and Divine Healing

A number of doctors did join the divine healing movement. A. B. Simpson, for example, tells of "one doctor who really believed the Bible to be the inspired Word of God [who] actually put his belief to the test by first saying to every patient at the first interview, 'Are you a Christian?'" If people answered in the affirmative, he would not prescribe anything but would ask them if they were willing to trust Christ. If so, he quoted Scripture for them and prayed. "He would treat with medicine only those who said they were not Christian." Apparently he was very successful.[17]

Two of the more famous physicians were Lilian Yeomans (1861–1942) and Finis Ewing Yoakum (1851–1920). Both experienced dramatic healings and both eventually joined the Pentecostal movement. Yeomans was born in Calgary, Alberta, the eldest of three daughters of physicians. During the American Civil War, the family moved to the United States and her father became an army surgeon. One of the first women to receive an M.D. degree from the University of Michigan in Ann Arbor, she returned home to go into practice with her mother, Amelia LeSueur Yeomans, a physician, surgeon, Women's Christian Temperance Union vice president, and Suffrage Club president. To deal with her afflictions and the stress of her practice, Lilian began to self-medicate with morphine and chloral hydrate. She was soon severely addicted. She tried various cures—the Keeley Gold Cure Institute, Christian Science, time in a sanitarium for nervous diseases. Finally on January 12, 1898, she found divine healing with Alexander Dowie in Zion City. In September 1907 she experienced sanctification and speaking in tongues. She wrote of her experience for *Way of Faith*, published by J. M. Pike in Columbia, South Carolina. He collected her letters into a book titled *Pentecostal Letters*. With encouragement from Carrie Judd Montgomery, Lilian spoke of her experiences across Canada. In later years she settled in Manhattan Beach, California, and became a faculty member at Aimee Semple McPherson's L.I.F.E. Bible College. She is buried at Forest Lawn.[18]

Finis Yoakum's father was also a physician in Texas who later became a Cumberland Presbyterian minister. His brother was president of several railroads. Finis graduated from the Hospital College of Medicine in Louisville, Kentucky, in 1885 and practiced medicine in Texas, Colorado, and California. He also taught at

Gross Medical College in Denver. In July 1894, on his way to a Methodist meeting, he was struck by a buggy with a drunken driver. A piece of metal pierced his back, broke several ribs, and caused internal bleeding. Thirty-two doctors pronounced his injuries fatal, but he survived, barely, suffering recurring bouts of infection, for antiseptic practices were just beginning to come into vogue. Hoping for some relief, he moved to California, where on February 5, 1895, an Alliance pastor prayed for him, and he made a remarkable recovery.

Yoakum resumed medical practice, though often offering his services free to the poor and outcast, and he became a frequent speaker on the subject of divine healing at Holiness camp meetings in the United States and Great Britain. For years he held weekly healing services at several locations. He founded Pisgah Faith Home in Pasadena, and a periodical called *Pisgah.* One announcement declared: "PISGAH Devoted to the Material Welfare, Bodily Healing, Moral Uplift, and Spiritual Life of the Stricken in Body, Victim of Drink, Outcast, Cripple, Hungry, Friendless and *Whosoever is in Need of the Water of Life.*" His ministry served more than eighteen thousand meals a month to the homeless and hungry. His work was widely publicized by Judd Montgomery, among others. When Pentecostal fire fell on Azusa Street in Los Angeles in 1906, Yoakum immediately visited. While sympathetic to the movement, he did not identify with any one denomination. He died of a heart attack in 1920.[19]

And not all believers in divine healing denigrated physicians. Dora Dudley in her book thanked several doctors for their efforts on her behalf, including Dr. B. (probably Dr. Botsford of Grand Rapids), who gave her "magnetic and homeopathic treatment," and Dr. Dolley of Albion, New York. But she also said, "I have heard physicians say that more deaths are caused by medicine than by disease."[20] And the statement contained a lot of truth.

James Bell, a local surgeon, spoke at an 1891 Holiness convention in Boston. Praising Simpson as a "wise and moderate voice," imbued with "sanctified common sense," Bell noted that it was the D.D.s and not the M.D.s who most often criticized divine healing. He too declared that many medicines did more harm than good, quoting Oliver Wendell Holmes as saying that if all medicines were thrown into the sea it would be bad for the fish but better for human beings. In Bell's opinion, the mortality rate would drop if no drugs were used, so adopting the tenets of divine healing would save lives even if it were not spiritually true.[21]

## No Drugs

Sarah Mix told Carrie Judd to "lay aside all medicine of every description" and "use no remedies of any kind for anything."[22] This was standard advice within the divine healing movement.

Maria B. Woodworth-Etter (1844–1924) quoted a Boston physician as saying, "I must warn you against the use of drugs by physicians. Narcotics, sedatives,
stimulants, tonics, quinine, antipyrine, and hundreds of others are injuring
brains and nerves, stomachs and livers, bringing on heart failure, and doing more
harm than good." Even drugs that have been proven beneficial should be avoided
because "unscrupulous manufacturers adulterated them with ingredients that
even doctors admit are positively dangerous to health and life." She cited a
study by the Illinois State Board of Pharmacy, which sent out 139 "decoy prescriptions." Twenty-three were filled with substances that bore no trace of the
drug prescribed; 69 were 80 percent impure; 10 were 20 percent impure. Only 31
were a pure version of the drug prescribed. And she was writing in the early twentieth century.[23]

Some avoided remedies of all kinds at all costs. Dora Dudley was once suffering from "la grippe and pneumonia," vomiting severely. Her aged aunt offered to
bring her a cup of warm water to settle her stomach, but Dudley refused, saying,
"Auntie, I should die before I would take anything to settle my stomach. If the
Lord does not settle it, it will never be settled." And then she added a comment for
the reader, "I believe, had I taken the water, I should have lost my faith, perhaps
my life."[24]

Others were more moderate. A. B. Simpson sometimes used cough drops to
ease his throat for speaking. Once while he was preaching, he pulled a handker-
chief from his pocket and several lozenges rolled across the floor like marbles. He
smiled and kept right on preaching. He also used eyeglasses later in life.[25]
Simpson left the issue of remedies up to the person: "Where a person sets any
value on them or is not clearly led of the Lord to abandon them, I never have advised him or her to do so." However, he also said, "Where people have real faith in
Christ's supernatural help, they will not want remedies."[26]

While giving up all medications sounds drastic to the modern reader, giving
up drugs in the nineteenth century may indeed have effected the cure in itself.
Mrs. Mix offers several good examples. For instance, she prints a letter from "Mrs.
Dr. J. A. Bassett," who had suffered from what appear to be severe migraine headaches for thirty years. Her husband, a physician, had administered all sorts of
remedies. Then she read of Mrs. Mix in Carrie Judd's *Prayer of Faith*, and her husband wrote to Mix in the fall of 1881. Upon receipt of Mix's reply, they stopped all
medications and began fasting and prayer. Mrs. Bassett's symptoms—pain, nau-
sea, blurred vision—disappeared completely.[27]

Mrs. Samuel Scranton, of Wallingford, Connecticut, was diagnosed by two
doctors as having cancer. Mrs. Mix came and prayed for her; she was able to dress
and eat. The real trial came, however, when she tried to discontinue the morphine
treatments that had kept her continuously drugged. She admitted that "the temp-

tation was terrible; it lasted a number of days," but eventually with God's help she overcame the addiction.[28]

Mary Cole, a Church of God (Anderson, Indiana) preacher, told of meeting two elderly sisters in Fresno, California, "one of whom was a habitual user of morphine. She was a doctor's widow and had acquired the habit by taking morphine as a remedy shortly after their marriage. . . . For nearly forty years she had been addicted to the morphine habit and had been given up by the doctors who had treated her." Cole realized that this case would take more prayer than she could give in one visit, so she sent her assistant Lodema Kaser. Kaser stayed and prayed with the woman for nearly two weeks, but in the end the woman was "like another person." Said Cole, "God had wrought a perfect deliverance."[29]

In the nineteenth century knowledge of several useful drugs was emerging: quinine from cinchona bark for the treatment of malaria and digitalis from foxglove for the heart. Beginning in 1897 something called salicylic acid (we call it aspirin) began to show promise in treating acute rheumatism and the reduction of fevers, but dosage and side effects were uncertain. Still the drug of choice for many of the regulars was calomel, a chloride of mercury and therefore poisonous, used as a strong emetic. Taken frequently and in large doses, it literally rotted the mouth, tongue, throat, and stomach.

Medications as we know them were not readily available until the 1950s and 1960s, and women were given Darvon and Midol as effective proprietary medicines for menstrual cramps; Valium, Librium, Elavil, and other drugs for depression and stress; Dexadrine to help with weight loss, the Pill for contraception, and hormone replacement therapy for hot flashes and other effects of menopause.[30] Sulfa drugs, discovered in the 1930s, and penicillin, developed by Alexander Fleming in the 1940s, along with other antibiotics, became common. Thorazine (chlorpromazine), the first synthetic tranquilizer, was accidentally discovered in the 1950s. Before that physicians had little to treat mental illness besides shock therapy and lobotomy. Prozac came on the market in 1988.

Despite medical developments, smallpox was still a scourge in the nineteenth century. Islamic doctors had inoculated against the disease for years. The wife of a British ambassador to the Ottoman Empire, Lady Mary Wortley Montague (1689–1762), who had been terribly disfigured by the disease in 1715, wrote friends in England about the practice. On the basis of the observation that cowherds who developed cowpox did not contract smallpox, Edward Jenner (1749–1823) began to develop a vaccine using a cowpox culture rather than a diluted smallpox one, as the Turks did. American Benjamin Waterhouse (1754–1846) was an enthusiastic advocate of Jenner's work, but the practice remained very controversial throughout the nineteenth century. While the work of Louis Pasteur (1822–1895) showed promise, it was not until the 1920s and 1930s that the medical community began to realize the power of bacteriology. Its first major therapeutic application was a diphtheria antitoxin developed in the 1890s that lowered mortality from 50 percent to 31 percent. A throat culture test was also developed to diagnose diphtheria more readily. The cause of syphilis was identified in 1905 and the Wasserman test for it was developed in 1906. In 1910 the drug Salvarson became available for treatment.[31] Many women's health problems were caused by syphilis and other venereal diseases, doctors having no clue about their transmission. When a man's symptoms cleared up, they assumed that the resumption of sexual relations was no problem. And all these new treatments cost money and involved access to knowledgeable physicians.

Tuberculosis, referred to always as "consumption," was the epidemic of the age, the leading cause of death. Robert Koch (1843–1910), a German bacteriologist, isolated the tubercle bacillus in 1889, but when the New York Health Department wanted to implement hygienic measures in the 1890s, physicians argued that the disease was not contagious. A test for TB was developed in 1890 and refined in 1907, but medications for treatment came much later.[32]

Those in the Holiness movement generally gave up a lot more than drugs and patent medicines in their quest for a holy lifestyle. All were temperance people, eschewing all forms of alcohol. For Church of God (Cleveland, Tennessee) leader F. J. Lee (1875–1928) that included most soft drinks, because "some one may see you drinking from a bottle and would not know but that you were drinking whiskey." And he added, "Now the Church is positively against dope drinks of which coca cola is one. Our members are not allowed to drink, make or sell it."[33] When Lee and Mary Lee Harris ([Cagle] 1864–1955) founded the New Testament Church of Christ in 1894, members were forbidden explicitly from using opium, morphine, tobacco, or any intoxicating drinks.[34]

In doing so they also had to tiptoe around several biblical texts. Generally they ignored Jesus' apparent consumption of wine at the Last Supper and his turning water into fine wine at the wedding at Cana (John 2:1–10). And Paul's explicit instruction to Timothy to "drink no longer water, but use a little wine for thy stomach's sake and thine often infirmities" (1 Timothy 5:23). Some suggested that this was just a specific word to Timothy because his geographic location had very bad water. A sermon by Lee countered that "wine doesn't mean fermented juice of grapes every time from a viewpoint of the Bible, but it also means the fresh juice just pressed from the grape."[35] The other troublesome story was that of Isaiah prescribing a fig poultice for King Hezekiah (2 Kings 20:7; Isaiah 38:21). Some suggested that this was just Isaiah's human suggestion, not God's direction, and that it happened under the dispensation of law, not grace.[36] Simpson noted that "in the still more elaborate prescriptions and prohibitions of Leviticus, even including procedures for dealing with the disease of leprosy, there is not even remote intimation of a doctor or a drugstore."[37]

## God's Remedies

Mary Mossman had her own views about remedies: "Some may say I do wrong in setting aside means. Most decidedly do I advocate means, but those only as given of the Lord"—laying on of hands, anointing with oil, and the prayer of faith.[38]

Having read James 5, many of the sick first asked their pastor for help. Carrie Judd Montgomery told of a woman with a tumor who read the passage and decided she needed to be anointed, so she wrote a note to her pastor, asking him to do it. He replied, "I would anoint you if I was *sure* that you would be healed, but as I am not sure of that fact, I do not feel that I can do that for you." Carrie and the woman rapidly concluded that with such lack of faith, his prayers probably would not be very effective anyway. So Carrie recruited a Methodist elder who was willing to do it.[39] Dora Dudley had a similar experience when she asked two deacons from her Congregational church to come anoint a crippled teenager. They told her the age of miracles was past.[40]

While the male clergy in the movement laid hands and anointed without much thought, for women doing so constituted a major step in claiming their own authority and ministries. Judd said, "I was too timid at first to even lay hands on the sick, although I could pray for them in faith. Later on, I was led by the Lord to realize that it was my privilege to lay hands on the sick according to Mark 16:18. . . . And I saw, that as a *believer* in the Lord Jesus Christ, I could have this privilege and authority."[41] After the deacons turned Dora Dudley down, she read Karl Andreas's *Healing of Sickness by Scriptural Means*. He said that if God gave gifts of faith, healing, or miracles to someone, then God also gave that person a call to ministry. "It came like a flash that the Lord had bestowed these gifts upon me and that I could use the oil in His name," Dudley concluded.

> I thought I could not; still the thought seemed pressed upon me that I was to do it. I prayed over it, and asked the Lord if it was His will that I should use the oil to let me remember to get it when I went up the street; if not, to take it from my mind. When I went, I forgot everything but the oil. I returned and asked God's blessing upon it, consecrating it to Him for this, and no other use. I then went to Miss Abbott [the crippled girl], telling her all about it. She replied, "I want you to use it." I asked the Lord to show His power, if it were pleasing to Him for me to anoint. I prayed with her and used the oil in His dear name.

Of course, Miss Abbott was healed forthwith. Interestingly, Dudley had met Miss Abbott through Abbott's mother, who had come to Dudley's door trying to sell one of the current medical books. Trying to be polite to a solicitor and testify at the same time, Dudley told her that she did not need the book since she had taken Christ as her Physician. The woman then told Dudley about her twenty-three-year-old daughter, crippled for twenty years by diphtheria that had settled in her spine and legs.[42]

"Some good Christian people objected to my praying with the sick and anointing with oil, because I am a woman," Dudley noted. But by the time she wrote her book, her arguments were well-honed: Jesus was anointed for burial by a woman. In Jesus Christ there is neither male nor female (Galatians 3:28). Jesus, not men, chose and sent out the disciples, instructing them to preach the gospel and heal the sick. And Jesus still chooses and sends willing and obedient followers. Plus, the word translated "elder women" in 1 Timothy 5:2 is the same as that translated "elders" in James 5:14. Said Dudley, "The Lord has honored my labors, obedience, and faith in Him and His Word by many wonderful signs which have followed."[43]

Mossman had the same struggle. She told of visiting a woman who had been confined to her bed for two years and was apparently near death. Mossman visited her regularly and prayed, "yet there was no visible change." Mossman asked God why, and God told her to lay hands on the woman. She hesitated but knew she must obey.

> The next time I called, I laid my hands on her, in prayer, and then calling her by name, reverently said, "In the name of the Lord, you are healed; He will not bless you any longer on that pillow. In the name of the Lord you must arise."

> The power of the Lord then came upon her and from that hour she began to amend, and the praises of God again filled her soul.

Her advice to others: "In regard to the anointing with oil, do you say that you are not an elder? I reply, you are, if the Lord so calls."[44]

Simpson seems to have encouraged women as well as men to lay hands and anoint for healing in his services. But, says his biographer A. E. Thompson, "Dr. Simpson was always careful to direct those who were anointed to look to the Lord and not to the anointing or the anointer, and very frequently took a very subordinate part in such services lest the eyes of any one should be turned to himself." As early as 1883, Simpson wrote, "It is very solemn ground and can never be made a professional business or a public parade. Its mightiest victories will always be silent and out of sight, and its power will keep pace with our humility and holiness."[45]

Some appear to have followed the reasoning that Charles Parham (1873–1929), the forerunner of Pentecostalism, articulated in *Apostolic Faith:* When people desire to be "anointed with oil in the seat of the particular malady," then "women must in every case anoint women and men must anoint men."[46] While most people today who do this ritual anoint the person's crown or forehead and lay hands simply on top of the head, numerous references from the nineteenth century indicate that hands were often laid at the site of the problem, whether that was chest, knee, or abdomen. For example, Mrs. Herbert Hall of West Haven, Connecticut, reported that when Mrs. Mix visited her, she knelt by the bedside and began to pray; it was a very simple prayer; she asked God to remove the pain and all inflammation; her prayer was as a child asking its parent for a piece of bread and butter; she anointed my bowels with oil in the name of the Lord; then placed her hand upon them, and also upon my heart; beseeching Him to make them all right; she directed my mind to the Great Physician that could heal both soul and body. I began to have a little more faith, and as she drew her hand over my bloated body I felt the swelling going down. I then laid my hand on my bowels to see if it was really so, and found it to be true; she then bade me in the name of the Lord to rise up and walk.[47]

The Reverend W. J. Laws wrote to Mix several times, requesting prayer for a young woman of fifteen in his congregation, Miss Susan Haden. He finally reported that she was fully healed. At the appointed time of prayer, "we read the Scriptures and sung [sic] and prayed, then I left the room, and my wife performed the anointing with oil in the name of the Father, Son and Holy Ghost, amen, commanding her to rise up by faith and walk, and she did, and as she began to walk, the power of God flowed into her soul, and she cried and praised God in the highest."[48] I have found no other instance where there seemed to be a hesitation to lay hands on someone of the opposite sex. In fact, in another case Edward Mix went to visit Vidella V. Cornell of New Haven, who was nearly dead. She later reported that "Mother came into the room with him. . . . He laid his left hand on my heart and his right hand on my eyes, and told my mother to pray." Then he prayed "as a child would to a tender parent." Her pain went away.[49]

## Prayer

In the Holiness movement, the prayer of faith was crucially important. For many leaders, their healing took place when they were able to pray a prayer of faith for themselves. Their ministries began when they were able to pray a prayer of faith for another. This was not a formulaic prayer; there are no particular words suggested in Scripture. The key element was that those doing the praying firmly and confidently believed that God heals people in response to prayer. The sick person did not always have to exercise faith. Children obviously fall into that category; often parents exercised faith for them. The same was true of spouses. But there are stories of people healed rather spontaneously when they stepped into a healing home or walked into a meeting devoted to healing. One could suggest, of course, that their actions in coming confirmed their faith.

Many commented on how simple and childlike the prayers of Mr. and Mrs. Mix were. They simply asked God for healing as a child would ask a parent for food or water. Mattie E. Perry's prayers were equally simple. As she commented, "The prayer of faith need not be long."[50]

## Testifying

Although James does not mention it, many believed that in order to gain and retain full healing, one must publicly testify to it. This paralleled Phoebe Palmer's insistence that one must testify to the experience of sanctification in order to maintain it. And it should be done at once. In *The Prayer of Faith*, Judd cautioned,

> We must beware lest we lose the blessing after it is once ours, by fearing to proclaim the victory until the battle is more fully won. "I will wait and see if it is really going to last, before I tell others what God has done for me," says unbelief, and because some of us yield to this temptation of Satan, we lose what we have gained.[51]

Simpson told a story to prove the same point:

> I know a dear brother in the ministry, now much used in the gospel and in the gospel of healing, who received a wonderful manifestation of God's power in his body and then went home to his church but said nothing about it. He was waiting to see how it would hold out.
>
> In a few weeks he was worse than ever. When I met him the next time, he wore the most dejected face you could imagine. I told him his error and it all flashed upon him immediately. He went home and gave God the glory for what He had done. In a little while his church was the center of a blessed work of grace and healing that reached far and wide, and he himself was rejoicing in the fullness of Jesus.[52]

The role of theological writings in the movement was to ground and strengthen believers' faith in divine healing.

## Notes

1. Andreas is cited by Dora G[riffin] Dudley, *Beulah: or Some of the Fruits of One Consecrated Life* (Grand Rapids, Mich.: published by the author, 1896), 50; and by Charles Ewing Brown, *When the Trumpet Sounded: A History of the Church of God Reformation Movement* (Anderson, Ind.: Warner Press, 1951), 73.

2. Carrie Judd Montgomery, *"Under His Wings": The Story of My Life* (Oakland, Calif.: Office of Triumphs of Faith, 1936), 206–7.

3. John Alexander Dowie, editorial, *Leaves of Healing*, June 14, 1895, 563, as quoted by Gordon Lindsay, *The Life of John Alexander Dowie* (Dallas: The Voice of Healing Publishing, 1951), 162.

4. Mrs. Edward Mix, *Faith Cures, and Answers to Prayer* (Springfield, Mass.: Press of Springfield Printing Co., 1882; repr. with critical introduction by Rosemary D. Gooden; Syracuse, N.Y.: Syracuse University Press, 2002), 156, 162–63, 85. Hereafter designated as Gooden.

5. R. Kelso Carter, *Divine Healing, or The Atonement for Sin and Sickenss* (new ed., re-written and enlarged; New York: John B. Alden, 1888), 83. His citations, using KJV English, are as follows: Genesis 50:2, where physicians embalm Joseph's father, Jacob; 2 Chronicles 16:12 concerning Asa; Mark 5:26 and Luke 8:43, concerning the woman with an issue of blood.

6. R. Kelso Carter, "Divine Healing," *The Century* 34 (March 1887), 777. Carter's articles ran along with critical articles by Methodist editor J. M. Buckley.

7. Carter, *Divine Healing*, 126.

8. Paul Starr, *The Social Transformation of American Medicine* (New York; Basic Books, 1992), 32; Guenter B. Risse, ed., *Medicine Without Doctors: Home Health Care in American History* (New York: Science History Publications, 1977), 1.

9. Joanna Pattterson Moore, *"In Christ's Stead": Autobiographical Sketches* (Chicago: Women's Baptist Home Mission Society, 1902), 16.

10. Risse, *Medicine Without Doctors*, 25; Starr, *The Social Transformation of American Medicine*, 33.

11. Risse, *Medicine Without Doctors*, 20.

12. Sarah Stage, *Female Complaints: Lydia Pinkham and the Business of Women's Medicine* (New York: Norton, 1979), 47–48.

13. Starr, *The Social Transformation of American Medicine*, 95.

14. Stage, *Female Complaints*, 51.

15. Risse, *Medicine Without Doctors*, 58.

16. Starr, *The Social Transformation of American Medicine*, 93–94, 98.

17. A. B. Simpson, *The Gospel of Healing* (1885; repr., Camp Hill, Pa.: Christian Publications, 1994), 64.

18. C. M. Robeck Jr., "Yeomans, Lilian Barbara," *Dictionary*, 907. Yeomans published a number of books, including *Healing from Heaven* (1926), *Divine Healing Diamonds* (1933), and *Balm of Gilead* (1935).

19. C. M. Robeck Jr., "Yoakum, Finis Ewing," *Dictionary*, 907–8. See "Founder of Pisgah Dies," *Los Angeles Daily Times* 2 (August 19, 1920), 7; Grant Wacker, *Heaven Below: Early Pentecostals and American Culture* (Cambridge, Mass.: Harvard University Press, 2001), 185; Douglas J. Nelson, "For Such a Time as This: The Story of Bishop William J. Seymour and the Azusa Street Revival" (Ph.D. diss., University of Birmingham, England, 1981), 204, 224.

20. Dudley, *Beulah*, 18, 33.

21. William Boyd Bedford Jr., " 'A Larger Christian Life'; A. B. Simpson and the Early Years of the Christian and Missionary Alliance" (Ph.D. diss., University of Virginia, 1992), 295–96.

22. Carrie F. Judd, *The Prayer of Faith* (1880; Oakland, Calif.: Office of Triumphs of Faith, 1917), 15.

23. Mrs. M. B. Woodworth-Etter, *Acts of the Holy Ghost, or The Life, Work, and Experience of Mrs. M. B. Woodworth-Etter* (Dallas: John F. Worley Printing n.d. [1912]), 421–22, 424.

24. Dudley, *Beulah*, 101–2.

25. Raymond Walter Schenk, "A Study of the New Testament Bases for the Teaching of Dr. Albert B. Simpson on Divine Healing" (master's thesis, Wheaton College, 1968), 62.

26. Simpson, *The Gospel of Healing*, 141.

27. Gooden, 63.

28. Mix, *Faith Cures*, 196; Gooden, 196.

29. Mary Cole, *Trials and Triumphs of Faith* (Anderson, Ind.: Gospel Trumpet, 1914), 217–18.

30. Stage, *Female Complaints:* 254–55.

31. Starr, *The Social Transformation of American Medicine*, 137, 138, 135, 139.

32. Ibid., 187, 191.

33. Mrs. F. J. Lee, *Life Sketch and Sermons of F. J. [Flavius Josephus] Lee* (Cleveland, Tenn.: The Church of God Publishing House, 1929), 191.

34. Robert Stanley Ingersol, "Burden of Dissent: Mary Lee Cagle and the Southern Holiness Movement" (Ph.D. diss., Duke University, 1989), 134.

35. Lee, *Life Sketch*, 11, 13.

36. Ibid., 17.

37. Simpson, *The Gospel of Healing*, 53.

38. M[ary] M[ossman], *Steppings in God; or the Hidden Life Made Manifest* (6th and rev. ed. with appendix; New York: Eaton & Mains, 1909), 107. Protestants tend to ignore James's injunction to confess one's sins to another person.

39. Montgomery, *"Under His Wings,"* 80.

40. Dudley, *Beulah*, 48, 50

41. Montgomery, *"Under His Wings,"* 80–81.

42. Dudley, *Beulah*, 50, 48–49.

43. Ibid., 50–51.

44. Mossman, *Steppings in God*, 123, 118.

45. A. E. Thompson, *A. B. Simpson: His Life and Work* (rev. ed.; Camp Hill Pa.: Christian Publications, 1960), 139–40.

46. *Apostolic Faith* (Kansas, December 1914), 4, as quoted by Wacker, *Heaven Below*, 109.

47. Gooden, 109.

48. Ibid., 140.

49. Ibid., 159.

50. Mattie E. Perry, *Christ and Answered Prayer* (Nashville: Benson Printing Company, 1939), 346.

51. Judd, *The Prayer of Faith*, 105.

52. Simpson, *The Gospel of Healing*, 128.

# 7

# Theology

Women founded healing homes; men wrote books on the theology of divine healing—with some doing both. As one might expect, these books began with scriptural example and were heavy with biblical citations. Examples of Jesus' healings loomed large, followed by the healing ministries of the apostles. These were usually followed by at least passing allusions to healings down through church history. The major theological rationale for divine healing held that healing was "in the atonement," purchased by Christ's redemptive act right alongside salvation. The prerequisites for individual healing were salvation, sanctification, and readiness to pray the prayer of faith.

Early books combined testimony with defenses of the practice. Charles Cullis published Dorothea Trudel's *Prayer of Faith* (1872), and Carrie Judd wrote *Prayer of Faith* (1880). In 1881 William Boardman published *The Great Physician* (alternately titled *The Lord That Healeth Thee*), and Ethan Otis Allen wrote *Faith Healing*. The 1880s saw a spate of books on the subject: A. J. Gordon's *Ministry of Healing* (1882), R. Kelso Carter's *Pastor Blumhardt* (1883) and *Divine Healing, or The Atonement from Sin and Sickness* (1884), Robert L. Stanton's *Gospel Parallels* (1883), A. B. Simpson's *Gospel of Healing* (1885), Otto Stockmayer's *Sickness and the Gospel* (2d ed., 1887), and R. L. Marsh's *"Faith Healing": A Defense* (1889). Alexander Dowie published *Divine Healing Vindicated* in 1893. Simpson published Andrew Murray's *Divine Healing* in 1900.[1] Others weighed in on the subject as well.

Gordon, as a Boston Baptist minister, worked out his theology within the milieu that also gave rise to Mary Baker Eddy's Christian Science. In the 1870s Gordon was a trustee for Cullis's institutions, and during the 1877 revival held in Boston by D. L. Moody, he witnessed several miraculous healings. He preached sanctification and wrote *The Ministry of the Spirit* (1894) and *The Two-Fold Life; or, Christ's Work for Us and Christ's Work in Us* (1895), as well as *The Ministry of Healing*.

Carter was a math and science teacher at a military academy. In *Divine Healing* Carter testified to his own healing. Five physicians—two in Philadelphia and three in Baltimore—had pronounced his heart disease incurable. After seven years of ineffective treatment, in 1879 he

> consecrated all to God, believed His word, called upon His servant, Dr. Chas. Cullis, and was prayed with according to James V., 14, 15, with the laying on of hands and the anointing with oil in the name of the Lord. From that day to this—over eight years—I have never touched any form of medicine or remedy. Praise the dear Lord alone! I am well.[2]

Carter often ministered with Simpson at early C&MA conventions. He published at least fourteen books, including two novels. A poet and hymnwriter, he collaborated with fellow hymnwriter Simpson on the church's first *Hymns of Christian Life*. At midlife, Carter went to medical school at Johns Hopkins and became a practicing physician. In 1897 Carter published *"Faith Healing" Reviewed after Twenty Years*, and he modified his position slightly after he was struck with "brain prostration" on March 1, 1887, and suffered for three years before taking a physician's remedy that brought relief.[3]

Robert. L. Stanton, brother to Elizabeth Cady Stanton's husband, Henry, was a former president of Miami University in Ohio and had been a moderator of the northern Presbyterian Church.

## The Bible

The Holiness movement's use of the Bible was precritical, sometimes resolutely noncritical. They saw it as a level playing field, with all verses potentially equally applicable to their situation. Thus they could cite and combine verses at random from the Hebrew Scriptures and the New Testament. Even in their day, some critics labeled this practice "grasshopper exegesis."[4] Sometimes they also used the Bible as a magical book, opening at random to find guidance.

From the Hebrew Scriptures in the King James Version, favorite citations included the following:

> Exodus 15:26: Moses at Marah told the people, "If thou wilt diligently hearken to the voice of the LORD thy God, and wilt do that which is right in his sight, and wilt give ear to his commandments, and keep all his statutes, I will put none of these diseases upon thee, which I have brought upon the Egyptians: for I am the LORD that healeth thee" ("Jehovah Rophi").

> Deuteronomy 7:15: And the LORD will take away from thee all sickness, and will put none of the evil diseases of Egypt, which thou knowest, upon thee; but will lay them upon all them that hate thee.

> 2 Kings 20:5: The prophet Isaiah to King Hezekiah: "Thus saith the LORD, the God of David thy father, I have heard thy prayer, I have seen thy tears: behold, I will heal thee."

Psalm 30:2: O LORD my God, I cried unto thee, and thou hast healed me.

Psalm 103:2–3: Bless the LORD, O my soul, and forget not all his benefits: Who forgiveth all thine iniquities; who healeth all thy diseases.

Isaiah 40:28–31: Hast thou not known? Hast thou not heard, that the everlasting God, the LORD, the Creator of the ends of the earth, fainteth not, neither is weary? There is no searching of his understanding. He giveth power to the faint; and to them that have no might he increaseth strength. Even the youths shall faint and be weary, and the young men shall utterly fall: But they that wait upon the LORD shall renew their strength; they shall mount up with wings as eagles; they shall run, and not be weary; and they shall walk, and not faint.

Isaiah 53:4–5: [The suffering servant] hath borne our griefs, and carried our sorrows: . . . But he was wounded for our transgressions, he was bruised for our iniquities: the chastisement of our peace was upon him; and with his stripes we are healed.

Jeremiah 30:17: For I will restore health unto thee, and I will heal thee of thy wounds, saith the LORD.

Malachi 4:2: But unto you that fear my name shall the Sun of righteousness arise with healing in his wings.

Carter argued that all of the patriarchs sought healing from God and that Moses knew the advanced medical knowledge of the Egyptians but also sought God's help.[5]

In the New Testament, the most important reference was Matthew 8:16–17's quotation of Isaiah 53:4: "When the even was come, they brought unto [Jesus] many that were possessed with devils: and he cast out the spirits with his word, and healed all that were sick: That it might be fulfilled which was spoken by Esaias the prophet, saying, Himself took our infirmities, and bare our sicknesses." Carter offered an extensive explanation of Isaiah 53:4, attempting to reconcile it with Matthew: "Neither of these words ['griefs and sorrows'] has reference to spiritual matters, but to bodily sickness alone. . . . The word translated *griefs* in Isaiah and *infirmities* in Matthew, means, properly, in the Hebrew and Greek, *diseases of the body*. In neither does it refer to the diseases of the mind or to sin." "Sorrows," Carter said, referred more to "the pains of the *mind*, . . . to anguish, anxiety, or trouble of the soul."[6] These writers also knew that the allusion was picked up in 1 Peter 2:24 as well: "Who his own self bare our sins in his own body on the tree, that we, being dead to sins, should live unto righteousness: by whose stripes ye were healed."

## Jesus and the Apostles

The Gospel accounts of Jesus' healing the sick provided and continue to provide fertile ground for sermonizing. Each story was analyzed for its lessons concerning Jesus' techniques, Jesus' intentions, the sick person's faith, the faith of others, the cause(s) of illness, the use of means. Authors returned again and again to Matthew 8:16 to emphasize that Jesus "healed *all* that were sick" and Luke 4:40, "Now when the sun was setting, all they that had any sick with divers diseases brought them unto him; and he laid his hands on every one of them, and healed them." As A. B. Simpson declared, "The personal ministry of Christ Jesus when on earth is our ground for claiming healing."[7]

While many of their contemporaries and later fundamentalists argued that Jesus' miracles, including the healings, were intended only to demonstrate his divine powers, William Boardman responded that "had His healing work been merely miraculous, as a sign of His Sonship, a seal of His plenipotentiary power and authority, a few signal instances of it would have sufficed."[8] Holiness writers also noted that Jesus commissioned his disciples to heal. Matthew 10:1 says, "And when he had called unto him his twelve disciples, he gave them power against unclean spirits, to cast them out, and to heal all manner of sickness and all manner of disease." The passage is paralleled in Mark 3:15 and Luke 9:1.

Critics noted that these were only the Twelve, those who would need supernatural warrants to plant the early church. In response, Holiness writers pointed out that Luke 10 also recorded the sending out of the Seventy. They too were given power to heal the sick (v. 9). In John 17:18 Jesus sent all of the disciples out into the world, having promised them in John 14:12 that "he that believeth on me, the works that I do shall he do also; and greater works than these shall he do; because I go unto my Father." Then Jesus repeatedly encouraged them to ask for whatever they needed and God would answer (John 14:13–14; 15:7; 16:23–24). Boardman declared that Jesus commissioned "without limit of time or office, age or sex, to do in His name, through faith in His name, what He had done in His own name as one with the Father."[9]

While Holiness writers were generally selective in their use of it, they often referred to the end of Mark 16:18: "they shall lay hands on the sick, and they shall recover" (judiciously ignoring v. 17 and the beginning of v. 18: "And these signs shall follow them that believe; In my name shall they cast out devils; they shall speak with new tongues; They shall take up serpents; and if they drink any deadly thing, it shall not hurt them"). Simpson quoted it as "Go ye. . . . In my name shall they cast out devils, . . . they shall lay hands on the sick, and they shall recover."[10]

For critics who argued that all this was about Jesus and did not apply today, advocates had two trump cards: Jesus' own promise, "Lo, I am with you always, even unto the end of the world" (Matthew 28:20), and "Jesus Christ the same yesterday, and to day, and for ever" (Hebrews 13:8). Stanton argued that

> when the primitive faith and practice of the Church shall be restored throughout Christendom, of putting the "healing of the sick" and "preaching the Kingdom of God" on the same plane of duty and privilege, the Church may expect "the Lord

working with them," and confirming the word with "signs following"; even restoring the Church's lost faith and power to its ancient measure.[11]

While Boardman had been convinced of the doctrine of healing by Psalm 103, Cullis found James 5 persuasive.[12] Gordon declared that "in James' epistle we find healing recognized as an ordinance, just as in Paul's epistle to the Romans and to the Corinthians we find Baptism and the Supper recognized as ordinances."[13] Simpson concurred: "The Lord Jesus has left for us in James 5:14 a distinct ordinance of healing in His name, as sacred and binding as any of the ordinances of the gospel." He said, "Observe the nature of the ordinance enjoined. It is 'the prayer of faith' and the 'anointing . . . with oil in the name of the Lord.' This is not a medical anointing, for it was not to be applied by a physician, but by an elder." Said Simpson, it was "a symbolic religious ordinance expressive of the power of the Holy Spirit, whose peculiar emblem is oil." He noted that the Greek Orthodox Church retained the practice but the Roman Catholic Church had changed it "into a mournful preparation for death."[14]

Interestingly, it is not until one gets into Pentecostal writers that one finds consistent references to the gift of healing as mentioned in 1 Corinthians 12:9, although Carter does refer to it in passing. Holiness writers also more or less ignored Jesus' work as an exorcist, especially in Mark. References to casting out demons begin to be found more frequently as these movements progress into the twentieth century.

## Church History

Protestants are not usually prone to trace church history prior to the Reformation, but Holiness writers on divine healing often referred to a certain litany of references. While they did not cite specific instances of healing, Gordon, for example, alluded to Justin Martyr, Irenaeus, Tertullian, Origen, Clement of Alexandria, Theodore of Mopsuestia, and Eusebius. He declared: "Whenever we find a revival of primitive faith and apostolic simplicity, there we find a profession of the chaste and evangelical miracles which characterized the apostolic age."[15] According to Simpson, "It remained in the church for centuries and only disappeared gradually in the church's growing worldliness, corruption, formalism and unbelief."[16]

Closer to the Reformation, Gordon cited a Waldensian source as saying, "concerning this anointing of the sick, we hold it as an article of faith." He went on to say of healing miracles, "These attend the cradle of every spiritual reformation, as they did the birth of the Church herself. Waldenses, Moravians, Huguenots, Covenanters, Friends, Baptists and Methodists all have their record of them."[17] He did give specific examples here, quoting from Count Zinzendorf's writings, George Fox's journals, and a Methodist magazine in London. Simpson biographer A. E. Thompson picked up the same lists.

## In the Atonement

Simpson coined the phrase "the fourfold gospel." The subtitle of his pamphlet on the subject was "The Fullness of Jesus." It became the motto and statement of faith for the Christian and Missionary Alliance and remains so: "Christ our Savior, Sanctifier, Healer and coming Lord." Without reference to Simpson, Dora Dudley spoke of "the grand fundamental doctrines of Christianity, the fourfold Gospel of Christ. These are Justification, Sanctification, Divine Healing and the Second Coming of Christ."[18] Aimee Semple McPherson worked with several versions before she settled on the themes of Jesus Christ as Savior, Healer, Baptizer with the Holy Spirit, and Soon-coming King as the theological summary for her International Church of the Foursquare Gospel.[19]

The core theological concept that all of these people agreed upon was that divine healing was "in the atonement," that just as Christ's work on the cross made salvation possible, so it made divine healing possible as well. This was the key concept disputed by their detractors. It was primarily based on their interpretation of Matthew 8:16–17 and Matthew's quotation of Isaiah 53:4 therein. As Harriette S. Bainbridge declared in *Life for Soul and Body* (1906), "Divine-healing and every other blessing we are authorized to ask from God, comes to us through virtue of the atonement of Jesus—it is purchased by His precious blood."[20]

Simpson declared that "griefs" in Isaiah 53:6 would better be translated as "sicknesses." He identified the use of "borne" with the scapegoat sent into the wilderness, bearing the people's sins on the Jewish Day of Atonement. "Isaiah must have meant healing, or Matthew would not have quoted it," Simpson declared. He buttressed this with an exegesis of Isaiah 53:5, which he and all of those cited uncritically read as describing Jesus. Simpson saw the four phrases in Isaiah as indicating that Christ died for our transgressions or actual sins; our iniquities or our moral and spiritual condition; the curse and consciousness of sin, giving us new life; and finally our healing through the agony on the cross. First Peter 2:24 in quoting Isaiah 53:5 reinforces this understanding.[21]

Mary Mossman offered another version: "We lay our indwelling as well as actual sin upon Jesus [sanctification as well as salvation] and recognize it as no longer ours (1 John 1:7). Does not the promise as fully include actual and hereditary diseases and physical ills, and shall they not be disposed of in like manner? . . . All we have to do is to claim the benefits of the atonement and wait on God until the full victory is wrought."[22]

Gordon began his argument, "In the atonement of Christ there seems to be a foundation laid for faith in bodily healing. . . . We have Christ set before us as the sickness-bearer as well as the sin-bearer of his people" and cited Matthew 8:17. He went on to note, "We hold that *in its ultimate consequences* the atonement affects the body as well as the soul of man. Sanctification is the consummation of Christ's redemptive work for the soul; and resurrection is the consummation of his redemptive work for the body. And these meet and are fulfilled at the coming and kingdom of Christ." He summarized his argument by saying that divine healing rests in the "testimony of scripture": it is grounded in the atonement, Christ's command in Mark 16:17–18, and in apostolic practice. "Thus this office like the great ordinances of Christianity rests on the three-fold support of promise and practice and precept."[23]

Carter also built his doctrine of divine healing on his understanding of the atonement and its personal application through salvation and sanctification. He said that the atonement

> embraces pardon from past sins and past uncleanness, and cleansing from all traces of inherited depravity, as well as the keeping power against sin in any form, outward or inward. The Atonement of Jesus Christ is a finished sacrifice, once for all, for my sins of commission and of omission, and for inbred sins; and of course provides for a maintenance of cleanness in my soul. . . . the Atonement has provided for the body all it has provided for the soul. . . . God now heals bodily sickness, precisely as He now heals soul sickness, by His power alone, unaided by any means whatsoever; and that He does it through and by virtue of the perfect Atonement of Jesus Christ.[24]

One of Elizabeth Baker's sisters, Nellie Duncan Fell, included a popular chorus that captured this emphasis:

> Healing for thee, healing for thee,
> In His atonement is healing for thee,
>  O, it is wonderful, how could it be
> Jesus brought healing for thee.[25]

Obviously this approach is based on the premise, as Simpson articulated it, that "the causes of disease and suffering are distinctly traced to the Fall and the sinful state of man. . . . if it be part of the curse of sin, it must have its true remedy in the great Redemption." Using the examples of Job and the woman bent over for eighteen years, Simpson declared that "sickness is distinctly connected with Satan's personal agency" and thus "the fundamental principle of divine healing . . . rests on Jesus' atoning sacrifice." Later he took up the case of Job again, stating, "The sickness came from Satan. . . . Job's sickness was divinely permitted. . . . Job's sickness was removed when he saw his sin and acknowledged it before God."[26] As a Pentecostal writer put it bluntly, "diseases originated from the devil."[27] On the theological level, this made sense; on the personal level it became problematic.

Based on this theology, most Holiness writers and preachers presented healing only within the context of deeper Christian experience. As Bainbridge cautioned, "Do not begin your quest for physical deliverance by praying to be healed."[28] Preachers presented divine healing only after they had preached salvation and sanctification. While some people testified that they got healed at the same time they found salvation, Simpson, for example, would not lay hands on anyone until he was sure that the person was saved and preferably sanctified or at least seeking sanctification. It was important that body, soul, and spirit all be fully consecrated to God.

Then one could take practical steps to seek healing. Simpson outlined them in *The Gospel of Healing:* be fully persuaded by what the Bible says about healing. "Be fully assured of the will of God to heal you. . . . Any doubt on this point will surely paralyze your prayer for definite healing. . . . Be careful that you are right with God"—confess sin, make restitution where appropriate, but do not let Satan paralyze you with a sense of unworthiness. "Commit your body to God and claim by simple faith his promise of healing in the name of Jesus. . . . Act your faith"— get up and walk. Be prepared for trials and setbacks. Use your newfound health and strength to serve God. Testify to others about your healing.[29]

Many declared that believers should ignore symptoms. Bainbridge spoke of symptoms as mere "temptations" to those who had truly accepted Christ as their Healer. In an article titled "Words of Counsel to Seekers After Divine Healing," Bainbridge also suggested that those who felt unable to pray the prayer of faith should confess that inability to God and wait for an "inward consciousness" that God had sent faith. She declared that too many seek anointing without first asking God's power to pray the prayer of faith—power which may not be given for months. Faith and health are joined: "If we are strong in faith, we may expect to be strong in body and soul. If we are weak in faith, we may expect to be weak in body and soul."[30]

## Resurrection Life

Simpson went beyond many of the other advocates of healing. Most focused on healing as an intervention for the acutely ill. Simpson certainly subscribed to that practice. But his experience led him to emphasize continuing health and strength. Said Simpson, "The risen and ascended Christ is the fountain of our strength and life." "There the gospel of healing finds the fountain of its deepest life. The death of Christ destroys sin—the root of sickness. But it is the life of Jesus that supplies the source of health and life for our redeemed bodies."[31] Simpson pointed to Romans 8:11, where Paul said that "if the Spirit of [God] that raised up Jesus from the dead dwell in you, [God who] raised up Christ from the dead shall also quicken your mortal bodies by his Spirit that dwelleth in you." In 2 Corinthians 4:11 Paul also said that "we which live are always delivered unto death for Jesus' sake, that the life also of Jesus might be made manifest in our mortal flesh."

Just as justification and sanctification involved definite experiences and continuing growth in a Christian's life, so accepting Christ as Healer resulted in ideally not only recovery from illness but also ongoing health. For Simpson it was a continuous process: "God works from within outward, beginning with our spiritual nature and then diffusing His life and power through our physical being."[32] Simpson spoke of experiencing the "fullness" of Christ in sanctification and healing. Healing was integral to the life of holiness and a foretaste of the resurrection. He often used terms most frequently associated with the mystics, such as "union" with Christ. For example, "We must live in [Christ]; we must take our healing as we do our life, breath by breath, from Jesus. We must live in His bosom under the shadow of His wings." But in language more familiar to the late twentieth century, he declared in the same passage that Christ's "death took away your liability to disease, but His resurrected body is a positive fountain of real vital energy. . . . His bodily energy vitalizes your body. . . . I think whole people need it as much as sick people. . . . I take it every morning and it has given me many times more the strength of my natural energy."[33]

Simpson stressed that one should not seek healing in itself but should always focus on Christ. This was obviously the theme of his impromptu sermon, "Himself," delivered at the international conference on healing in London and widely reprinted even today. Simpson also wrote a hymn with the same theme and title. The first verse summarizes the thought:

Once it was the blessing,
    Now it is the Lord;
Once it was the feeling
    Now it is His Word.
Once His gift I wanted,
    Now the Giver own;
Once I sought for healing,
    Now Himself alone.[34]

Bainbridge spoke in a more pragmatic way. A person "can lose the grace of divine healing, just as easily as he can lose a fortune, by neglecting to attend to the conditions of its maintenance." These include living in obedience to God's laws; correcting one's bad habits; obeying the leading of the Holy Spirit in all things, including eating, resting, and working; and learning how "to constantly co-operate with the Spirit in habits of thought, speech, will, and conduct." Her slogan was "Christ in us, in our Health, now and always."[35]

## Faith

The key element in divine healing is faith and praying the prayer of faith. This is why Simpson said, "I have never felt I could claim the healing of anyone until he or she first accepted Jesus as Savior. But I have several times seen the soul saved and the body healed in the same hour."[36] Healing faith cannot be manufactured or conjured up. Most advocates relied on the quotation of the Bible and the theological logic of healing in the atonement to generate faith in those seeking healing. Faith was seen as a gift of God and not merely a result of the believer's actions. However, the seeker must come to a place of faith without the slightest taint of doubt. Carter noted that "inquirers are instructed to believe they do receive, *when* the Spirit witnesses within that their consecration and obedience are complete and the prayer has been offered. They are to believe this on the simple warrant of the Word."[37] Healing evangelist F. F. Bosworth put it another way: "Getting things from God is like playing checkers. Our move is to expect what he promises . . . before we *see* the healing . . . He always moves when it is His turn."[38]

Parents could exercise faith on behalf of their children. Rarely are there accounts of people exercising faith on behalf of the unconscious or incapacitated. In the vast majority of cases within the Holiness movement, no one taught that there is any special merit or personal power in the teacher or preacher or elder praying for healing, anointing, or laying on hands. Certainly they needed to believe in divine healing, but their actions did not convey divine power. Healing came by faith, but it was not the faith that healed. God healed, Christ healed. Faith received the healing.

Those praying with doubts could, however, inhibit a healing. Carrie Judd declared, "Doubt is fatal to faith."[39] As Simpson said, "One doubt will destroy the efficacy of faith. . . . A faith that is going to wait for signs and evidence will never be strong."[40] Jennie Smith (1842–1924), the railroad evangelist, had been confined to a reclining position for many years by a very painful leg malady. She gained her nickname by traveling on her bed in railroad baggage cars and sharing her faith with railroad men. Although she accepted the possibility of healing for others, she had not felt led to claim it for herself. She even had an experimental surgery to correct the problem. It alleviated some symptoms but not the entire problem. Finally in April 1878 she gathered a small group to pray for her healing. After an hour of prayer,

> some were obliged to leave. One brother, whom I had not met before, as he shook hands on leaving, said,

> "My sister, you are asking too much; you are too anxious to get well. The Lord can make better use of you upon your cot, than upon your feet."

"No, I am not anxious to get well; I have gained the victory over that. If the heat of the furnace was increased a thousand-fold, I could say, 'Thy will be done,' and feel, pain would be sweet if *fully* shown to me that it is the Father's will that I should suffer. But I believe the time has come for me to know that will."

Up to this point in the meeting, there was not that oneness of mind that I felt there must be.[41]

She then asked who was willing to pray through the night with her if need be. Her physician was the first to agree. As the group continued to pray, she sat up, stood up, and walked.

Judd advised,

When we have made every effort to believe, and have acted out our faith as far as possible, it is sometimes the dear Lord's will not to give us, at once, the blessing which we know we have claimed by faith. But we must not let anything make us doubt, for any waiting on *His* part, to give us according to our faith, is productive of the highest good. He alone knows how precious is the trial of our faith.[42]

## God's Will

Apparently many people inserted into their prayer the caveat "if it be thy will," presumably as a gesture of humble submission to God's sovereignty. Jennie Smith on her cot and Smith Platt on his canes had plenty of time to prayerfully consider their physical and spiritual conditions. Both had come to terms with their physical disabilities as part of God's plan for their lives. Yet each later reconsidered, prayed for healing, and received it. A number of authors, however, caution against praying "if it be thy will," seeing it rather as a sign of doubt. They argue that Scripture is crystal clear: healing is included in the atonement, so God's will is plain. To those who said that "we are presumptuous to claim the healing of disease absolutely," Simpson replied that we "don't have to wonder" if it is God's will because Scripture is clear. In the Gospels Jesus was willing to heal all who came to him. God's will for every true Christian is perfect health. We do not have to ask if this applies to us.[43] Said Simpson, "We can only know His will from His Word and Spirit. And we must not expect a special revelation from His Spirit where His Word has clearly spoken."[44]

Apparently William Boardman initially used the phrase "thy will be done," but in an essay published after his death in an Alliance publication, Boardman said that he had changed his mind and no longer included that in his prayers.[45]

To those unable to pray the prayer of faith, Bainbridge offered "Words of Counsel to Seekers After Divine Healing." She suggested that they confess their inability to God and wait for an "inward consciousness" that God had sent faith—which she said might take a while, even months. It was foolish to ask for anointing without first seeking God's power to pray the prayer of faith.[46]

And this leads to the admonition Mrs. Mix gave Carrie Judd: "*act faith*. It makes no difference how you feel, but get right out of bed and begin to walk by faith." This advice certainly had a biblical ring. As Jesus commanded, "Stretch forth thy hand" (Luke 6:10). "Arise, and take up thy bed, and walk" (Mark 2:9). Testimonies to healing are rife with examples of those who took that first step or climbed that first hill. Some were healed instantaneously and completely; others spoke of being healed and gradually recovering full strength and vigor.

But beyond that are one's response to the symptoms of illness. "Faith, not feeling, is the victory," declared Martha Wing Robinson. She noted that "many people lose their healing because, after they have taken the healing, they look at the symptoms."[47] Simpson counseled that "we must steadily believe that back of all symptoms God is working."[48] One must regard symptoms as ploys from Satan, tempting one to doubt. Bainbridge declared:

> Symptoms of sickness are to be regarded as temptations by people who have truly accepted the Lord Jesus Christ as Healer. But they need to see them as temptations, or trials of their faith in the finished work of Christ—proving to their own selves whether they believe *they have* the sickness indicated by such symptoms, or whether they believe *they have*, through a living and availing faith in the blood of Christ, which was shed for us, the promise of a divine deliverance from their ailment on the authority of His infallible Word.[49]

Mossman quoted Cullis as telling those whom he had just anointed at one of his conventions:

> We have claimed out and out a distinct promise. The position for us now to assume is, "I am healed, praise God," Praise Him. That He has healed you in this hour. Do not look at your symptoms, they may not have disappeared, but what of that? They are not the disease, but only its effects. They will change in God's own time, but He has touched the root of the disease."[50]

One should not mention one's symptoms to others to garner sympathy. One should continue to have faith and ignore them. One must not only pray the prayer of faith but also keep on praying it daily.

# Notes

1. See bibliography.
2. R. Kelso Carter, *Divine Healing, or The Atonement for Sin and Sickness* (new ed., rewritten and enlarged; (New York: John B. Alden, 1884, 1888), 27.
3. Donald W. Dayton, *The Theological Roots of Pentecostalism* (Grand Rapids, Mich.: Frances Asbury Press, Zondervan, 1987), 130.

4. J. Kevin Butcher, "The Holiness and Pentecostal Labors of David Wesley Myland: 1890–1918" (master's thesis, Dallas Theological Seminary, 1983), 73.

5. R. Kelso Carter, "Divine Healing" *The Century* 34 (March 1887): 777.

6. Carter, *Divine Healing*, 40.

7. John Sawin, "The Fourfold Gospel," in *The Birth of a Vision* (ed. David F. Hartzfeld and Charles Nienkirchen, Regina, Sask.: His Dominion Supplement no. 1, 1986), 12.

8. William E. Boardman, *The Great Physician (Jehovah Rophi)* (Boston: Willard Tract Repository, 1881), 60.

9. Ibid., 72.

10. A. B. Simpson, *The Gospel of Healing*, (1885; repr., Camp Hill, Pa.: Christian Publications, 1994), 8.

11. Robert L. Stanton, *Gospel Parallelisms: Illustrated in the Healing of Body and Soul* (Buffalo, N.Y.: Office of Triumphs of Faith, 1884), 174, as quoted by Dayton, *The Theological Roots of Pentecostalism*, 127.

12. Boardman, *The Great Physician*, 13.

13. A. J. Gordon, *The Ministry of Healing or, Miracles of Cure in All Ages* (3d ed.; Chicago: Fleming H. Revell, 1882), 48.

14. Simpson, *The Gospel of Healing*, 10, 18, 19.

15. Gordon, *The Ministry of Healing*, 64.

16. Simpson, *The Gospel of Healing*, 8.

17. Gordon, *The Ministry of Healing*, 65, 64.

18. Dora G[riffin] Dudley, *Beulah: or Some of the Fruits of One Consecrated Life* (Grand Rapids, Mich.: published by the author, 1896), 95, and she refers again to "fourfold gospel" on 100.

19. Edith Blumhofer, *Aimee Semple McPherson: Everybody's Sister* (Grand Rapids, Mich.: Eerdmans, 1993), 190–93.

20. Harriette S. Bainbridge, *Life for Soul and Body* (Brooklyn, N.Y.: Christian Alliance Publishing Co., 1906), 8. The back cover offers Simpson's *Gospel of Healing*, A. J. Gordon's *Ministry of Healing*, and Andrew Murray's *Divine Healing* for sale. This book appears to be columns she wrote for a periodical because sometimes she seems to be answering readers' questions.

21. Raymond Walter Schenk, "A Study of the New Testament Bases for the Teaching of Dr. Albert B. Simpson on Divine Healing" (master's thesis, Wheaton College, 1968), 20–27.

22. M[ary] M[ossman], *Steppings in God; or, the Hidden Life Made Manifest* (6th and rev. ed.; New York: Eaton & Mains, 1909), 107–8.

23. Gordon, *The Ministry of Healing*, 16, 18, 30.

24. Carter, *Divine Healing*, 25–27.

25. Elizabeth V. Baker and co-workers, *Chronicles of a Faith Life* (1915; repr., New York: Garland 1984), 93.

26. Simpson, *The Gospel of Healing*, 23, 24, 26, 75–76.

27. Bert H. Doss, "A Wonderful Healer, a Wonderful Physician," *Church of God Evangel* (March 4, 1922) in *Healing in the Church* (ed. James A. Cross, Cleveland, Tenn.: Pathway Press, 1962), 47.

28. Bainbridge, *Life for Soul and Body*, 72.

29. Simpson, *The Gospel of Healing*, 59, 61, 64–65, 66, 69, 70, 71.

30. Harriette S. Bainbridge, "Words of Counsel to Seekers After Divine Healing," *Christian Alliance and Foreign Missions Weekly* 15 (September 25, 1895), 199, as quoted by Bedford, "'A Larger Christian Life,'" 299, 284.

31. Simpson, *The Gospel of Healing*, 27. I have reversed the sentences for clarity.

32. Ibid., 34–35.

33. Sawin, "The Fourfold Gospel," in *The Birth of a Vision*, 12.

34. A. B. Simpson, "Himself," *Hymns of the Christian Life* (Harrisburg, Pa.: Christian Publications, 1936), 154.

35. Bainbridge, *Life for Soul and Body,* 142, 144.

36. Simpson, *The Gospel of Healing,* 139.

37. Carter, *Divine Healing,* 19.

38. F. F. Bosworth, *Christ the Healer,* 98–99, as quoted by Grant Wacker in *Heaven Below: Early Pentecostals and American Culture* (Cambridge, Mass.: Harvard University Press, 2001), 26.

39. Carrie Judd, *The Prayer of Faith* (Buffalo, N.Y.: H. H. Otis, 1880, 1882), 106.

40. Bedford, " 'A Larger Christian Life,' " 283, quoting *The Gospel of Healing,* 75–77.

41. Jennie Smith, *From Baca to Beulah* (Philadelphia: Garrigues Brothers, 1880), 198–99.

42. Judd, *The Prayer of Faith,* 107.

43. Simpson, *The Gospel of Healing,* 48.

44. Bedford, " 'A Larger Christian Life,' " 281; Schenk, "A Study of the New Testament Bases for the Teaching of Dr. Albert B. Simpson on Divine Healing," 48–49, quoting from Simpson's *Inquiries and Answers,* 4–5.

45. Bedford, " 'A Larger Christian Life,' " 281. See *Christian Alliance and Foreign Missionary Weekly* 6 (January 16, 1891), 39.

46. Bedford, " 'A Larger Christian Life,' " 284. This quotation is from a column with that title that Bainbridge published in *Christian Alliance and Foreign Missionary Weekly* 15 (September 25, 1895), 199.

47. Gordon P. Gardiner, *Radiant Glory: The Life of Martha Wing Robinson* (Brooklyn, N.Y.: Bread of Life, 1962), 298.

48. Bedford, " 'A Larger Christian Life,' " 297.

49. Bainbridge, *Life for Soul and Body,* 39–40.

50. Mossman, *Steppings in God,* 109; also referred to by Bedford, " 'A Larger Christian Life,' " 262–63.

# 8

## Pentecostalism

Pentecostalism began with a healing.

In February 1906, black Holiness preacher William Seymour (1870–1922) was invited by a friend, Neely Terry, to come from Houston to Los Angeles and preach to her small congregation. They had been expelled from Second Baptist Church because of their Holiness ideas. However, when he shared the notion that the baptism of the Holy Spirit was evidenced in the book of Acts by speaking in tongues, the leader of the congregation, Julia W. Hutchins, suggested he preach elsewhere.

Part of the interracial group decided to gather weekly in homes to pray and to listen to Seymour. He began to fast, seeking God's will in the situation. On Monday, April 9, 1906, about 6 P.M., Seymour dropped by to visit Mr. and Mrs. Edward S. Lee on South Union Avenue. "Irish" Lee, a bank custodian, had a splitting headache and asked Seymour to pray for his healing so that he could attend the evening's meeting. After Seymour prayed, Lee immediately felt much better and so asked Seymour to pray also that he might receive the Holy Spirit. To their surprise and delight, Lee at once began to speak in tongues. Seymour had not yet experienced the blessing himself.

Together they walked over to the home of Richard and Ruth Asberry at 214 North Bonnie Brae, where the group was to meet. Seymour opened the meeting with a song; several people prayed and gave testimonies. Then Seymour began to preach on Acts 2:4 ("and [the disciples] were all filled with the Holy Ghost and began to speak with other tongues, as the Spirit gave them utterance"). He shared what had just happened with Edward Lee—how Lee had been healed, filled with the Holy Spirit, and spoke in tongues. As if on cue, Edward Lee raised his hands in praise and a strange language poured from his mouth.

Others received the gift as well. Even though she was musically untrained, Jennie Evans Moore (1883–1936) spontaneously started playing the piano and singing in Hebrew[1]—the first woman there to receive the blessing. (Seymour later married her on May 13, 1908.) For three days the joyous celebration continued,

attracting widespread attention. The meeting became so exuberant that the
porch floor collapsed. The group immediately knew they needed a building, and
they found it at 312 Azusa Street. Built in 1888 by First African Methodist Episcopal Church, the now-vacant building had been a tenement above and livery stable
below. On Maundy Thursday, April 12, Seymour received the Holy Spirit and
spoke in tongues—he described the Spirit as a fiery radiance that melted him.
The next couple of days groups of men—Anglo, Asian, black, and Mexican—all
worked to clear debris from the building and ready it for services. By Tuesday,
April 17, the *Los Angeles Times* had gotten word and sent a reporter. The rest
is history.[2]

Born May 2, 1870, in Centerville, St. Mary Parish, Louisiana, sugarcane
country eighty miles southwest of New Orleans, Seymour was the eldest son of
Simon and Phillis Salabar Seymour. They had been freed from slavery less than
five years before, not by the Emancipation Proclamation but by ratification of the
Thirteenth Amendment.[3] Around 1900 William Seymour left the bayou for Indianapolis, where he worked as a hotel waiter and joined a Methodist church. He
soon moved on to Cincinnati, where he became involved in the Holiness movement through the teaching of white evangelist Martin Wells Knapp (1835–1901).
A nearly fatal case of smallpox blinded Seymour's left eye and prompted a deeper
spiritual journey.

Seymour returned to the South about 1904, eventually settling with some
relatives in Houston. That winter he felt led to visit Charles Price Jones in Jackson, Mississippi, a visit that again nourished his spirit. In the summer of 1905
Seymour was asked by the Reverend Lucy F. Farrow to pastor her Holiness church
while she worked in Kansas as a governess to the children of Charles Parham, a
white Holiness and healing evangelist. Neely Terry came by the church while in
town from Los Angeles to visit her family. From Farrow, in October 1905 Seymour learned that Parham believed that speaking in tongues was the evidence of
the baptism of the Holy Spirit. Farrow had spoken in tongues while in Kansas.
When Parham returned to Houston in December 1905 to open a Bible school,
Seymour asked to become a student (Farrow was the school's cook). Parham,
sympathetic to the Ku Klux Klan, agreed only to let Seymour listen from the hall.
During evening services, blacks sat in the back of the room and were not welcome
at the altar. In January 1906 Seymour left for Los Angeles.[4]

## Charles Parham

Charles Fox Parham (1873–1929) was born June 4, 1873, to William M. and
Anne Maria Eckel Parham in Muscatine, Iowa, the third of five sons. A sickly
child, he contracted a difficult fever at six months, rheumatic fever at nine, and

then a tapeworm. At age twenty-five, he said he suffered from dyspepsia, catarrh, sick headaches, a "stigmatized" eye, an abscess on his liver, and bouts with angina.[5] He felt called to ministry even before his conversion in 1886, perhaps in response to his mother's death in December 1885. By age fifteen he was preaching in local Methodist churches. At seventeen he enrolled in college to become a Methodist minister. However, in college he began to think that perhaps becoming a physician was a better way to help people and make money. When he changed majors, his religious life suffered and his rheumatic fever flared up. Finally in late 1891 he renewed his vow to preach and experienced complete healing.[6]

In September 1897 Parham and his young son Claude Wallace experienced healing again. From then on the Parhams decided to avoid drugs and doctors, relying on God alone for healing. In 1898 Parham committed himself to including divine healing in his public ministry. After holding meetings in Topeka, Kansas, in the summer of 1898, the Parhams relocated there and opened the Bethel Healing Home. "The object of the house is to provide home-like comforts to all who seek healing and a temporary stopping place for a friend while in the capital city."[7] By 1900 healing homes in Emporia, Ottawa, and Eskridge, Kansas, had a loose affiliation with Parham's. At Bethel there were four services on Sunday: morning worship at 11 A.M., Sunday school and Bible study at 2 P.M.; teaching on healing at 3, and an evangelistic service at 7:30. Eventually Parham's work included Bethel Bible School, a temporary orphanage, employment services, a rescue mission for transient men, and a shelter for prostitutes and poor working girls.[8] He also published a newspaper titled *Apostolic Faith.*

In 1900 Parham visited A. B. Simpson's Missionary Training Institute in Nyack, New York. Simpson encouraged his work. At least one of Parham's students had attended Simpson's Institute before coming to Topeka: Agnes Ozman (1870–1937).[9] Parham also traveled to Chicago to meet Alexander Dowie and to Shiloh, Maine, to meet Frank Sandford.[10] Around Christmas 1900, when he went off to hold meetings, he left Bible-school students with an assignment: to study the New Testament and to see what happened when a person received the Holy Spirit. Concentrating on the book of Acts, they concluded that people spoke in tongues (see Acts 2:4; 10:45–46; 19:6).

During the watch-night service on New Year's Eve, students prayed that they, too, might receive this evidence of the Holy Spirit. Around midnight Agnes Ozman asked that Parham lay hands on her and pray. As he did, just after midnight, January 1, 1901, she began to speak in what she said was Chinese.

In a sermon soon after, Parham declared:

> Now all Christians credit the fact that we are to be recipients of the Holy Spirit, but each have their own private interpretations as to his visible manifestations; some claim shouting, leaping, jumping, and falling in trances, while others put stress upon inspiration, unction, and divine revelation. . . . How much more reasonable it would

be for modern Holy Ghost teachers to first receive a Bible Evidence, such as the Disciples, instead of trying to get the world to take their word for it.[11]

However, after the flurry of speaking in tongues around New Year's 1901, activity trailed off. Parham and Ozman went back to preaching about salvation, sanctification, and divine healing. During a fall 1903 revival that Parham held in Galena, Kansas, the newspaper reported that eight hundred were converted and more than a thousand healed.[12]

In the Azusa Street revival, tongue speaking, or glossolalia, became the definitive evidence for many of the baptism of the Holy Spirit. Initially advocates of the phenomenon believed that it was xenolalia and meant that they would be able to evangelize the world by speaking different languages miraculously without study. While some may have been able to speak languages known to others (and early Pentecostal literature contains many testimonies attesting to that), it soon became obvious to those in the United States and those who rushed to mission fields abroad that speaking in tongues most often resulted in verbalizations that were spiritually satisfying to speakers but unintelligible to outsiders.[13]

Seymour acknowledged his debt to Parham in the first issue of *Apostolic Faith,* but when Parham arrived at Azusa Street in late October 1906, Parham's racism eclipsed his sanctification. As Amanda Berry Smith once said, "Some people don't get enough of the blessing to take prejudice out of them, even after they are sanctified."[14] Parham apparently felt that he could assume theological authority or perhaps white privilege. Shocked by the mingling of blacks and whites and by the exuberance of the worship, Parham began his sermon by declaring "God is sick at his stomach!" He went on to denounce their activities as "animalism" and the glossolalia as "white people imitating unintelligent, crude negroisms of the Southland, and laying it on the Holy Ghost."[15] While many outsiders, upon discovering Pentecostal worship, assumed that it was a novel phenomenon, a close reading of Holiness texts throughout the nineteenth century reveals that all of the behavior had been in evidence especially in camp meetings for a century or more. In the fall of 1906 Parham had already tried and failed to seize control of Zion, Illinois, after Dowie suffered a stroke. In the summer of 1907 Parham was arrested in San Antonio, Texas, on a charge of sodomy, a charge later dropped by the police. Although details of the incident never surfaced, rumors concerning it were another blow to his reputation. His followers drifted off into other groups.

## Revival on Azusa Street

Seymour sought to publicize the Azusa Street revival through a paper he too called *Apostolic Faith* (Parham was no longer publishing under the title). The first issue contained a statement of faith on page 2, which spoke of the "First Work—Justification" and the "Second Work—Sanctification" with "The Baptism of the Holy Spirit." Next came "Seeking healing—I must believe that God is able to heal," followed by a string of biblical references. In a page 1 report of the meetings, Seymour noted, "In about an hour and a half, a young man was converted, sanctified, and baptized with the Holy Ghost, and spoke with tongues. He was also healed from consumption, so that when he visited the doctor he pronounced his lungs sound." Another article on page 2 asserted, "Canes, crutches, medicine bottles and glasses are being thrown aside. . . . No need to keep . . . after God heals you." Yet another story on page 3 told of an incident on August 11, 1906, when an Indian man from central Mexico heard a German woman speaking his native dialect. Happily converted, he gave his testimony, and it was translated by a man who had been a missionary in the area. Then the young Indian, under the power of the Holy Spirit, laid hands on a woman nearby in the congregation, and she was healed of consumption.[16] Subsequent issues of the paper contained many similar stories of healings.

Typical was the story of eleven-year-old Lawrence F. Catley, suffering from tuberculosis. His African-American family had migrated to Los Angeles from San Antonio, looking for a better climate. His suffering was so intense that he would often go to bed, praying not to wake up. One day in 1906 a neighbor told his mother that she should take him to Azusa Street where people would pray for him. She did; they did. He was healed in a moment. As a young man Lawrence passed the physical and served in World War I. After the war he became a pastor. And that is what he was still doing when newspaperman Russell Chandler interviewed him for the *Los Angeles Times* in 1976.[17]

Seymour saw the work on Azusa Street as a continuation of God's outpouring. In the first issue of *Apostolic Faith* he declared, "We preach old-time repentance, old-time conversion, old-time sanctification, and old-time baptism with the Holy Ghost, which is the gift of power upon the sanctified life, and God throws in the gift of tongues." In response to the question, "What is the real evidence that a man or woman has received the baptism with the Holy Ghost?" Seymour wrote, "Divine love, which is charity. Charity is the Spirit of Jesus." Then they exhibit the fruits of the Spirit as listed in Galatians 5:22–23: "love, joy, peace, longsuffering, gentleness, goodness, faith, meekness, temperance." Then they speak in tongues, with signs following such as healing the sick and casting out demons.[18] Seymour believed that the result would be a new manifestation of the kingdom of God, marked by spiritual power, interracial reconciliation, and a new level of Christian unity. Many wanted power, but few in the age of Jim Crow were ready for racial reconciliation. The hope of unity turned into deeper fragmentation.

## Dividing the Faithful

Although Seymour remained true to the principles enunciated by many
Holiness and early Pentecostal advocates and did not found a new church or denomination, many people did start new organizations. By 1907 more than
twenty-five Holiness denominations had been formed,[19] and Pentecostals began
to create their own divisions. In 1908 Seymour's white administrative assistant,
Clara E. Lum (d. 1946), departed Los Angeles with his national and international mailing lists. She took them to Portland, Oregon, where Florence Crawford (1872–1936), a married white woman who had been sanctified, Spirit
baptized, and healed at Azusa Street, had already set up her own ministry. Lum
and Crawford started publishing *Apostolic Faith* from there, ignoring protests
from Seymour and his church's board of directors. Crawford's denomination is
still called the Apostolic Faith.

On March 2, 1907, white Chicago evangelist William H. Durham (1873–
1912) visited Azusa Street, received the baptism of the Holy Spirit, and spoke in
tongues. Seymour prophesied that Durham's preaching would result in the Holy
Spirit's descent on many people. When Durham returned to Chicago, the prophecy appeared to be fulfilled. Thousands came to hear him preach. In January 1910
Aimee Semple was instantaneously healed of a broken ankle in one of his services.
Those blessed by his preaching took the Pentecostal message to Italy, Scandinavia,
and South America.[20] In 1911 Durham preached at Azusa Street in Seymour's absence and taught that there was no need for a "second work of grace," that is,
sanctification. Stressing that the "finished work" of Jesus Christ on Calvary included sanctification along with justification, he urged people to find salvation
and then seek baptism of the Spirit with speaking in tongues. Seymour was ap-
palled and locked him out of Azusa Street. The controversy divided Pentecostals,
even though Durham died within a year—Seymour having prophesied that he
would perish unexpectedly if he ever deviated from God's will![21]

Those from more Wesleyan or Methodist backgrounds retained all three
blessings—salvation, sanctification, and baptism of the Spirit. Others from Presbyterian and Baptist or Reformed backgrounds tended to take Durham's "Finished Work" position that once a person was justified, then all he or she needed
was baptism of the Spirit with speaking in tongues.

## Unraveling the Alliance

Members of A. B. Simpson's Christian and Missionary Alliance already
leaned toward a more Reformed view of sanctification, rather than the Wesleyan
emphasis, and did not find Durham particularly disturbing. They were in their

own debate over the validity of the Pentecostal message and experience. Most receptive were Alliance people in northern Ohio—as my grandmother once surreptitiously confessed, "In the early days, everyone spoke in tongues." In 1906 Miss Ivey Campbell (1874–1919) returned home from a visit to Los Angeles and preached Pentecostalism in Akron and Cleveland branches of the Alliance.

David Wesley Myland (1858–1943), though born near Toronto on April 11, 1858, grew up near Cleveland. His father was called "a walking Bible cyclopaedia." His mother taught him Bible stories and helped him memorize Scripture. He was converted on November 20, 1877, the same year his father died. His dying mother dedicated him to the ministry, although at the time he was a businessman. By 1885 he was a Methodist local preacher. By 1891 he was leading an Alliance group in Cleveland. A very talented musician, Myland began to write hymns with James M. Kirk. They and two other pastors formed the famed Ohio Quartette.[22] Myland eventually published numerous songbooks.

Miraculously healed seven different times when close to death, Myland became a strong advocate of Holiness teaching and healing. Emphasis on the latter moved him from Methodism to the C&MA in 1890. His healing home, which operated for three years in Cleveland, was called El Shaddai. Following Simpson's lead, he spoke of healing as based not so much in Christ's atoning work on the cross as in Christ's resurrection power.[23] At the formation of the C&MA in 1897, Myland was appointed the first central district superintendent. By the end of his service with the Alliance, he had established churches in eighty of Ohio's eighty-eight county seats. Having heard about the Azusa Street revival almost immediately, he received the baptism of the Spirit and his seventh healing on November 3, 1906. He began preaching Pentecostalism.

Ivey Campbell's message was also affirmed by her district superintendent, W. A. Cramer, who received the baptism in Cleveland and wrote about it for the *Christian and Missionary Alliance Weekly*, April 27, 1907 issue, under the title "Pentecost in Cleveland." Simpson sent Dr. Henry Wilson to investigate. That summer's district convention at Beulah Park, Ohio, on Lake Erie was a hotbed of Pentecostal activity.[24]

In July 1912 the Mylands left the Columbus, Ohio, C&MA congregation and the denomination and moved to Plainfield, Indiana, fourteen miles west of Indianapolis. There he founded the Gibeah Bible School. It did not last very long, but included such students as J. Roswell Flower, Alice Reynolds Flower, Fred Vogler (1888–1972),[25] and Flem Van Meter, all of whom became leaders in the Assemblies of God.[26]

Carrie Judd's husband, George Montgomery, a very successful businessman, went to investigate the Azusa Street revival almost immediately. He was impressed, but she was more cautious. She felt that many people had become prideful. However, as friends began to experience the blessing and find increased power to pray and witness, she became more open. She had always thought of her experience of the Holy Spirit at her healing as her baptism. While on a trip back East (with C&MA friends in northern Ohio) in the summer of 1908, she took time to "tarry," to wait on God. She prayed, "By the blood of Jesus my whole being is open to the fulness of God, and by that same precious blood I am closed to any power of the enemy." The Spirit said, "Take," and finally she received the Spirit by faith, "to take complete possession of spirit, soul and body." A week later, in Chicago, on June 29, 1908, she spoke in tongues. She wrote about her "pentecostal" blessing in a tract titled "The Promise of the Father," reprinted in her autobiography, *"Under His Wings."* Following a trip to visit Alliance missions around the world in 1909, she spoke in two services at Simpson's New York church and then ministered at the Alliance conventions in Beulah Park, Ohio, and in Chicago, where many more spoke in tongues, sang in tongues, and were slain in the Spirit.[27] Like many others, Montgomery and Myland characterized the blessing as an outpouring of the "latter rain" prophesied in Zechariah 10:1 ("Ask ye of the LORD rain in the time of the latter rain; so the LORD shall make bright clouds, and give them showers of rain, to every one grass in the field"). Montgomery even gave her testimony to "pentecostal fulness" at a Friday healing meeting at Simpson's New York Gospel Tabernacle.[28] As late as 1918 Simpson was still inviting her to speak; she gave a weeklong series of messages at Old Orchard that year, even though she had joined the Assemblies of God in 1917.

Healing continued to be an issue. At an Ohio camp meeting (probably Beulah Park), Montgomery reported Mrs. Frances Kies sought healing but felt she did not receive it became she had rejected the "Pentecostal baptism of the Holy Spirit." She was healed when she finally "yielded to God, and told Him she was willing to speak in tongues as the Spirit gave utterance, even though she should meet great persecution because of it." Kies wrote of her experience in "The Miracle-Working Power of the Living God": "There was a conflict in my body as if another being was struggling within, but after a definite command in the almighty Name of Jesus, I was delivered."[29]

One of Montgomery's friends was Elizabeth Sisson. Healed of an incurable disease during her sojourn at Bethshan in London, she returned to the United States in 1887 to spread the teaching of divine healing. She became associate editor of Judd's *Triumphs of Faith.* When George Montgomery invited Judd to visit him in California in 1889 so he could propose to her (the Montgomerys were married May 14, 1890), Sisson went along. But she too was seeking a deeper experience of Holiness. One morning during a camp meeting in the 1890s (possibly Old Orchard, Maine), her "whole being let go to God" and she found herself "imbedded in God." "Heaven opened above my soul, and from the throne of God came flowing down great streams of love in hot tides." As she tried to preach, she "staggered about the platform, filled with unutterable glory." "I could but say to myself, 'Oh, this is the

Holy Ghost *and fire*. Why, I am drunk—drunk with God and glory." Known for her high-decibel preaching, Sisson traveled the United States and Canada, preaching the Word, often accompanied by her sister Charlotte W. Sisson. She preached in the British Isles in 1908. Sisson was the keynote preacher at the fifth General Council of the Assemblies of God, held in 1917. In 1915 she ministered for four months with healing evangelist F. F. Bosworth in Dallas.[30]

At Elim in the winter of 1906–1907, Elizabeth Baker and her sisters "were waiting on God for a fresh outpouring of His Spirit. The news of the movement called 'Pentecost' had reached us and we were questioning over it," wrote Olivia Work Bruce. "Personally I shrank from it, although believing it was from God. I argued that it was not necessary for everyone to speak in tongues, for I failed to see the real meaning as God has since shown us." Then one day her husband came into the kitchen where she was working and announced that her sister Marguerite was speaking in tongues. She went to see what was happening, and the Spirit "took possession, first with holy laughter, then with an overmastering desire to sing. I never could carry a tune without the notes, so it did not occur to me to yield to that desire, until it came with such force I just started singing."[31]

Simpson's Gospel Tabernacle in New York witnessed all kinds of signs and wonders in October 1907. In a widely reported incident, Miss Grace Hanmore sang heavenly melodies in tongues while suspended five or six feet above the floor. "Caught away in the Spirit," she did not know that she was singing. "She was raised bodily from the floor three distinct times. She afterwards stated she had seen a vision of a golden ladder and had started to climb it."[32] She later married Harold Moss, the principal of the Beulah Heights Bible and Missionary Training School in North Bergen, New Jersey. Even platform ministers were slain in the Spirit at Gospel Tabernacle.

The C&MA was in turmoil, and Simpson was ambivalent. Publicly he was trying to remain open to new truth and to quell defections from his movement. He did not want to quench the Spirit, but he also did not want the movement destroyed by unbridled enthusiasm. He wanted to say that the baptism of the Spirit can take many forms, but Pentecostals were beginning to say that those who did not speak in tongues had not received the Spirit and perhaps were not sanctified either. Other leaders read him as hostile to the movement, but Charles Nienkirchen's research into Simpson's personal diary revealed that Simpson was earnestly seeking Pentecostal baptism. At Old Orchard in August 1907 during his annual renewal of his personal covenant with God concerning healing, he was led to "believe and claim it all and rest in Him." Back home in Nyack, New York, "God revealed to [him] the NAME of JESUS in special power." A few days later the diary noted a divine visitation, "a very mighty and continued resting in the Spirit [came] down upon my body until it was almost over-powering and continued during much of the night." He renewed his personal disciplines of prayer and fasting. On a visit to Hamilton, Ontario, to celebrate the forty-second anniversary of his ordination, "the Spirit came with a baptism of Holy laughter for an hour or more." The next day his diary reported that he was "immersed for six hours in 'a distinct sense of . . . warmth . . . a penetrating fire.'" And then there was a five-year gap in the diary. He resumed it on October 6, 1912, with an entry that made it clear he had been seeking the gift of tongues, but it never came. With resignation he wrote: "No extraordinary manifestation of the Spirit in tongues or similar gifts has come."[33]

Finally in 1912 Simpson drew the line, and the C&MA remained a Holiness denomination. Many of those Alliance people convinced of the Pentecostal message helped to found the Assemblies of God. Simpson rejected the notion that speaking in tongues is required as "initial evidence" that a person has received the baptism of the Holy Spirit and is thus more important than other gifts. He was alarmed at how divisive the phenomenon had become, especially within the Alliance, and at the waves of fanaticism and extremism that it seemed to breed. He warned against seeking "experiences" rather than God.[34]

C&MA leaders defecting to the Assemblies included Carrie Judd and George Montgomery, healing evangelists F. F. Bosworth and B. B. Bosworth, and Daniel W. (1856–1927) and Mattie Kerr, a leading Alliance pastor in Dayton, Ohio, who experienced the Pentecostal blessing at Beulah Park in 1907. Alice Reynolds Flower (1890–1991) was sanctified and received the gift of tongues at the C&MA Tabernacle in Indianapolis, which her mother (after being healed) had helped to establish. Roswell Flower (1888–1970) was a member of the same congregation. Married in 1911, they teamed up to preach with the Mylands. Eventually they founded the *Pentecostal Evangel,* and Roswell held various executive positions in the Assemblies.[35]

Other leaders such as the Mylands and Minnie T. Draper became Pentecostal but remained independent of denominations. Draper was sanctified and healed at Simpson's Gospel Tabernacle and ministered beside him in many healing services including those in New York, Old Orchard, and Rocky Springs, Pennsylvania. Her testimony, "A Threefold Prescription: James 4:7,8," appeared in Montgomery's *Triumphs of Faith.* She was serving on the executive board of the Alliance when she received the Spirit baptism in 1906. Remaining on the board until 1912, she also helped organize the Bethel Pentecostal Assembly in Newark, New Jersey, and the Ossining (New York) Gospel Assembly, both of which eventually affiliated with the Assemblies of God.[36]

## Struggle in Zion

Plagued by charges of gross financial mismanagement and felled by a stroke, Alexander Dowie died in 1907, leaving Zion City with a power vacuum at a critical moment. Various factions struggled for power while the community's traditional Holiness and healing beliefs were being confronted with new Pentecostal experiences. Leaders were able to rebuff Charles Parham, and they officially rejected Pentecostalism. But many community members were attracted to it.

One of those was Martha Wing Robinson (1874–1936). She was born in Sand Spring, Iowa, to parents with deep New England roots: Harriet Tuttle (1846–1938) and Charles Orin Wing (1846–76). Converted at age twelve in a revival, she joined the Methodist church. At sixteen she went to live in Smith Falls, Ontario, with the aunt for whom she was named, now married to William Blair, a Methodist minister. There she completed her education. In 1893 she returned to teach in Iowa. In poor health, she tried allopathic and homeopathic physicians. Nothing helped. Her troubles included "stomach, liver, and kidney trouble, palpitation of the heart, continuous and severe headaches, female weakness with a partial paralysis of all lower organs, all resulting in a diseased state of the nerves that kept the entire flesh" of her body in constant pain "resembling inflammatory rheumatism, especially at nerve centers, such as wrists and ankles." On November 17, 1897, she began a three-month stay in a Davenport hospital, "taking massage and electrical treatment under the care of Dr. W. D. Middleton, one of the best physicians" in the city. Eventually doctors concluded that her maladies were incurable and that she was dying.

Her uncle had told her, "Mattie, something seems to tell me the Lord wants you to live and work just for Himself," but she had her mind set on a literary career. Through more than five years of struggle, it became clear that she could not find healing without a full surrender to God's will. In 1898 she gave up reading novels and took up Hannah Whitall Smith's *The Christian's Secret of a Happy Life* and Frances Ridley Havergal's *Kept for the Master's Use*. Havergal, a favorite poet of many Holiness advocates, was an invalid. Then a friend of the Wing family was healed. Mrs. H. E. Penley went to Dowie's healing home in Chicago. Her testimony was published in his *Leaves of Healing*.

Mrs. Penley visited Martha and left a copy of the paper. Martha politely read it but dismissed the testimonies. "I was afraid of getting into something absurd and fanatical," she said. But eventually she prayed about it and studied the Bible. On January 1, 1899, she sent Dowie a letter, requesting prayer. At the appointed time she and her sister prayed together. Nothing happened. She asked God to show her what needed to be done, and confession of certain things came to mind. So she repented. Still nothing happened. Finally in February she gave it all up to God. And the pain left. Her swollen liver subsided. On April 15, she went to the Zion Home in Chicago. At one meeting, Dowie had people pray with him clause by clause: "Take me as I am and make me what I ought to be in spirit, soul, and body, no matter what it costs." She agreed and was baptized but still felt that her surrender was incomplete. She stayed in Chicago for two months. Returning to Davenport at the end of June, she was completely well.[37]

In Davenport, Robinson worked for a year as the general secretary of a club for young working women. Then she worked with Tri-City Electric. Her Christian boss gave her flexible hours to accommodate her ministry. During a trip to Moline, Illinois, she prayed for a woman whose body had already been prepared for burial. The woman opened her eyes, smiled, and sat up. Robinson was present at the 1899 watch-night service when Dowie unveiled his plans for Zion City. On May 24, 1901, she, along with several women who became her lifelong friends, was ordained by Dowie. In November 1901, she moved to Zion City. Secretary to the manager of its largest commercial enterprise, she was also responsible for the spiritual welfare of all female workers. She also began working with Sarah M. Leggett. Carried to Chicago on a stretcher, suffering from a "blood tumor," Sarah had been instantly healed by Dowie's prayers.[38]

When Henry Walker Robinson (1874–1916), who had come to Zion from Toronto, first proposed marriage, Martha refused. The effectiveness of her prayers for healing was becoming known, and many people were coming to her. She was still working as a secretary and producing a biweekly payroll for five hundred workers. Early in 1903 she was put in charge of the spiritual welfare of her housing subdivision as well. Exhausted, she began to have health problems and spiritual fatigue as well. Realizing that if she married, she could quit her job and devote herself to ministry full time, she married Robinson on August 10, 1905.[39]

Harry was immediately assigned to an Apostolic Catholic Church congregation in Detroit, with a second small congregation in Toledo. Hearing that there was trouble in Zion, Martha returned to visit in 1906 about the same time that Parham arrived and news of the Azusa Street revival was taking hold. Seeing music director F. F. Bosworth receive the baptism of the Holy Spirit, Martha began to seek it, too. She felt she received the baptism in December 1906 but did not speak in tongues until February 1907. Harry also sought Spirit baptism but never did seem to find it, which caused major crises in their marriage and ministry. He resigned from Dowie's group. They moved to Toronto, where Zion friends were starting a Pentecostal ministry. Feeling that he should not minister until he had been baptized with the Spirit, Harry tarried and Martha was left to cope. She sang in the Spirit and experienced automatic writing. One day she played the organ under the Spirit's influence. She felt God had given her multiple gifts of wisdom, knowledge, and prophecy. For a while her ministry blossomed, and then suddenly all of her gifts seemed to disappear, precipitating not only poverty but also a dark night of the soul. Under various circumstances, the Robinsons began to live apart.[40]

Eventually her gifts returned. Martha and several other couples felt the call to move into a home together in downtown Toronto in 1909. In 1910 several of the group felt called to return to a very troubled Zion City and hold tent meetings. For a while the ministry was divided between Zion and Toronto, but eventually all moved to Zion in June 1911. Although they were not exactly welcomed by Zion's leadership, which had rejected the Pentecostal experience, they took up a ministry of healing, reconciliation, and restoration.

Eventually the group had three faith homes in Zion City, where Mrs. Robinson ministered for the last twenty-five years of her life. The inner circle included Robinson, Eva MacPhail (1876–1958, who eventually married William Leggett); Lydia Leggett (1871–1953) and her husband, George A. Mitchell (1861–1933); Sarah Leggett (1866–1949) and her husband, Elder Eugene Brooks (1856–1954). Their plan was to work together totally under God's direct guidance. They did not advertise, announce services, or send out a newsletter. There were no signs on their buildings or even any nameplates over the doorbells. As in other faith homes, people could come and stay for a day or a week. If they wished to stay longer, the leaders would ask God if that were a good thing. It God said yes, people were expected to help with the chores. All financial matters were strictly by faith. They took offerings only the first Sunday of the month and that all went straight to foreign missions. Healing was a constant in the ministry.[41]

Later in life, Martha Robinson was in pain, but God did not let her pray for her own healing. Instead Christ called her "into tune" with himself. "Jesus is my Life. Jesus is above pain," she said. From time to time "a flow of glory and life" would go through her and the pain was relieved.[42] She died, in Zion, on June 26, 1936.

## Pentecost in the South

The Azusa Street revival spread nationwide, and indeed around the world. The April 1907 edition of *Apostolic Faith* contained a letter from evangelist G. B. Cashwell, dated March 24 and sent from West Union, South Carolina: "Pentecost has come to the South. The power is falling from the Atlantic to the Mississippi River. The cities and country are filled with the glory of God, healing, working of miracles, diverse kinds of tongues, interpretation of tongues. Oh, how I praise God."[43]

Cashwell (1862–1916), known as the "Pentecostal apostle to the South," was a Methodist preacher who joined the newly formed Holiness Church of North Carolina in 1903. After reading reports by Frank Bartleman (1871–1946) about the Azusa Street revival in J. M. Pike's *Way of Faith,* he went to Los Angeles to check it out. Initially racial prejudice held him back, but eventually his desire for the blessing overcame his reluctance and he asked Seymour and others to lay hands on him. Receiving the gift of tongues, Cashwell said he spoke "English, German and French."

Returning to North Carolina, in January 1907 he rented a tobacco warehouse in Dunn to hold meetings, and Pentecostal revival ensued. In February 1907 he visited Fire-Baptized Holiness Church leader J. H. King (1869–1946) in north Georgia, and King received the Pentecostal experience. In March Cashwell held meetings in the South Carolina Piedmont, and former Presbyterian minister N. J. Holmes (1847–1919) and his students at the Altamont Bible and Missionary Institute spoke in tongues. Cashwell also introduced the Pentecostal message to A. J. Tomlinson. These men were all Holiness leaders in the Southeast.[44]

Across the South virtually all Holiness churches became Pentecostal. The largest denomination was and is Charles Harrison Mason's Church of God in Christ (COGIC), headquartered in Memphis. Mason visited Azusa Street and received the baptism at Seymour's hands. COGIC had already been incorporated in 1897, and between 1907 and 1914 many white Pentecostal ministers, including Carrie Judd Montgomery,[45] held credentials in the denomination in order to continue their ministries outside their previous affiliations and to enjoy such perks as ministerial railroad passes. However, in April 1914 the "white wing" of COGIC, led by Howard A. Goss (1883–1964), called a meeting in Hot Springs, Arkansas, to form the Assemblies of God. No blacks were invited.[46]

In the Southeast, Benjamin Hardin Irwin's Fire-Baptized Holiness Association evolved toward two denominations. William E. Fuller (1875–1958) became bishop of the predominately black Fire-Baptized Holiness Church of God of the Americas after whites withdrew to form the Pentecostal Holiness Church.[47] In Cleveland, Tennessee, A. J. Tomlinson helped to found the Church of God (Cleveland, Tennessee), and then the Church of God Prophecy, also headquartered there.

A few southern groups remained Holiness. Charles Price Jones separated from Mason's Church of God in Christ to form the Church of Christ (Holiness), U.S.A. Mary Lee Cagle and her New Testament Church of God joined with Phineas Bresee's (1838–1915) Southwestern churches to become the Church of the Nazarene in 1915. So did J. O. McClurkan's Nashville Holiness group called the Pentecostal Mission that formed in 1898 within the ranks of Cumberland Presbyterians. While McClurkan (1861–1914) had affirmed divine healing and the premillennial second coming, as well as a Reformed view of sanctification as the "indwelling" of the Spirit, and had at one time been aligned with Simpson's Christian Alliance, he rejected speaking in tongues.[48] Holiness revivalist William B. Godbey (1833–1920) also rejected speaking in tongues as essential. When asked if he spoke in tongues, the erudite Godbey quoted from the New Testament in Greek. Southern Holiness advocates A. B. Crumpler (1863–1952) and G. B. Cashwell returned to the Methodist Episcopal Church, South.

# Oneness

In 1914 the Assemblies of God were wracked by yet another controversy. It began in April 1913 at an international Pentecostal camp meeting in Arroyo Seco, California, when Canadian evangelist R. E. McAlister (1880–1953) noted in a sermon that in Acts 2:38 the apostles baptized people in the name of the Lord Jesus Christ, rather than the traditional trinitarian formula of Matthew 28:19. Southern California pastor Frank J. Ewart (1876–1947) began to study the issue and on April 15, 1914, he preached the Oneness of God as opposed to the doctrine of the Trinity as outlined in the Nicene Creed of 325. He and Glenn A. Cook (1967–1948), who had worked beside Seymour at Azusa Street, rebaptized each other "in Jesus' name." Cook also baptized Garfield Thomas Haywood (1880–1931), an African-American pastor in Indianapolis, and 465 members of his congregation.

As Oneness teachings spread, leaders of the Assemblies of God were divided. A Third General Council, convened October 1–10, 1915, in St. Louis, tried to find a middle ground with respect for the rights of conscience for pastors and local churches, but this proved unworkable. A Fourth General Council in the fall of 1916 finally set doctrinal limits in a "Statement of Fundamental Truths" that affirmed the traditional view of the Trinity. Haywood, one of the few blacks who had even participated in the formative meetings of the Assemblies, proceeded with his Pentecostal Assemblies of the World, the largest black Oneness group. Whites formed a variety of denominations, some of which eventually became the United Pentecostal Church. First general superintendent was Howard Goss, converted under the ministry of Charles Parham and one of the primary leaders in the formation of the Assemblies of God.[49]

# Aftermath

After the hubbub subsided, William Seymour and the still interracial group on Azusa Street kept the apostolic faith. The crowds had come and gone. A group of about twenty struggled to keep the doors open. On September 28, 1922, Seymour was working in his office when he experienced severe heart pains. A worker ran to get a physician, who examined Seymour and left him resting comfortably. But about 5 P.M. Seymour was sitting up and dictating a letter when a second massive heart attack felled him.

After the funeral his wife, Jennie, carried on as pastor. In the winter of 1930–1931 a white self-styled bishop tried to take control, precipitating a legal battle. A white judge chose to lock the church's doors while he deliberated. Trustees of the church borrowed $2,000 from Mrs. Seymour to pay the legal bills and in return gave her title to the building. In the meantime, the city took the opportunity in 1931 to condemn the now-empty building as a fire hazard and raze it. So she went back to leading the small congregation in her home at 217 North Bonnie Brae, across the street from the Asberrys' at 214, the place where it all began. She died on July 2, 1936.[50]

# Notes

1. Vinson Synan, *The Holiness-Pentecostal Tradition: Charismatic Movements in the Twentieth Century* (Grand Rapids, Mich.: Eerdmans, 1971, 1997), 96.
2. Douglas J. Nelson, "For Such a Time as This: The Story of Bishop William J. Seymour and the Azusa Street Revival: A Search for Pentecostal/Charismatic Roots" (Ph.D. diss., University of Birmingham, England, 1981), 59–62. The story of Lee's healing is on p. 60.
3. Ibid., 151–53.
4. Ibid., 32–37. See also C. M. Robeck Jr., "Azusa Street Revival" and "Seymour, William Joseph," in *The New International Dictionary of Pentecostal and Charismatic Movements* (ed. Stanley M. Burgess; Grand Rapids, Mich.: Zondervan, 2002), 344–50, 1053–58. Hereafter *International Dictionary*.
5. James R. Goff Jr., *Fields White unto Harvest: Charles F. Parham and the Missionary Origins of Pentecostalism* (Fayetteville: University of Arkansas Press, 1988), 23. See also Goff, "Parham, Charles Fox," in *International Dictionary*, 955–57.
6. Ibid., 26–29.
7. Ibid., 39, 40, 45. See also David E. Gray, "'Lean Not Thou on the Arm of Flesh,'" *Shawnee County Historical Bulletin* 57 (November 1980): 143–50.
8. Goff, *Fields White unto Harvest*, 47. 48, 45, 48.
9. William Boyd Bedford Jr., "'A Larger Christian Life': A. B. Simpson and the Early Years of the Christian and Missionary Alliance" (Ph.D. diss., University of Virginia, 1992), 223. See Sarah Parham, *The Life of Charles F. Parham: Founder of the Apostolic Faith Movement* (Joplin, Mo.: Tri-State Printing Co., 1930), 48. See also Edith L. Blumhofer, "Ozman, Agnes Nevada," in *International Dictionary*, 952.
10. Synan, *The Holiness-Pentecostal Tradition*, 90. Synan says that Parham first heard speaking in tongues at Shiloh.
11. Ibid., 112.
12. Parham, *The Life of Charles F. Parham*, 88–99.
13. See Felicitas D. Goodman, *Speaking in Tongues: A Cross-Cultural Study of Glossolalia* (Chicago: University of Chicago Press, 1972). In a cross-cultural study of the phenomenon, this cultural anthropologist found that it can be discovered in a variety of religious settings, that it is not a language in terms of grammar and syntax, but that it is a form of ecstatic vocalization marked by certain acoustic patterns.
14. Amanda Berry Smith, *An Autobiography: The Story of the Lord's Dealings with Mrs. Amanda Smith, the Colored Evangelist* (Chicago: Meyer & Brother, 1893), 226.
15. Nelson, "For Such a Time as This," 208–9.
16. *Apostolic Faith* (Los Angeles) 1 (September 1906): 2, 1; 2; 3. The September 1907 issue, 2, reprints the statement of faith found above but adds two long paragraphs headed "Healing" offering a narrative history of healing in Scripture.
17. Nelson, "For Such a Time as This," 206; see Russell Chandler, "Pasadena Cleric Recalls Mission," *Los Angeles Times*, January 11, 1976.
18. Iain MacRobert, *The Black Roots and White Racism of Early Pentecostalism in the U.S.A.* (New York: St. Martin's, 1988), 85, quoting *Apostolic Faith* 1:1 (September 1906); William Seymour, "Questions and Answers," *Apostolic Faith* 1:11 (January 1908): 2.
19. Robert Mapes Anderson, *Vision of the Disinherited: The Making of American Pentecostalism* (New York: Oxford University Press, 1979), 37.

20. R. M. Riss, "Durham, William H.," *Dictionary,* 255–56; *International Dictionary,* 594–95.

21. Nelson, "For Such a Time as This," 39.

22. J. Kevin Butcher, "The Holiness and Pentecostal Labors of David Wesley Myland: 1890–1918" (master's thesis, Dallas Theological Seminary, 1983), 37, 39, 42, 48, 52–53. See also E. B. Robinson, "Myland, David Wesley," *International Dictionary,* 920–21.

23. Ibid., 47.

24. Charles W. Nienkirchen, *A. B. Simpson and the Pentecostal Movement: A Study in Continuity, Crisis, and Change* (Peabody, Mass.: Hendrickson, 1992), 81–84. Nienkirchen also discusses all of the people covered in this section, as well as others not mentioned.

25. See chapter on Vogler in Edith L. Blumhofer, *"Pentecost in My Soul": Explorations in the Meaning of Pentecostal Experience in the Early Assemblies of God* (Springfield, Mo.: Gospel Publishing House, 1989), 100–116.

26. Butcher, "The Holiness and Pentecostal Labors," 4, 107.

27. Carrie Judd Montgomery, *"Under His Wings," The Story of My Life* (Oakland, Calif.: Office of Triumphs of Faith, 1936), 164-69, 187.

28. Bedford, " 'A Larger Christian Life,' " 227–28.

29. Montgomery, *"Under His Wings,"* 200.

30. Grant Wacker, *Heaven Below: Early Pentecostals and American Culture* (Cambridge, Mass.: Harvard University Press, 2001), 55, quoting from Sisson's article in *Latter Rain Evangel* (May 1909), 10; Wacker, 166. See also C. M. Robeck Jr., "Sisson, Elizabeth," *Dictionary,* 788–89; *International Dictionary,* 1071–72.

31. Elizabeth V. Baker and co-workers, *Chronicles of a Faith Life* (1915; repr., New York: Garland, 1984), 103–5.

32. Nienkirchen, *A. B. Simpson,* 84–85. He quotes from Stanley Frodsham, *With Signs Following* (Springfield, Mo.: Gospel Publishing House, 1926), 51–52. Frank Bartleman, *How Pentecost Came to Los Angeles* (Los Angeles: the author, 1925), also mentions it, p. 103. His mother was Virginia E. Moss (1875–1919); see G. B. McGee, "Moss, Virginia E.," *International Dictionary,* 909.

33. Nienkirchen, *A. B. Simpson,* 104–6. The entries from Hamilton are for September 12 and 13, 1907.

34. Ibid., 93.

35. Concerning Daniel Kerr, see Nienkirchen, *A. B. Simpson,* 109–10. Concerning Alice and Roswell Flower, see Nienkirchen, 34–35, and G. B. McGee, "Flower, Joseph James Roswell and Alice Reynolds," *Dictionary,* 311–13. See also the chapter on the Flowers in Blumhofer, *"Pentecost in My Soul,"* 40–60. For a history of the Assemblies of God, see Edith L. [Waldvogel] Blumhofer, *Restoring the Faith: The Assemblies of God, Pentecostalism, and American Culture* (Urbana: University of Illinois Press, 1993). This is an expansion of Edith Waldvogel, "The 'Overcoming Life': A Study of the Reformed Evangelical Origins of Pentecostalism" (Ph.D. diss., Harvard University, 1977).

36. Nienkirchen, *A. B. Simpson,* 112–13; G. B. McGee, "Draper, Minnie Tingley," *Dictionary,* 250; *International Dictionary,* 587–88.

37. Gordon P. Gardiner, *Radiant Glory: The Life of Martha Wing Robinson* (Brooklyn, N.Y.: Bread of Life, 1962), 5–69.

38. Ibid., 77, 80, 81, 91, 94.

39. Ibid., 92–93, 95–100.

40. Ibid., 112–18, 121–22,140–42, 170, 178–83.

41. Ibid., 213–17.

42. Ibid., 291–92, 302.

43. *Apostolic Faith* (Los Angeles) 7 (April 1907), 4.

44. H. V. Synan, "Cashwell, Gaston Barnabas," *International Dictionary,* 457–58; C. M. Robeck Jr., "Pike, John Martin," Ibid., 988–89; H. V. Synan, "King, Joseph Hillery," Ibid., 822–23; N. J. and Lucy Holmes, *Life Sketches and Sermons: The Story of Pentecostal*

*Pioneer N. J. Holmes* (Royston, Ga.: Press of the Pentecostal Holiness Church, 1920; repr., Franklin Springs, Ga.: Advocate Press, 1973); H. D. Hunter, "Tomlinson, Ambrose Jessup," *International Dictionary,* 1143–45.

45. Daniel E. Albrecht, "Carrie Judd Montgomery: Pioneering Contributor to Three Religious Movements," *Pneuma* 8 (fall 1986), 118. The credential was dated January 11, 1914.

46. Synan, *Holiness-Pentecostal Movement,* 69–70; MacRoberts, *The Black Roots and White Racism of Early Pentecostalism,* 64, 117, 120. Montgomery's first credentials from the Assemblies were dated November 30, 1917 and probably issued on the basis of her prior COGIC affiliation. She is listed among the charter members.

47. H. V. Synan, "Fuller, William E.," *International Dictionary,* 652–53; "Fire-Baptized Holiness Church," *Ibid.,* 640.

48. Synan, *The Holiness-Pentecostal Movement,* 70–71.

49. See D. A. Reed, "Oneness Pentecostalism," *Dictionary,* 644–51; E. A. Wilson, "McAlister, Robert Edward," *International Dictionary,* 852; J. L. Hall, "Ewart, Frank J.," *Dictionary,* 290; C. M. Robeck Jr., "Haywood, Garfield Thomas," *Dictionary,* 349–50; J. L. Hall, "Goss, Howard Archibald," *Dictionary,* 343.

50. Nelson, "For Such a Time as This," 46–47, 262–70.

# 9

# Healing Evangelists

A. B. Simpson, in *The Gospel of Healing*, declared, "I have never allowed anyone to look to me as a healer. I have had no liberty to pray for others while they placed the least trust in either me or my prayers—or in anything or anyone but the merits, promises and intercessions of Christ alone."[1] Others were less restrained.

Healing played a large part in the evangelism of Charles Parham, although he does not seem to have represented himself as a healer, per se. After the events of January 1, 1901, at Bethel Bible School in Topeka simmered down, Charles Parham and Agnes Ozman went back to holding evangelistic meetings in which divine healing played a significant part. Others continued to do the same.

Perhaps it was a natural evolution that some Holiness and Pentecostal preachers who featured divine healing as part of their ministry came to be seen as healers by the press and by their constituencies. All of them continued to follow the revivalist format outlined in 1835 by Charles Grandison Finney in his *Lectures on Revivals of Religion*. They held "protracted meetings," usually nightly for weeks at a time, in which they urged sinners to repent of their sins and the previously saved to deepen their commitment through the baptism of the Holy Spirit in sanctification and/or speaking in tongues. Public evening meetings were supplemented with various types of prayer meetings, "inquirers' meetings," and instructional sessions. Divine healing was a topic usually approached toward the end of the week. Following Simpson's example, healing was often the topic of Friday's sermon, followed by the laying on of hands or mass prayers for the sick. Those who were successful with this type of ministry gained the reputation of healers.

## Mattie E. Perry

Mattie Perry was born May 15, 1868, in Oconee County, South Carolina, the second of nine children. Her father, J. A. Perry, the son of Baptist parents, became a local Methodist preacher. Her mother, Jane Holden, was from a Methodist family. Mattie was "gloriously saved at Bethel camp meeting" when she was twelve. In July 1887 she "consecrated myself and my all for time and for eternity, without reserve, so far as I knew, to the Lord to be used as He saw fit." She began by doing "altar work" (praying with seekers) during the Twelve Mile Camp Meeting in Pickens, South Carolina, that October. She attended the Williamston Female College, graduating in 1892.[2]

Perry hoped to be a charter student at the Methodists' Scarritt Training School, but there was no money. She felt called to go to China as a missionary, and she applied to the Methodist Episcopal Church, South, Board of Missions, but they turned her down. They termed her a "hindered volunteer." Whether the hindrance was money, health, or family responsibilities is unclear. She applied to the South Carolina Methodist Conference to be a city missionary. They told her there were no openings. She heard that J. M. Pike was looking for agents to solicit subscriptions to his Holiness paper *The Way of Faith*, published in Columbia. So she applied. Pike sent her a stack of papers but assigned her no territory.

Understandably discouraged, Perry began to make her own way. Her family having moved to Spartanburg, she began her own city mission work, especially in the textile mill hill section of town—nursing the sick, visiting house to house, passing out Christian literature, teaching a temperance Sunday-school class at her church, assisting in revival services, often with her brother Samuel (1875–1960). Having read George Müller's *Life* as a child, she learned to trust God for her material needs and her family's as well. Since she had become the support of her mother, her invalid father, and two younger siblings, she began holding revival meetings on her own or with a brother or sister as traveling companion.[3]

In 1895 Perry traveled from Laurinburg, North Carolina, to Keuka, New York, with less than $12 in her purse, even though the train ticket cost $22. God always provided the money. Her goal was to attend the New York State convention of Simpson's Christian Alliance. When Simpson preached on missions, she stood and pledged to support a missionary to China. That fall she attended Simpson's Bible Institute and undertook the support of a friend she met there, Amy Brown, who arrived in China in January 1896 and stayed until driven out during the Boxer Rebellion. Perry had been sanctified for some time but found a "deeper death to self" when Simpson and Stephen Merritt (1833–1917) held a Holiness convention in Columbia.[4]

When the Christian and Missionary Alliance was formed in 1897, Mattie Perry became its pioneer superintendent for the Southeast—North Carolina, South Carolina, Georgia, Florida, and Tennessee. For the rest of her life, she held meetings under its auspices. She also reached out to Pentecostal groups after a "Pentecostal baptism of the Holy Spirit" that she alluded to but did not describe in her autobiography.[5]

Sometime in her early life Perry considered herself an invalid, suffering from a number of diseases—"heart, lungs, blindness, neuralgia, and other diseases." Under the treatment of physicians, she grew worse. She "submitted cheerfully to the suffering, thinking it was His will," but she kept praying that if God had a lesson for her to learn that she would learn it quickly. Then, she said, "the first person I saw who taught divine healing prayed with me and I was instantly lifted out of the invalid life to perfect health." Unfortunately she did not disclose in her book under what circumstances it took place, though it appears to have happened in the early 1890s. Apparently for three years after her healing, she neglected to preach on the subject. After the Spirit convicted her on the subject, she expressed remorse that she had not shared this good news earlier and had thus deprived others of healing they might have received.[6]

From 1898 to 1926 Perry conducted "a faith school for poor boys and girls," including an orphanage, in Marion, North Carolina. Called the Elhanan Training Institute and Orphanage and averaging 150 students and staff, the school was run on Müller's faith principle. Perry was not only its founder and administrator but also its spiritual leader and chief fundraiser. Not surprisingly, "as a result of excessive work, taking many of the sleeping hours," she "went down with exhaustion." For many years she ran the school from either her "invalid's couch" or a "rolling chair." Yet even while she was bedridden, people would come for her to lay hands on them, and they would find healing. She suffered a variety of ills: "I broke out with smallpox and was healed in a night. Had cancer, fever, tumor, throat and lungs affected, asthma, carbolic acid by mistake one night." She claimed the promise of Mark 16:18 ("if they drink any deadly thing, it shall not hurt them") and "was instantly healed and went to sleep and had no further ill effects from it." Another time, "My heart failed again and I was thought to be dying." She had pellagra—"my whole body was affected and I was a physical wreck, but I anointed myself for healing, in the absence of anyone to do it for me, and I was healed that night. All pain was gone, and within eight days the tender new flesh had come back in the affected parts of my hands and feet, and I was made whole." She speaks of "fourteen years of invalid life."[7]

The timing is unclear, but eventually Perry had a "Pentecostal baptism of the Holy Spirit," and after that "the old, tired feeling went like the dropping of an old garment. My memory was quickened and my nerves steadied instantly." Later she said that on November 19, 1919, she left North Carolina for the West with $6 and within six months she had traveled alone more than twelve thousand miles, holding meetings. "And as I went I was healed and soon holding some of the greatest campaigns of my life." Eventually the Elhanan buildings burned, and she closed the school in 1927. Her health improved when she went back to her evangelistic and healing ministry.[8]

In the 1920s Perry held numerous meetings across the country, often in C&MA churches. In Sharon, Pennsylvania, in 1921, headlines read "Hundreds Healed." Newspapers called her a "healer" and "a woman of unusual power." She preached in Ohio and New York and across the South to Texas. She held four campaigns in Washington, D.C. In Pittsburgh and in Dallas she assisted the Bosworth brothers.[9]

Finally in 1937 she retired to teach at God's Bible School (Martin Wells Knapp's school) in their Christian worker's course and to write for their publication, *God's Revivalist*. For several years she had been publishing her own Elhanan Correspondence Bible School and developing a "harmony" of the whole Bible, matching Old Testament Scriptures with what she perceived as their fulfillments in the New Testament.[10] She died November 14, 1957.

## Maria B. Woodworth-Etter

Maria B. Underwood Woodworth-Etter (1844–1924; she pronounced her name "Mariah") took another route. Born in Lisbon, Ohio, she was converted, baptized, and felt a call to ministry at age thirteen. But she married Philo H. Woodworth and gave birth to six children. After five of the children died and her marriage proved difficult, at thirty-five she renewed her spiritual commitment and began to preach. In 1884 she affiliated with the Winebrennerian Church of God (Findlay, Ohio). During March 1885 meetings in Columbia City, Indiana, she later wrote that "the Lord showed me while there that I had the gift of healing, and of laying on of hands for the recovery of the sick."[11] Beginning with a January 1885 revival at the Methodist Episcopal Church in Hartford City, Indiana, her meetings attracted national attention with more than twenty newspaper reporters in attendance—including reporters from the *Cincinnati Enquirer,* the *Indianapolis Journal,* the *Fort Wayne Gazette,* and the *New York Times.* Apparently, due to her lack of education, her speaking abilities in the beginning were meager, but later stories attributed more eloquence. Many stories focused on trance behavior by Mrs. Woodworth, those in the congregation, and others in their homes—she was often dubbed the trance evangelist. The *Indianapolis Journal* (September 9, 1885) told the story of Mrs. C. P. Diltz of Madison County, who had been healed that spring after Mrs. Woodworth prayed at her bedside.[12]

Crisscrossing the country for the next two decades, Woodworth drew crowds of twenty-five thousand people. In 1891 she divorced Woodworth, charging him with adultery; he died a year later. In 1902 she married Samuel Etter, hyphenating their two last names. Then she dropped out of sight. Amazingly, her biographer W. E. Warner was unable to document her activities between 1905 and 1912.[13] One might suggest that since she turned sixty in 1904 and her new husband was in poor health (he died in 1914), perhaps she retired to care for him. Yet in 1912 she re-emerged on the public scene, holding revivals as a full-fledged Pentecostal. At age sixty-eight she held meetings from July into December at F. F. Bosworth's church in Dallas. The next spring Woodworth-Etter was a featured speaker at the Worldwide Camp Meeting of Pentecostals in Arroyo Seco, California.

In March 1913 she held six days of meetings in Oakland, California, which Carrie Judd Montgomery attended and described favorably in her paper, *Triumphs of Faith.*

> The altar services were remarkable, large numbers crowding forward for spiritual blessing and healing of the body. So many desired healing that it was impossible for Mrs. Etter to pray personally with each one, but she laid hands on a large number at nearly every altar service and prayed the prayer of faith for them. . . .
>
> We conversed with a young woman who was instantly healed of deafness. She said she had been deaf for fifteen years and very deaf for three years. She heard me as I conversed with her in an ordinary tone, and she seemed very happy and full of praise. Mrs. Etter had commanded the deaf demons to come out of her ears in the name of Jesus. A man whom we knew was healed of deafness with which he had been afflicted for more than fifty years.[14]

Note that Mrs. Woodworth-Etter was praying the prayer of faith *for* the sick rather than encouraging them to pray it for themselves. Pentecostals were also beginning to speak about casting out demons, whereas one seldom finds references to demons in nineteenth-century Holiness literature. In 1918 Woodworth-Etter established her own local church in Indianapolis.[15] Despite her divorce and sometimes eccentric behavior, Maria Woodworth-Etter completed her life journey with dignity and respect from many quarters.

## Aimee Semple McPherson

Woodworth-Etter's successor in many ways was Aimee Semple McPherson (1890–1944), whose story is much better known. Born in Canada to a Methodist church musician father and a Salvation Army lassie mother, she came by Holiness naturally. At seventeen she married Pentecostal evangelist Robert Semple in a Salvation Army ceremony. Both were ordained in 1909 in Chicago by William Durham. Understanding China to be their mission field, they had only begun language study in Hong Kong when Robert contracted malaria and died. Their daughter, Roberta, was born shortly thereafter.

Aimee returned to the United States, to New York City, where she met Harold Stewart McPherson (1890–1968). They married in 1911. Aimee resumed her ministry, even during her pregnancy with their son Rolf Potter Kennedy McPherson (1913–). On October 30, 1918, Aimee visited Woodworth-Etter in

Indianapolis.[16] Although the McPhersons ministered together for a time, he eventually returned to Rhode Island, and they divorced in 1921. In 1919 Aimee was ordained as an evangelist by the Assemblies of God. She returned those credentials in 1921, not because of her divorce but because she wanted to hold full financial title to the church she was building in Los Angeles, the Angelus Temple. Out of that grew the International Church of the Foursquare Gospel. Echoing Simpson, Aimee's gospel focused on Jesus Christ as Savior, Baptizer with the Holy Spirit, Physician and Healer, and Coming King.[17]

After Aimee was wonderfully healed of a badly dislocated ankle as a young adult, she made healing services a part of her ministry. During a 1921 crusade in San Diego, crowds clamoring for healing prayers grew so great that she held two outdoor services in Balboa Park. U.S. Marines volunteered to help control the crowd, estimated by the police at thirty thousand.[18] A revival that same year in Denver saw thousands seeking healing. Sister Aimee even proclaimed July 10, the last day of the crusade, Stretcher Day. The mayor's wife, a prominent lawyer, and a state Supreme Court justice were among those who claimed healing during her visit.[19]

Sister Aimee's fame spread, and her obligations multiplied. In addition to being pastor of a church and leader of a denomination, she was the first woman to obtain a radio station license to broadcast the gospel. She baptized Marilyn Monroe. And healing remained a major emphasis throughout her ministry. Despite critics and some self-inflicted scandals, she remained a beloved figure and force to be reckoned with until her death on September 27, 1944.[20] Fifty thousand mourners paid tribute.

Sister Aimee bridged the gap between the early days of Pentecostalism and the healing revivals of the 1940s and 1950s. She represents an earlier period of individual healers than those whom David Edwin Harrell Jr., lifted up in *All Things Are Possible* (1975).[21] He wrote of the post-World War II healing evangelists, but no one has similarly focused on those active during and after World War I. Nor are they the subject of this book. But one can point to several men who were Sister Aimee's colleagues.

## The Bosworth Brothers

My grandmother used to talk about the time the Bosworth brothers set up their revival tent two blocks from her home in the field where my senior high school came to stand. She swore they visited her home and played her old upright piano. Fred Francis Bosworth (1877–1958) and his younger brother Burton B. Bosworth, along with their wives, held healing revivals across the country. Born in Nebraska, F. F. Bosworth learned to play the cornet. When the family moved to

Fitzgerald, Georgia, he eventually followed, suffering from pulmonary disease that doctors diagnosed as hopeless. In Fitzgerald he wandered into the Methodist Episcopal Church, South, where evangelist Mattie E. Perry was preaching Holiness. When he began to cough during the service, she laid hands on him and prayed, and he received healing. He bought a barber shop, was appointed the assistant postmaster, and elected city clerk. In his spare time he directed two bands.[22]

Eventually he moved to Dowie's Zion City, where he became band director. When Charles Parham visited in 1906, Bosworth received the Pentecostal blessing, including speaking in tongues. He also felt called to preach and began receiving invitations across the country from South Bend, Indiana, to Austin, Texas; from Conway, South Carolina, to Waco, Texas. Beginning in 1910 he pastored the Christian and Missionary Alliance Church in Dallas where Woodworth-Etter held a major revival in 1912. F. F. was a delegate to the First General Council of the Assemblies of God, but eventually he withdrew because he could not affirm the gift of tongues as the *only* initial sign of Spirit baptism. The brothers then held healing crusades under the auspices of the Christian and Missionary Alliance, including the one in my hometown, Lima, Ohio.

The August 1920 meetings in Lima were a turning point. B. B. was the musician for the meetings—soloist, song leader, playing slide trombone in duet with F. F.'s cornet. Although F. F. had preached on healing for many years, just before the Lima meetings he did a "Spirit-illumined study of the Bible on the subject of Healing" and "began boldly to emphasize in the Lima meetings that sick people, both saints and sinners, should be invited from far and near, to hear what the compassionate Christ longs to do for their pain-racked bodies as well as their sin-burdened souls." The sick came in droves.[23] The Bosworth brothers also became pioneers in radio evangelism. When William Branham (1909–1965) began his healing ministry, F. F. Bosworth came out of retirement to join him.[24]

## Other Healers

Charles Sydney Price (1880–1947) came to Pentecostalism via Canada. An Englishman, trained as a lawyer at Oxford, he became a Methodist and then Congregational pastor on the West Coast. He was baptized with the Holy Spirit after attending one of Sister Aimee's meetings in 1920. Healing soon became a part of his message. After successful crusades in the Pacific Northwest and across Canada, he traveled to many other parts of the world.[25]

Raymond T. Richey (1893–1968) was another of the healing evangelists of the 1920s and 1930s. He published a book titled *Helps to Young and Old* (1922). A childhood injury caused his eyes to fail, but his eyesight was restored when he committed his life to Christ in 1911. During World War I he ministered to troops near Houston and contracted tuberculosis. Seeking a better climate, he moved to southern California, where he found healing again in 1919. His healing ministry began almost by accident when another evangelist that Richey was scheduled to assist became ill and left Richey to pray for the sick.[26]

John G. Lake (1870–1935), a very successful businessman, came into his healing ministry through a series of healings in his family. In 1898 his wife was healed of consumption under the ministry of Alexander Dowie. Lake became an elder in the Zion Catholic Apostolic Church. Receiving the Pentecostal blessing in 1906 during Parham's visit to Zion, Lake became a faith missionary to South Africa, where his wife died in 1909. He returned to Spokane, Washington, in 1914, and continued his healing ministry. Relocating to Portland, Oregon, in 1920, he continued to preach healing until his death in 1935.[27] Lake often said that he could "feel the Spirit flow" down his arm, into his hand, and across to the person seeking healing.[28]

Smith Wigglesworth (1859–1947) was a British evangelist, trained only as a plumber, who also had a strong healing ministry around the world in this period. He learned to read as an adult and then claimed to read nothing but the Bible. He experienced Pentecost under the ministry of Anglican vicar Alexander Boddy (1854–1930) and his wife, Mary, in their Sunderland parish. His healing ministry began shortly thereafter when he was healed of appendicitis. He conducted numerous meetings in the United States.[29]

This group of healing evangelists moved divine healing beyond the local church and camp meeting settings into the more public realm of tent and auditorium revivals. Some brought it to radio and eventually television. Woodworth-Etter and McPherson, because they were women, had to evolve strong personal styles; the men slipped easily into the ministerial mode of public ministry. But focusing more directly on one person as a dispenser of healing, despite all of their efforts to give God the credit, changed perceptions of divine healing. However, within local Holiness and Pentecostal churches divine healing continued to be practiced, even if more muted.

## Denominational Commitments

Divine healing was written into the initial statements of faith in many Holiness and Pentecostal denominations. Although emphasis shifted away from healing and sanctification in the C&MA, it has always maintained Simpson's "fourfold gospel" in its logo: Jesus Christ as Savior, Sanctifier, Healer, and Coming King. Likewise, Aimee Semple McPherson's International Church of the Foursquare Gospel has remained committed to Jesus Christ as Savior, Baptizer with the Holy Spirit, Healer, and Coming King.

In 1907 the General Assembly of the Church of God (Cleveland, Tennessee) debated the question, "Shall we use drugs in case of sickness or take Jesus alone?" They concluded to "take Jesus as our Physician." Some people carried a card in their wallet with the following:

| | |
|---|---|
| **Medical Card** | |
| Name: _____ | |
| Name of Firm: | Church of God |
| My Physician Is: | Jesus |
| Address: | Heaven |
| Phone: | By Way of Prayer[30] |

The *Discipline of the Holiness Church* in 1902 declared that "healing of the body of its sickness is a blessed provision of the atonement. . . . We do not consider it an evidence of sin or a mark of divine displeasure because a person is sick or employs medical aid. Neither do we believe that it is an evidence in itself that a person is of God because he is healed in answer to prayer." *The Constitution . . . of the Fire-Baptized Holiness Church* in 1905 said, "we believe also in divine healing as in the atonement." Eventually uniting to form the Pentecostal Holiness Church, they continued to affirm divine healing and in fact began to declare after World War I that anyone who saw a doctor or took any form of medication was demonstrating unbelief. Even the use of glasses, dental work, or aspirin for a headache were denounced. This led to a split in 1920. Two north Georgia pastors withdrew and formed the Congregational Holiness Church. They noted that Isaiah applied a "fig poultice" to King Hezekiah (2 Kings 20:7), Jesus put clay on a man's eyes (John 9:6), Paul told Timothy to "take a little wine for the stomach's sake" (1 Timothy 5:23), and the Good Samaritan poured oil and wine into the man's wounds (Luke 10:34). The CHC statement of faith affirmed, "We believe in divine healing for the body (but we do not condemn Medical Science)."[31]

# Notes

1. A. B. Simpson, *The Gospel of Healing* (1885; repr., Camp Hill, Pa.: Christian Publications, 1994), 139.

2. Mattie E. Perry, *Christ and Answered Prayer* (Nashville: Benson Printing Company, 1939), 25, 27, 28, 35, 40.

3. Ibid., 46, 42, 53, 83. 133. See D. G. Roebuck, "Perry, Samuel Clement," *International Dictionary*, 982–83.

4. Perry, *Christ and Answered Prayer*, 95–98,

5. Ibid., 145, 72.

6. Ibid., 69, 59.

7. Ibid., 72, 202–3.

8. Ibid., 72, 204, 227, 271.

9. Ibid., 231, 217, 227, 249, 230, 237.

10. Ibid., 266, 307.

11. Mrs. M. B. Woodworth-Etter, *Acts of the Holy Ghost, or The Life, Work, and Experience of Mrs. M. B. Woodworth-Etter* (Dallas: John F. Worley Printing, n.d. [1912]), 107–8.

12. Roberts Liardon, comp., *Maria Woodworth-Etter: The Complete Collection of Her Life Teachings* (Tulsa, Okla.: Albury Publishing, 2000), 68–79, 177–78.

13. W. E. Warner, *The Woman Evangelist: The Life and Times of Charismatic Evangelist Maria B. Woodworth-Etter* (Metuchen, N. J.: Scarecrow, 1986), 163. See also Warner, "Woodworth-Etter, Maria Beulah," *International Dictionary*, 1211–13.

14. Liardon, *Maria Woodworth-Etter*, 447. From Carrie Judd Montgomery, ed., "Mrs. Etter's Meetings in Oakland," *Triumphs of Faith*, March 1913. November and December 1912 issues of the magazine had carried stories about Woodworth-Etter's meetings in Dallas. The November report was from a letter by Mrs. C. Nuzum. The second was a first-hand report from the editor—apparently she and her husband went to visit the meetings. Carrie wrote, "Mrs. Etter is an old-time friend of ours," 443.

15. W. E. Warner, "Woodworth-Etter, Maria Beulah," *Dictionary*, 900–901.

16. Edith L. Blumhofer, *Aimee Semple McPherson, Everybody's Sister* (Grand Rapids, Mich.: Eerdmans, 1993), 147.

17. C. M. Robeck Jr., "International Church of the Foursquare Gospel," *Dictionary*, 461–63.

18. Blumhofer, *Aimee Semple McPherson*, 83, 160–62.

19. Ibid., 171–72.

20. Ibid., 375.

21. David Edwin Harrell Jr., *All Things Are Possible: The Healing and Charismatic Revival in Modern America* (Bloomington: Indiana University Press, 1975).

22. Eunice M. Perkins, *Fred Francis Bosworth: The Joybringer* (2d ed. (n.p.: n.p., 1st ed., 1921; 2d ed., 1927), 15–31.

23. Ibid., *Fred Francis Bosworth*, 36–37, 48, 63, 69, 84, 88–89, 85–86.

24. R. M. Riss, "Bosworth, Fred Francis," *Dictionary*, 94.

25. R. M. Riss, "Price, Charles Sydney," *Dictionary*, 726–27.

26. R. M. Riss, "Richey, Raymond Theodore," *Dictionary*, 758.

27. J. R. Zeigler, "Lake, John Graham," *Dictionary*, 531; Roberts Liardon, comp., *John G. Lake: The Complete Collection of His Life Teachings* (Tulsa, Okla.: Albury Publishing, 1999), 9–23. In addition to volumes on Woodworth-Etter and Lake, Liardon has published a similar volume on Smith Wigglesworth.

28. Grant Wacker, *Heaven Below: Early Pentecostals and American Culture* (Cambridge, Mass.: Harvard University Press, 2001), 94.

29. W. E. Warner, "Wigglesworth, Smith," *Dictionary*, 883–84. The Boddys were major Pentecostal leaders in England. See D. D. Bundy, "Boddy, Alexander Alfred," *International Dictionary*, 436–37.

30. Mickey Crews, *The Church of God: A Social History* (Knoxville: University of Tennessee Press, 1990), 70.

31. Vinson Synan, *The Old-Time Power: A History of the Pentecostal Holiness Church* (rev. ed.; Franklin Springs, Ga.: Advocate Press, 1973, 1986), 166, 167, 168; B. L. Cox, *History and Doctrine of the Congregational Holiness Church* (2d ed.; n.p.: n.p., 1959), 7, 42.

# 10

## When Healing Fails

New Englander Frank Sandford (1862–1948) was once a local baseball star. Originally a Freewill Baptist minister, he began to preach Holiness after reading Hannah Whitall Smith's *The Christian's Secret of a Happy Life.*[1] He became convinced of the doctrine of divine healing after an 1887 visit to A. B. Simpson's camp meeting at Old Orchard. His widowed sister Maria had come home from the meeting the year before claiming healing from lifelong crippling back pain, but he had been skeptical even though she was able for the first time to do her own housework, caring for her five children.[2] At Old Orchard he also met and courted Helen Kinney, daughter of wealthy Simpson supporters, student at Simpson's Missionary Training Institute, and vowed missionary candidate. Simpson presided at their 1892 wedding.[3]

Over the winter of 1895 Sandford founded The Holy Ghost and Us Bible School; then he built a community named Shiloh, near Durham, Maine.[4] He began to publish a journal titled *Tongues of Fire.* But all was not well. On January 23, 1904, Sandford was arrested and charged with cruelty to children and manslaughter in the death of Leander Barrett, who died of diphtheria when the Shiloh community depended on prayer rather than administer a relatively new antitoxin serum that might have quelled the disease. Six others in the community died of smallpox the same winter. One jury could not decide; a second found him guilty.[5]

Eventually Sandford proclaimed himself to be the prophet Elijah. He bought a yacht and set out to save the world. But when food and water failed, he refused to admit defeat and put into port. He was sentenced to a ten-year term in the Atlanta federal penitentiary for starving to death six members of his crew.

Those for whom divine healing failed seldom left testimonies, but eventually Holiness and Pentecostal communities had to come to terms with their failures as well as their successes.

# Who to Blame?

The most vexing issue concerning divine healing is how to respond to the fact that not everyone is healed. This was especially difficult for many Holiness and Pentecostal people because they were convinced that all sickness is the result of sin; Christ's atonement makes total healing possible for all believers; and it is clearly God's will that all of God's people live healthy lives until God calls them home. Although occasionally there were reports of people being raised from the dead, most Holiness and Pentecostal people were clear that the Bible never promised that people would not die. Their understanding was that people could live in a state of health until the time of their deaths. To be healed is to be delivered from sickness and suffering.

The first option always considered when healing did not take place was to blame the victim, to look for sin in the life of the sick person. Lutheran pastor Johann Christoph Blumhardt had offered the traditional Christian sacrament of penance. The sacrament is suggested in James 5:16: "Confess your faults one to another, and pray for another, that ye may be healed." American revivalists stressed confession of one's sins to God as the repentance necessary for justification. Thus Holiness leaders stressed that one must be fully converted, and better yet entirely sanctified (completely surrendered, consecrated to God), before seeking healing. Simpson usually would not anoint or pray for someone who did not affirm a Christian commitment. Sandford required public and repeated confession before the entire community, and he became the judge as to whether repentance was thorough, sincere, and acceptable. Church of God (Cleveland, Tennessee) leader F. J. Lee put it another way: "If you are sick and desire to get through to God, you should not leave a single fault unconfessed. . . . If this isn't done, God is not under any obligation to hear the prayers."[6] Note the attempt to put God under obligation. Many did speak as though their theology involved some kind of airtight contractual arrangement in which God was obligated to heal if human beings completed the required preparation. This echoed Phoebe Palmer's approach to sanctification in *The Way of Faith*.

There were variations on the theme. Dora Dudley offered nearly thirty reasons why some were not healed. The first was "lack of entire consecration. . . . God does not invade the will without our consent." The second was that the sick must give up self-pity, being "sensitive," and their desire to be catered to. The third was to be sure they were not withholding their tithe. She also suggested that people suffer because they are cruel to animals—keep birds in cages or beat their horses.[7]

Taking another tack, Dudley suggested that some people lack patience. They go to doctors for years, but if Jesus does not heal them at once, they lose heart.

Rather than following up on their prayer of faith with joy and gladness, they grumble, murmur, and find fault. They forget that God's timetable may not be their timetable; just because a person is ready to be healed is no sign that God is ready to heal.[8] Testimonies, in fact, do reveal many examples of people who were healed gradually, over a period of time.

Going further, Dudley examined other motives. Some seek healing for their own glory or for their own enjoyment and not for the glory of God alone. Some compare their healing with that of others and are either proud or disappointed. Some try to bargain with God. Some go it alone when their symptoms are slight and seek God's help only when they are beyond human hope. Some are too timid, too afraid of ridicule, and do not give public witness to what God has done for them, so they lose it. Some are still mourning over lost blessings in the past. Some would only abuse good health if they had it. The reasons are myriad.[9]

When reporters asked Maria B. Woodworth-Etter about her husband's declining health, she was quick to answer. Headlines in *The Atlanta Journal* for April 13, 1914, summarized her reply:

Divine Healer Tells Why Husband's Ills Defy Her Treatment

"He Lacks Faith and God Has Purpose in Keeping Him Sick," Declares Mrs. Woodworth Etter

Has Tried to Cure Him But Fails Every Time

Woman Says Weather Aggravates Attack of Rheumatism, but Blames Absence of Faith for Its Continuance

She explained that "he is more than seventy years old," and "traveling as we do from coast to coast, he is constantly exposed to the weather and this, I think, has brought it on. Yes, I have tried to give him faith, and I think I have kept him alive by working over him and have kept his mind clean." She admitted that doctors had seen her husband and that he was taking medicine. She noted, "I don't tell people not to see doctors, you know, but I do tell them when doctors have failed to cure them: 'Come to the Lord.'"[10] Mr. Etter died in August 1914.

Sandford was a master at blaming others. After several people at Shiloh had died of smallpox, he wrote in the *Everlasting Gospel*, "We have not the slightest doubt that each one of these people were cut down directly or indirectly to the judgment hand of God."[11] Since three older boys had run away from the authoritarian community just before a terrible winter when smallpox, mumps, and diphtheria descended, the children and their parents became the focus of blame. As Shirley Nelson put it, "If a child misbehaved, it was as if the parents had directly disobeyed God, and God might punish the parents by punishing or even killing the child." One of the children, Nelson's father, Arnold, later said, "We were frightened to the point of spinal chills by the talk of leaders about the danger, unless we each lived close to God and made sure all faults were confessed 'one to another,' . . . There were no grey areas. You were on God's side or Satan's."[12]

R. Kelso Carter in *Divine Healing* spoke in equally harsh tones. "Many good people, who are most undoubtedly saved, fall into sin through a variety of causes, and in consequence, while forgiven, are taken from the world or prostrated beneath chronic diseases. . . . Many earnest working Christians of full habit sin frightfully through intemperance in the marriage relation. . . . The extent of this evil, amongst the best people in the churches, is simply appalling" (other authors ignored this "problem"). "Parents are very frequently responsible for the sickness in their children. . . . It may seem a hard thing to say, but it is plain that the saintly reputation of many lingering invalids cannot be built upon their years of suffering, for these are rather the evidence either of some great sin in the past, or of a persistent lack of conformity to the will of God in one way or another."[13]

Virtually never does one read about ministers, leaders, or healers who hesitated to lay hands on someone or anoint or lead in prayer because *their* faith was weak or their spirit discouraged. Leaders almost always project the blame outward, and the sick usually internalize it.

A more neutral response to the question "Who is to blame?" came from discussions of the prayer of faith. All agreed that a person seeking healing should have sufficient knowledge of the biblical and theological grounding for divine healing as well as a sure belief in it. That is why healing conventions and faith homes had days of instruction leading up to the anointing service.

To pray the prayer of faith effectively required a great deal from sick persons and the ones ministering to them. The faith of both must be strong. The minister must be confident and persuasive; the sick person must have faith, be willing to take a risk, and exhibit great courage. Simpson declared, "Faith for divine healing is not mere abstinence from remedies, an act of intellect or will, or a submission to the ordinance of anointing, but it is the real, spiritual touch of Christ, and it is much more rare than many suppose."[14] Elsewhere he spoke of the need for "aggressive and victorious faith."[15] Dudley suggested that some people never get beyond their own faith, but it is the "faith of Jesus within us" that heals. Both comments suggest the interplay of that perennial theological conundrum between human agency or free will and God's sovereign gift of grace.

Some do admit that God may have a variety of reasons for withholding healing. Lee declared, "Doubtless God permits sickness and suffering to come to some because of sin. He doubtless allows the enemy to attack some because of sin in order to cause them to fall in line, but I am sure there are thousands of real sanctified, upright, conscientious Christians who are living daily free from sin, yet have been subjected to real suffering and sickness."[16]

Simpson clearly understood the complexity of the issue, but his explanations ran the gamut. For example, he sometimes attributed sickness to a direct attack by Satan. At other times he blamed the victim: "Not always, yet often such long and terrible disorders are the direct result of sinful indulgence. Many today are physically powerless because of secret, youthful sins."[17] He also wrote, "Physical suffering, unless you are in God's full will, will come as Divine Chastening. We do not in Divine Healing teach—we would not dare to teach—that there is no place in God's economy for sickness. When you get on the devil's territory, it is permitted by God to bring you back."[18] Others also spoke of sickness as sometimes coming from God not only as chastening but also to teach a lesson. Sometimes Simpson could leave it in the hands of God:

> First of all, . . . we do not know and probably you do not know and will not know absolutely, until "we know even as we are known."
>
> It is quite shocking how some people get upon the throne and sit in judgment on God's providences, dealing His judgments upon the heads of their brethren, and explaining the mysteries of His will as though they were His special interpreters and vicegerents.
>
> One of His supreme thoughts in many of His dealings is to teach us to be still, and know that He is God.

He went on to note that some are not healed because their lifework is completed. "Sometimes a person or their friends do not understand God and feel disappointed, but if they wait on God, they will find understanding and peace."[19] When Mattie E. Perry was asked, "Why do some people not receive healing?" she answered, "My Father knows what hinders. We may not know always."[20]

Essentially there is no answer to the question why some are healed and others are not, why the righteous sometimes suffer and sinners live long and healthy lives. Despite the best attempts of Holiness and Pentecostal people to find the secret of divine healing, they uncovered no magic formula, no surefire cure. Medicine had and has the same problem. Some people did and do find their suffering eliminated through spiritual means. And some do not. A modern antibiotic or a particular surgery may cure many people with a specific condition, but some will experience no relief. There are no guarantees. The answer to the question is still a mystery. For religious persons, it is a mystery locked in the inscrutable mind of God.

Another option that seemed to open up as these groups moved into the twentieth century was to blame physical maladies on demonic activity. While casting out demons or exorcism is clearly evident in Jesus' ministry, especially in the gospel of Mark, it is very rarely mentioned by nineteenth-century Holiness writers. But as one moves into Pentecostalism, references to demons become more frequent. For example, Lee, at one time general overseer of the Church of God (Cleveland, Tennessee), said that "a man of intelligence and a worker in the church, resisted us when we began several years ago to teach on the line of demonology," but the man later saw demons leaving his body in healing. Lee declared, "I do not say that everyone that loses eyesight is caused by a demon, for we know that some have lost their eyesight by some accident," but some do. He also spoke of "floating demons" that "cause temporary disease, pains, etc." If not cast out, the person will develop a chronic disease, and the demons "will be much harder to expel."[21]

## Why Healing Declined

The reasons that the emphasis on divine healing declined in Holiness and Pentecostal churches in the first half of the twentieth century are numerous. Or perhaps one should ask how and why the emphasis on healing shifted. Were anyone counting, perhaps the same numbers of people continued to be healed through prayer, but the landscape changed.

The most obvious shift is that public perceptions of divine healing came to be focused on individual healers, the healing evangelists mentioned in the previous chapter and spotlighted in David Edwin Harrell's *All Things Are Possible*. With the advent of radio and then television, healing became the province of showmen whom the general public often regarded as fakes, frauds, and con men. The fact that some became involved in public scandals and even criminal behavior further stigmatized the subject as the century progressed.

Prayers for the sick, including the laying on of hands and anointing with oil, continued within many, if not most, Holiness and Pentecostal congregations. But they began to retreat, to downplay, to minimize the doctrine and practice of divine healing. The reasons are far deeper than bad publicity. They were responses to developments in secular medicine, in culture, in theology, and in their organizational evolution.

## Medicine Progressed

Around the beginning of the twentieth century, medicine began to make significant progress. It became more scientific and found more effective remedies and therapies. This improved its status and clout. In 1869 Charles Eliot became president of Harvard University and reorganized its professional schools. As a chemist, he presided over the medical faculty. He expanded the standard medical curriculum from two four-month terms to three nine-month terms. The University of Pennsylvania followed suit. Johns Hopkins University and Medical School opened in 1893 with a rigorous scientific four-year curriculum—though this was still only in addition to a high-school education. The regulars adopted the new practices, reorganized the American Medical Association in 1901, worked for standardized licensing of medical schools and individual physicians, and drove all alternatives to the fringes.[22]

The Pure Food and Drug Act was passed on June 30, 1906, and took effect January 1, 1907. The act was passed in response to two series of muckraking articles in the *Ladies' Home Journal* in 1903 and *Colliers' Weekly* in 1905. It stipulated that all information on the labels of patent medicines must be accurate and true. It did not require the listing of all ingredients, only the disclosure of certain dangerous substances: "cocaine, opium, morphine, heroine, chloroform, alcohol, cannabis indica, chloral hydrate, and acetanilide." Patent medicines could still contain these ingredients; they just had to disclose them on the label. However, in 1905 the *Journal of the American Medical Association* finally closed its pages to patent medicine advertising and set up a Council on Pharmacy and Chemistry to set standards for drugs and to evaluate their effectiveness. In 1924 the AMA forced drug companies to choose between producing what are now called over-the-counter drugs and those medicines prescribed by doctors. Until the 1990s the latter drugs were advertised only in *JAMA*.[23]

The smallpox vaccination was available, and an antitoxin for diphtheria had been developed. My mother, born in 1912, and her siblings acquired smallpox vaccinations sometime during their childhood. However, when I entered a country school at the end of World War II, I was not required to have any immunizations. I had chicken pox as an infant. I survived scarlet fever, measles, mumps, and whooping cough during grade school. It was not until we entered city schools in the early 1950s that my brothers and I were required to get smallpox vaccinations and diphtheria and tetanus shots. My parents had no scruples against such things; they just had little money for things that were not absolutely required. Polio vaccines were developed in the 1960s. Today, of course, most children by age two have had sixteen to twenty doses of various vaccines to avoid all of these childhood ills.

## Prosecutions Increased

Organized medicine began to attack legally those who practiced divine healing. A number of people were charged with practicing medicine without a license and other charges. At first this strategy did not hold up in court, but as medicine became more effective and physicians more closely regulated, the courts began to side with physicians' associations and county health officials.

In Chicago, Alexander Dowie was charged a number of times with practicing medicine without a license. Legislation was passed governing hospitals, and then his healing homes were cited for not complying with the law. One of his reasons for moving to Zion City was to be free of such legal harassment.

Maria B. Woodworth-Etter was arrested on several occasions. In August 1913 she was arrested in Framingham, Massachusetts, on charges that she was obtaining money under false pretenses because she promised healing, which the authorities considered a fraud. After a four-day trial in which thirty-five people testified to their healings in her defense, she and two others were found innocent.[24] In September 1920 the seventy-six-year-old evangelist was arrested in Fremont, Nebraska, for "practicing medicine and surgery without a license and unlawfully treating and professing to heal." Along with three other evangelists in her party, she was arraigned on charges brought by the county attorney. After posting bail, she conducted the evening service and then moved on to Omaha. There reporters asked her about the charges, and she replied, "I'm fighting the battle of the Lord. They may arrest me every day. It doesn't matter. I'm always ready for the next mission." The charges were later dismissed.[25]

As medicine developed inoculations and vaccinations against diseases, issues around children began to surface. First there was the smallpox vaccination, then the diphtheria and tetanus inoculations. As these became effective, common, and finally required by law, the ability of parents to make decisions about their children's care based on religious principles were increasingly challenged. Holiness and Pentecostal groups were intimidated by legal actions.

In 1907 the *New York Times* reported that a Christian and Missionary Alliance member on Staten Island had been arrested in the death of an infant. The *Times* noted that manslaughter charges would have "beneficial effect on the infatuated folks who hold themselves superior to medical science and the law."[26]

In 1915 Walter Barney, a Church of God (Cleveland, Tennessee) pastor in Foster Falls, Virginia, was tried and convicted on involuntary manslaughter charges for refusing medical aid for his sick daughter. Leaving a wife and five other children without support, he served four months at hard labor before petitions convinced the governor to pardon him.[27]

Another Church of God member, James Bradley of Brandon, Florida, was similarly charged in 1918. His fifteen-year-old daughter Bertha had a seizure and fell into the fireplace, severely burning her body on April 26. A month later the state stepped in and took her to a hospital for the insane, where she died of blood poisoning from the burns. Her father was convicted of manslaughter on May 22, 1919, and sentenced to ten years. The decision was overruled on appeal. As the states began to tighten laws protecting children, churches modified their stands.[28]

This obviously continues to be a problem that some Holiness and Pentecostal groups share with such groups as Christian Science and Jehovah's Witnesses. In the 1980s a radical Holiness group in northern Indiana, a breakaway from the Church of God (Anderson), incurred legal prosecution after several children in the group died without medical care.[29]

## On the Mission Field

Holiness groups such as the Christian and Missionary Alliance had been deeply involved in foreign missions from their beginnings. The Pentecostal out-pouring of tongues initially excited many who believed they could go to a foreign land and share the gospel in the language of the people immediately. In the late nineteenth century, in addition to denominational mission programs, there were a number of faith missions around the world, missionaries who raised their financial support from people at home. Mainline denominational missions paralleled the development of scientific medicine—sharing new medicines; training nurses, doctors, and public health specialists; building hospitals and medical schools. In 1883 Simpson denied any value to medical missionaries. He would send only those who "know Christ's healing power" and have "direct faith in the Great Physician." But a decade later he announced that the Alliance would send to Africa doctors and nurses, or at least those with a short-term course in some form of medicine, because "the heathen" were not able to trust God for healing.[30]

Divine healing presented an increasing quandary for mission candidates in groups who practiced it. Even people whose health was good in North American and European settings suffered seriously when sent to India, China, or Africa, for example. After scientists discovered the value of quinine in fighting malaria, should missionaries take it? Within the Alliance, there was debate. Some felt missionaries should uphold the group's doctrine and live by faith. And some missionaries preached divine healing and reported miraculous healings among the groups they served. Others said it was a shame to have dedicated and trained personnel die within their first year on the field. Mortality was especially high for missionaries in West Africa. Thirty-three Alliance missionaries who entered the Congo between 1884 and 1898 died, eighteen within the first year of their arrival. In 1900 the Alliance required all missionaries to believe and affirm the four-fold gospel, but in the matter of divine healing, the use of medications was left to individual discretion. The missionary was free to use medicines and give them to others, as long as she or he did not oppose the doctrine.[31] But the Alliance continued to lose missionaries: one in the Philippines to cholera in 1903; another in India to typhoid; a China missionary in 1904 to smallpox; and more in West Africa, even though some did take medicine and get treatment from physicians. The *Christian Alliance Foreign Missions Weekly* carried stories of missionaries who survived the same health problems while refusing medical help and relying on faith. There were also testimonies to healing among native workers and children in orphanages operated by missionaries. Bedford suggests that all of this affected denominational commitment to healing.[32]

# Early Clerical Critics

Divine healing always attracted critics, and early Holiness people had already attracted a host of critics among Methodist churchmen before they
adopted healing. One of the most vocal and tireless was J. M. Buckley (1836–
1920), Methodist minister and editor of *Christian Advocate* from 1880 to 1912.
In September 1875 he delivered *An Address on Supposed Miracles.* In June 1886
his article "Faith-Healing and Kindred Phenomena" was published in the popular magazine, *The Century.* This was followed by a second article in *The Century*
with the same title, plus a pro-healing article by R. Kelso Carter. Simpson answered Buckley with an article "Divine Healing and Demonism Not Identical"
in his publication *Word, Work and World.* Buckley gathered his articles and
more into a book in 1892 titled *Faith-Healing, Christian Science and Kindred
Phenomena.*[33]

Buckley had a litany of criticisms. First, laypeople really do not understand
their diseases, and women are prone to hysteria, which can bring on symptoms
that mimic real disease but can also instantaneously disappear. He also argued (as
recent scientific experiments have now demonstrated) that "spiritualist healers,
mesmeric and magnetic healers" plus those of other religious sects can all produce results similar to those of faith healers and "mind curers." This incensed Holiness people, who considered their brand of Christian cures unique and all
others bogus. Then Buckley pointed out the limitations of divine healing: no one
can raise the dead; no one claims to cure anyone *born* blind or deaf like the Gospels claim for Jesus; no one restores amputated limbs or lost eyes; no one seemed
to be able to cure even all occurrences of the same disease. Healers may have some
success with "functional" mental illness but not with "dementia or idiocy." He attributed any successes to the power of suggestion: "subjective mental states, as
concentration of the attention upon a part with or without belief, can produce effects either of the nature of disease or cure." Indeed, "concentrated attention, with
faith, can produce very great effects."[34]

Buckley then listed reasons why he considered divine healing detrimental.
First, "its tendency is to produce an effeminate character which shrinks from
any pain and to concentrate attention upon self and its sensations." Second, it
becomes a question of whom God likes best. Third, it opens the door to all sorts
of superstitions, such as considering dreams prophetic and using the Bible as a
Ouija board by opening it at random for guidance, which Holiness people often
did. Fourth, it opens the door "to other delusions which claim a supernatural
element." And finally, "it greatly injures Christianity by subjecting it to a test
which it cannot endure." In his second article he added two more complaints. It
had influenced women to leave their husbands and families to visit healing

homes, and it was "a means of obtaining money under false pretenses," especially from gullible women.[35]

In 1883 and 1884 a major debate on divine healing raged in the pages of the *Presbyterian Review* between Robert L. Stanton and Marvin R. Vincent. Stanton, a former moderator of the Presbyterian Church, had just published *Gospel Parallelisms: Illustrated in the Healing of Body and Soul.* Vincent was a New York City pastor on the faculty of Union Theological Seminary

We have already written of the case being made against divine healing by William McDonald, president of the National Camp Meeting Association for the Promotion of Holiness, in the pages of the *Advocate of Christian Holiness.* In 1897 the Association agreed that speakers should not preach on healing or dispensationalism at national camp meetings.

## The Rise of Fundamentalism

Holiness and Pentecostal groups were also challenged in the early twentieth century by the rise of fundamentalism. Today the media have succeeded in lumping all three groups and more together under the umbrella of "evangelicals" or "conservative Christians," but the three groups began with rather clear and sharp divisions.

Fundamentalism developed as an East Coast phenomenon. What it had initially in common with Holiness and Pentecostal groups was the acceptance of Darby's dispensational premillennarianism. Ministers, educators, and laypeople imbibed the teaching at revivalist D. L. Moody's conferences in Northfield, Massachusetts, and Bible and prophecy conferences at Niagara-on-the-Lake, Ontario, from 1883 to 1897 (commonly referred to as the Niagara Conferences). The teaching was codified by the Reverend C. I. Scofield (1843–1921) in the notes to the Scofield Reference Bible (1909)—King James Version, of course—complete with Bishop James Ussher's dating.

Fundamentalism was in essence an intellectual, theological response to the rise of science and of German biblical criticism, which were beginning to have significant influence on Eastern universities and seminaries. Resistance was most pronounced at the Presbyterian stronghold, Princeton Seminary in New Jersey. There theologians A. A. Hodge (1823–1886) and B. B. Warfield (1851–1921) developed two significant theological affirmations that they thought would answer German higher criticism of the Bible. They argued for the "verbal" and "plenary" inspiration of the Bible—each and every word of the original is "God-breathed." And the Bible is "inerrant in the original autographs"—the Bible is without error as originally written with regard not only to historical events and theological principles but also numerical statements and scientific observations. And it is taken to be "infallible" not only in terms of the worldviews of the centuries in which it was written but also in terms of twentieth-century worldviews—at least in principle, though most did not argue that the world is flat even if biblical writers did seem to describe it that way. On the other hand, if the biblical writers said the sun stood still for Joshua (Joshua 10:13), it stood still.

These views were novel and creative, despite the assurances of fundamentalist leaders that they were just rewording what had been believed by Christians down through the centuries. For example, in limiting the focus of inspiration to the text, they ignored the complementary traditional affirmation of the Holy Spirit's inspiration of the reader as well. In concentrating infallible truth in the "original autographs," they ignored the fact that we have no original manuscripts of biblical books to verify their theory (for the New Testament, the earliest complete manuscripts we have are fourth- and fifth-century codexes) and the church's complementary theological affirmation that God has also preserved a sufficiently reliable text down through the centuries.[36]

Between 1910 and 1915 a series of twelve volumes of essays titled *The Fundamentals* was published, funded by wealthy oilmen Lyman Stewart and Milton Stewart. Three million copies were sent to every English-speaking Christian leader in the world. Essays included theological treatises on a wide variety of topics and personal testimonies.

The northern Presbyterian Church in the U.S.A. general assembly in 1910 adopted a five-point "Deliverance" that became the basic "Fundamentals." They affirmed the plenary inspiration and verbal inerrance of the Bible, the virgin birth of Jesus, the substitutionary view of the atonement, the bodily resurrection of Jesus, and the reality of Jesus' miracles. These were reaffirmed by the denomination in 1919 and 1923, causing major conflicts. Eventually fundamentalists withdrew, forming such groups as the Orthodox and the Bible Presbyterian churches. In 1929 a colleague of Hodge and Warfield, J. Gresham Machen (1881–1937), left Princeton Seminary to found Westminster Seminary in Philadelphia. The fundamentalist controversy also fractured the American (Northern) Baptist Convention, spawning such groups as the Conservative Baptists and the General Association of Regular Baptists, as well as many independent Baptist churches. Holiness, Pentecostal, and fundamentalist divisions left missionaries and indigenous Protestant churches around the world reeling.

While many Pentecostals were in agreement with many fundamentalist teachings, especially concerning the Bible and the second coming, fundamentalists were adamantly opposed to Pentecostalism. Indeed the 1928 convention of the World's Christian Fundamentals Association, founded in 1919, barred Pentecostals from attendance and condemned their theology. The statement particularly denounced Pentecostalism's "wave of fanatical and unscriptural healing."[37]

## Fundamentalist Critics

Warfield, professor of didactic and polemic theology at Princeton and editor of *The Princeton Review* from 1890 to 1903, was a vehement critic of Holiness and divine healing. *Counterfeit Miracles* (1918) was originally his Thomas Smyth Lectures delivered in October 1917 at Columbia Theological Seminary, Columbia, South Carolina. Warfield denounced Holiness teachings in a two-volume work titled *Perfectionism* (1931). While staunchly defending the miraculous elements of Jesus' life and other miracles recorded in the Bible, Warfield just as vigorously denounced Holiness and Pentecostal testimonies to miraculous healing. He saw no promise of such miracles in Scripture, and he declared that the miraculous is contrary to God's usual modus operandi. Biblical miracles, for Warfield, were designed only to authenticate the divinity of Jesus and the commission of the apostles and were thus uncalled for thereafter. He also argued that such teaching involved unscriptural doctrines equating sickness with sin, which he interpreted Jesus as denying in John 10:3 (to the disciples who asked why a man had been born blind, Jesus answered, "Neither hath this man sinned, nor his parents: but that the works of God should be made manifest in him"). In Warfield's view, "Sickness is often the proof of special favor from God, and it always comes to His children from His Fatherly hand, and always in His loving pleasure works together with all other things which befall God's children, for good." God has appointed human means for healing, and healing advocates should not hold them in contempt. Besides, divine healing "leads to the production of 'professionals' standing between the soul and God" (hence the sacerdotal apparatus of the Roman Catholic Church, according to Warfield), tempting people to pride and autocracy.[38]

Another fundamentalist critic was H. ("Harry") A. Ironside (1876–1951). His father was a Plymouth Brethren street preacher who died when Harry was an infant. Born in Toronto, as a teenager Harry ended up in Los Angeles, in a local church, teaching a Sunday-school class while still unsure of his own salvation. In February 1890 he read John 3 and Romans 3 and claimed salvation: "Then I expected to feel a thrill of joy. It did not come. . . . I expected a sudden rush of love for Christ. It did not come either." Still he was sure of salvation. After he decked another young man in a fight, he decided that perhaps he needed sanctification. For months he was a regular at Salvation Army meetings and sought holiness. Finally one morning he took a train twelve miles out of Los Angeles to a deserted arroyo, sat down under a sycamore tree, and prayed until 3 A.M. the next morning. Fully surrendered, he experienced holy ecstasy. He walked back to the church and testified at the 7 A.M. service. He rose in the Army ranks. But when he confessed his continued struggles and temptations as a young man to an older leader, he was told that they were only temptations, that temptations are not sin, so not to worry about it. He became disillusioned, decided that all who professed Holiness were hypocrites, and resigned his post. He went to Carrie Judd Montgomery's Beulah Home of Rest near Oakland. There, "sick people testified of being healed by faith, and sinning people declared they had the blessing of holiness. I was not helped but hindered, by the inconsistency of it all." Those who profess Holiness, he declared "are frequently cutting, censorious, uncharitable and harsh in their judgment of others"[39] (he was about twenty at the time of this discovery and was writing this a decade later, having obviously achieved perfect charity).

Ironside had an equally harsh assessment of Pentecostalism, as did many other fundamentalists:

> Superstition and fanaticism of the grossest character find a hotbed among "holiness" advocates. Witness the present disgusting "Tongues Movement," with all its attendant delusion and insanities. An unhealthy craving for new and thrilling religious sensations, and emotional meetings of a most exciting character, readily account for these things. . . . In the last few years hundreds of holiness meetings all over the world have been literally turned into pandemoniums where exhibitions worthy of a madhouse or a collection of howling dervishes are held night after night. No wonder a heavy toll of lunacy and infidelity is the frequent result.[40]

Ironside went on to become pastor of Moody Bible Church in Chicago, one of the nation's leading fundamentalist pulpits, from 1930 to 1948. Completely self-taught (his formal education ended in grade school), he published forty-six books and thirty-one pamphlets, many still in print. His authoritative writing style and clearcut exposition of Scripture made him the premier authority on the Bible for many fundamentalists.[41]

Another fundamentalist critic of divine healing was A. C. Gaebelein (1861–1945), influential editor of *Our Hope* magazine and a consulting editor on the Scofield Reference Bible. An ardent dispensationalist, he fostered missions to Jews. In 1925 he published *The Healing Question: An Examination of the Claims of Faith-Healing and Divine Healing Systems in the Light of the Scriptures and History.*[42] Gaebelein agreed with healing advocates that healing is included in the atonement, but he declared that it would not be experienced until the body is glorified at the second coming of Christ. He denied that it is the privilege of Christians in the present life.[43]

# Class

Although it is seldom admitted by believers, American churches form a social hierarchy. Some churches project an aura of high social class, and others are considered low class. Some perceptions can be backed up with sociological data. For example, in the nineteenth-century South the slave owners and textile mill owners tended to be Episcopalians, the managerial class Presbyterians, the workers Methodists, Baptists, and Holiness folks. There are also regional perceptions of class. Southerners (except for Charlestonians) are at the bottom of that hierarchy; New England Yankees at the top.

Fundamentalism began as a movement in the Northeast among Presbyterians. It was financed by oil wealth. Fundamentalism had colleges and several seminaries. It also projected an image of being the genuine antique faith. They called it Princeton theology. Is it any wonder that the New York-based Christian and Missionary Alliance—former Presbyterian Simpson having already attracted a number of Episcopal clergy—would move toward fundamentalism? Especially since Pentecostalism originated on the spiritually dubious West Coast and had been embraced by Southerners, pictured as ignorant, benighted, backwoods bigots. Although Pentecostalism had its fair share of people of means (the Montgomerys, for example), the public seemed to conclude that Pentecostalism was the faith of poor, ignorant, country people. In fact it was a quite urban movement, with no particular corner on ignorance. Holiness and Pentecostal groups initially opened the ministry to women and men without regard to formal education. Both groups criticized educated clergy as having heads full of vain knowledge but empty hearts. They disdained seminary education in favor of short-term Bible schools. Early Methodists and Baptists had done the same—Presbyterians had always valued an educated clergy.

Initially Holiness and Pentecostal groups violated the color line. White evangelists sometimes stayed with black families; black musicians often ministered at predominately white camp meetings. The Azusa Street revival was fully integrated, as were many of the groups elsewhere that it nurtured. This did not elevate the social status of the groups involved among either whites or blacks. Whites soon began to withdraw into their own denominations, but this did not necessarily improve their social status, already set by the revival's origins and by its increasing identification with the South.

Robert Mapes Anderson argued that the 1916 census showed 81 percent of all Pentecostals resided in the South and the 1926 census still listed 55 percent in the South. Pentecostalism was an urban phenomenon only in the West and Midwest. In the South, white Pentecostalism was strongest in the Appalachian and Ozark mountain regions. He noted that the majority of early Pentecostal leaders were rural born, usually in the South, and that the majority of their fathers were farmers or blue-collar workers. Many were reared in abject poverty.[44]

To many Christians and many nonreligious people, Pentecostalism represented fanaticism, extremism, and emotionalism. Holiness and Pentecostal people were labeled Holy Rollers. Extreme emotionalism did mark some worship services—as it had for centuries. But some Holiness and Pentecostal groups also became known for their strict and legalistic lifestyles. For example, some prohibited the eating of meat, sweets, and "medicinal foods." Churches divided over the wearing of wedding rings and neckties by men. Rules for women were particularly strict: no cutting of hair, no jewelry whatsoever, no decoration on hats (such as feathers, ribbons, or artificial flowers), no hair curlers, no cosmetics. Members were not to attend any public entertainment such as sporting events, circuses, dances, plays, or even concerts. Divorce was highly discouraged, and re-marriage was prohibited as long as the spouse was alive. Although some still ob-serve elements of this lifestyle, succeeding generations more often rebelled against it. Divine healing was seen as just another example of their irrationality and primitivism.

As the twentieth century progressed, members of many Holiness and Pente-costal churches modified the emotionalism of their services and modulated to-ward fundamentalist rationalism and control. They stressed separation from worldliness but became more moderate in terms of dress and entertainments. They began to convert three-year Bible schools into four-year liberal arts colleges, which now have taken the title "university." Some have their own seminaries. Clean living and responsible lives led to steady jobs, better pay, and hence upward social mobility. Subsequent generations also yearned to fit in, and become middle class. Hard work made that possible, although Holiness and Pentecostal people still sometimes exhibit surprising inferiority feelings with regard to fundamental-ists and mainline Protestants. The desire for upward mobility has kept many motivated for education and job advancement and sometimes celebrity.

## Retreat

Thus under fundamentalist criticism and social pressures, as Holiness people began to draw back from Pentecostalism, they also drew back from divine heal-ing. For example, the 1906 annual report of the Christian and Missionary Alli-ance declared that "many forms of fanaticism and extravagance" had discredited healing. The 1909 report noted that the C&MA practice of divine healing contin-ued, but it was "less sensational and spectacular and more a matter of habitual experience and normal Christian living."[45] Even before Simpson's death in 1919, people were talking about a spiritual decline in the church. Typically, as in any movement, the second generation affirmed the tenets of the faith but often did not experience the deeper life. Much of the retreat from divine healing could be laid up simply to the dynamics of the second generation. Simpson's close associ-ate Kenneth Mackenzie acknowledged that Simpson's healing ministry had "slowed down" in later years. The weight of denominational machinery on his shoulders left less time and energy for healing.[46] For many years the Christian and Missionary Alliance had a Department of Healing as part of its national bureaucracy, but eventually it was disbanded and mention of it removed from the church's official manual. Until the Depression, many local congregations had two midweek services, one for prayer and one for healing. The healing service was dropped.[47] Despite such efforts as C&MA president Kenneth Mackenzie's *Divine Life for the Body* (1926), Bedford concludes:

> The proclamation of healing became muted, however, in reaction to Pentecostalism and with the deaths of foreign missionaries who succumbed to disease despite their "prayers of faith." The diminishing attention to the original doctrinal positions [Holiness and healing] left the Alliance known primarily as a missionary-sending agency.[48]

Some groups tried to hold the line. Declared A. J. Tomlinson, "the Church of God will not compromise. Some individuals may wear the white feather of cowardice and compromise, but the Church as a whole will not do it." Lee refused all drugs and medical treatment in his long battle with cancer that ended in 1928. A church historian noted that "he suffered a painful death,"[49] but even with full medical attention today many cancer patients still suffer very painful deaths.

In 1939 Mattie Perry was asked by an interviewer, "Many people are opposed to what they term 'healing rackets.' What, in your opinion, is the acid test of a true healing ministry?" Perry answered, "Blood and money. If they plead the blood of Jesus and make no charge for the service."[50] She kept it simple, and she lived the life of faith.

## Notes

1. Shirley Nelson, *Fair, Clear, and Terrible: The Story of Shiloh, Maine* (Latham, N.Y.: British American Publishing, 1989), 15, 35, 43–44. Nelson's parents were members of the Shiloh community; her uncle Leander died there.
2. Ibid., 46–47.
3. Ibid., 57.
4. Ibid., 72, 78.
5. Ibid., 203–41. Sandford was also charged with cruelty to his son John as well as four other children. The charges stemmed from his harsh and sadistic discipline within the community, including a seventy-two-hour fast that denied even water to children sick with diphtheria and smallpox. In 1911 Sandford was arrested on six counts of manslaughter in the deaths of six crewmen of his ship. Convicted, he served seven years of a ten-year prison term. He was released in 1918. See Nelson, *Fair, Clear, and Terrible*, 343, 347, 379.
6. Mickey Crews, *The Church of God: A Social History* (Knoxville: University of Tennessee Press, 1990), 74.
7. Dora G. [Griffin] Dudley, *Beulah: or Some of the Fruits of One Consecrated Life* (Grand Rapids, Mich.: published by the author, 1896), 60, 62, 63, 64.
8. Ibid., 63, 64, 65.
9. Ibid., 64–69.
10. Roberts Liardon, comp., *Maria Woodworth-Etter: The Complete Collection of Her Life Teaching* (Tulsa, Okla.: Albury Publishers, 2000) 477.

11. Grant Wacker, *Heaven Below: Early Pentecostals and American Culture* (Cambridge, Mass.: Harvard University Press, 2001), 25, quoting from *Everlasting Gospel* (July 1, 1903), 19.

12. Nelson, *Fair, Clear, and Terrible*, 205.

13. R. Kelso Carter, *Divine Healing, or The Atonement for Sin and Sickness* (new ed., rewritten and enlarged; New York: John B. Alden, 1884, 1888), 88, 89, 153, 139.

14. A. E. Thompson, *A. B. Simpson: His Life and Work* (rev. ed.; Camp Hill, Pa.: Christian Publications, 1960), 149.

15. William Boyd Bedford Jr., "'A Larger Christian Life': A. B. Simpson and the Early Years of the Christian and Missionary Alliance" (Ph.D. diss., University of Virginia, 1992), 287.

16. James A. Cross, ed., *Healing in the Church* (Cleveland, Tenn.: Pathway Press, 1962), 66.

17. A. B. Simpson, The *Gospel of Healing* (1885; repr., Camp Hill, Pa.: Christian Publications, 1994), 89.

18. Raymond Walter Schenk, "A Study of the New Testament Bases for the Teaching of Dr. Albert B. Simpson on Divine Healing" (master's thesis, Wheaton College, 1968), 19, quoting from *The King's Business* (1886), 156.

19. Thompson, *A. B. Simpson*, 147–48. The quotations are from a Simpson editorial.

20. Mattie E. Perry, *Christ and Answered Prayer* (Nashville: Benson Printing Company, 1939), 346–47.

21. E. C. Clark, ed., *Marvelous Healings God Wrought among Us* (Cleveland, Tenn.: The Church of God Publishing House, n.d. [c. 1944]), 30, 32.

22. Paul Starr, *The Social Transformation of American Medicine* (New York: Basic Books, 1982), 112–15.

23. Ibid., 129–34.

24. Wayne E. Warner, *The Woman Evangelist: The Life and Times of Charismatic Evangelist Maria B. Woodworth-Etter* (Metuchen, N.J.: Scarecrow, 1986) 216–17.

25. Liardon, *Maria Woodworth-Etter*, 551, quoting from the *Fremont Evening Tribune*, September 30, 1920; Warner, *The Woman Evangelist*, 243.

26. Bedford, "'A Larger Christian Life,'" 293.

27. Crews, *The Church of God*, 74–75; Vinson Synan, *The Holiness Pentecostal Tradition: Charismatic Movements in the Twentieth Century* (Grand Rapids, Mich.: Eerdmans, 1971, 1997), 192; Wacker, *Heaven Below*, 186.

28. Crews, *The Church of God*, 75, 78.

29. Faith Assembly, Wilmot, Ind., founded by Hobart Freeman (d. 1986). See Julia Mitchell Corbett, *Religion in America* (4th ed.; Upper Saddle River, N.J.: Prentice Hall, 2000), 330–31.

30. Bedford, "'A Larger Christian Life,'" 321.

31. Ernest G. Wilson, "The Christian & Missionary Alliance: Developments and Modifications of Its Original Objectives" (Ph.D. diss., New York University, 1984), 184. Wilson did a content analysis on Alliance publications on the elements of the fourfold gospel for selected periods from 1887 to 1978. From 1887 to 1892 there were 338 articles on divine healing; from 1931 to 1936 there were 53. In the 1908 edition of the denomination's hymnal *Hymns of Faith* there were 24 hymns about divine healing; in the 1936 edition there were 13, reduced to 11 in the 1978 edition. See Wilson, 318.

32. Bedford, "'A Larger Christian Life,'" 323, 326, 332–33. Bedford notes that the Alliance was always forthright in its reporting of the causes of missionary deaths.

33. J. M. Buckley, "Faith-Healing and Kindred Phenomena," *The Century* 32:27 (June 1886), 221–36; J. M. Buckley, "Faith-Healing and Kindred Phenomena," supplementary article, *The Century* 33:99 (1887), 781–87; A. B. Simpson, "Divine Healing and Demonism Not Identical," *Word, Work and World* 7 (1886), 52–114; J. M. Buckley, *Faith-Healing, Christian Science and Kindred Phenomena* (New York: Century, 1892). See Raymond J.

Cunningham, "Ministry of Healing: The Origins of the Psychotherapeutic Role of the American Churches" (Ph.D. diss., Johns Hopkins University, 1965), 26.

34. Buckley, 224, 226, 227, 232, 233.

35. Buckley, 236, 785, 786.

36. For background see Ernest R. Sandeen, *The Roots of Fundamentalism: British and American Millenarianism, 1800–1930* (Chicago: University of Chicago Press, 1970), and Timothy Weber, *Living in the Shadow of the Second Coming: American Premillennialism, 1875–1925* (Grand Rapids, Mich.: Zondervan, 1983).

37. Synan, *The Holiness-Pentecostal Tradition*, 208.

38. B. B. Warfield, *Counterfeit Miracles, or Miracles True and False* (New York: Charles Scribner's Sons, 1918), 193–95.

39. H. A. Ironside, *Holiness: The False and the True* (1912; repr., Neptune, N. J., Loizeaux Brothers, n.d.), 8–25, 28.

40. Ibid., 38–39.

41. J. A. Carpenter, "Ironside, Henry ('Harry') Allen (1876–1951)," in *Dictionary of Christianity in America*, ed. Daniel G. Reid et al. (Downers Grove, Ill.: InterVarsity Press, 1990), 582.

42. A. C. Gaebelein, *The Healing Question: An Examination of the Claims of Faith-Healing and Divine Healing Systems in the Light of the Scriptures and History* (New York: Publication Office of "Our Hope," 1925).

43. Schenk, "A Study of the New Testament Bases for the Teaching of Dr. Albert B. Simpson on Divine Healing," 15.

44. Robert Mapes Anderson, *Vision of the Disinherited: The Making of American Pentecostalism* (New York: Oxford University Press, 1979), 114, 115, 99–100.

45. *Annual Report* (1906), 6–7, as quoted by Bedford, "'A Larger Christian Life,'" 336–37.

46. K. Mackenzie, "My Memories of Dr. Simpson," *Alliance Witness* 7 (July 24, 1937), 56, as quoted by Charles N. Nienkirchen, *A. B. Simpson and the Pentecostal Movement: A Study in Continuity, Crisis, and Change* (Peabody, Mass.: Hendrickson, 1992), 135.

47. Wilson, "The Christian and Missionary Alliance," 179.

48. Bedford, "'A Larger Christian Life,'" abstract iii.

49. Crews, *The Church of God*, 76, 79.

50. Perry, *Christ and Answered Prayer*, 345.

# 11

## Healing for Today

Health is an obsession in today's society. Newspapers, magazines, and television programs are filled with the latest medical study, wonder drug, surgical innovation, and health warnings. We are constantly urged to watch our diets, exercise more, take the appropriate medications, and wear sunscreen and mosquito repellent. We monitor ourselves for signs of breast, prostate, and skin cancers. We medicate ourselves with vitamins, minerals, and herbal products to enhance our health.

And increasingly, religion is part of the prescription.

### Religion Is Good for Your Health

Numerous scientific studies have now shown that religion is good for one's health. Harold G. Koenig, M.D., director of the Duke University Center for the Study of Religion/Spirituality and Health, has compiled the results in *The Healing Power of Faith* (1999). Whatever the faith to which they are committed, people with stronger religious commitments report greater satisfaction with their lives. They have stronger marriages and family ties. They live healthier lifestyles—they are less inclined to smoke, drink, use illicit drugs, or engage in risky sexual behaviors. They cope well with stress and suffer less depression. They have stronger immune systems and use fewer expensive hospital services. They live longer. Koenig devotes a chapter to each of these subjects, detailing how they are documented.[1]

Herbert Benson, director of Harvard Medical School's Mind/Body Medical Institute, has been prescribing meditation to his patients for years and scientifically testing the results. He has written about it in *Timeless Healing: The Power of Biology and Belief* (1996) and *The Relaxation Response* (1975). He found that patients who repeat a mantra of their choice—"Om," "God is good," "peace," "Lord, have mercy," "green"—can lower the stress levels within their body, lower their blood pressure, relax their muscles (including the heart), and lower their pulse rate. While any word with pleasant connotations can work, Benson found that those who used words to which they attached religious meaning were more successful at reducing their stress.

This would suggest that the people I have introduced in this study were on the way to better health when they committed themselves to the religious life and took steps to become more serious in their faith. For some that did mean giving up bad health habits such as using tobacco or drinking spiritous liquors. It often meant becoming more involved with their local church congregations and prayer groups. It meant attending camp meetings, which usually involved camping out in the woods. The fresh air, relaxing schedule, enjoyable social interaction, inspiring worship, and emotional altar services contributed to physical, emotional, and spiritual refreshing.

## Prayer Changes Things

Scientists have also been studying the effects of prayer. One of the earliest studies done was reported in *Prayer Can Change Your Life* by William R. Parker and Elaine St. Johns. Their study, conducted at the University of Redlands, California, in 1951, compared three groups: one that participated in a therapy group using psychology alone for help with their ordinary life problems, another that agreed to pray for themselves and their problems every night for nine months, and the "prayer therapy group" that met each week to pray together for two hours about their problems. All were given a set of psychological tests before the experiment began, which revealed certain aspects of personality that might be contributing to their problems. Leaders of the first group were given this information to guide their therapy. Members of the last group were given a sealed envelop each week containing a paper listing one trait in their personality that they might want to pray about improving. Repeating the battery of tests at the end of nine months revealed that the psychotherapy group had a 65 percent improvement. Those who just prayed for themselves showed no improvement. But the "prayer therapy group" had a 72 percent improvement.[2]

While Parker's and St. Johns's methodology was questionable and their conclusions therefore difficult to interpret, their book made a lasting impression on me, and apparently on many others. It suggested that prayer might have results that could be studied and tested in the laboratory. Since then many researchers have devised ingenious experiments to test the expression of human intentions and requests that religious people call prayer. Many of these fascinating experiments are recounted by Larry Dossey, M.D., former chief of staff at Humana Medical City in Dallas; co-chair of the Panel on Mind/Body Interventions, Office of Complementary and Alternative Medicine at the National Institutes of Health; and editor of *Alternative Therapies*. His books include *Healing Words* (1993), *Prayer Is Good Medicine* (1996), and *Reinventing Medicine* (1999).

Skeptics want to say that any effects of prayer are due to the power of suggestion or the placebo effect. The placebo effect is the well-known medical phenomenon in which a fair number of those who think they are receiving medications
but who are really being given inert sugar pills show the same improvement as
those receiving the real medication. A study not involving prayer reported in
2002 that people who had make-believe knee surgery became pain-free and
walked with more freedom than many of those who had undergone knee surgery
for real. But the placebo effect is not a negative thing. Indeed, it shows that the
human body (perhaps in concert with the Universe, the Divine, or whatever one
wants to term it) can heal without medical help. But those who have structured
the scientific experiments to test the effects of prayer have tried to eliminate suggestion or placebo in order to focus on the effects of prayer alone. Interestingly,
some researchers have done this by using plants, animals, and objects, thus reducing the chance that "subjects" might be swayed by the prestige of the experiment-
ers' white lab coats or the university name on the front of the building.

The research indicates a number of things. Validating at least in part the
theme of this book, sick people who are intentionally prayed for have better medical outcomes than people who are not prayed for. Double-blind experiments
have verified this. These are experiments where the sick persons did not know
they were being prayed for and those praying knew little more than the sick person's first name; there was no physical contact between them. The people described in this book would probably be disturbed by many things about these
experiments. While anointing with oil and laying on of hands is recommended in
James 5, prayer alone seems to do a fairly good job. The sick persons need not
have any faith of their own—these tests made no measure of the religiosity of the
patients involved. Certainly the research Koenig describes would suggest that the
patient's religious resources might bolster healing as well. Research on prayer has
also found no distinct merit in Christian prayers as opposed to Buddhist, Hindu,
or Muslim prayers. In fact, usually in these experiments those doing the praying
come from a variety of religious traditions.

These experiments do show that prayer works. With AIDS patients and those
admitted to hospitals who are suffering with cardiac difficulties, those assigned
randomly to be prayed for needed less antibiotics, less pain medication, and fewer
procedures. Their hospital stays were shorter, and fewer died.[3]

## Healing Traditions Today

With or without this scientific verification, Christian traditions of divine
healing continue today.

Perhaps most obvious are faith healers on television and in civic auditoriums
and arenas, usually working within the Pentecostal tradition. Perhaps best known is

Benny Hinn (b. 1952), who traces his spiritual heritage to television healer Kathryn Kuhlman (1907–1976). Many are also familiar with Oral Roberts (1918–), who began his work as a tent evangelist in the Pentecostal Holiness Church. Roberts eventually joined the United Methodist Church, had a significant television ministry, and founded Oral Roberts University and the City of Faith Medical and Research Center in Tulsa, Oklahoma. Richard Roberts (1948–) carries on his father's work today.[4] Better known globally is the Osborn family, Tommy Lee Osborn (1923–) of Oklahoma and Daisy Washburn (1924–1995), from California, whom he married in 1941. They began a ministry of healing in 1948 and have preached the message around the world. Their daughter LaDonna also ministers.

Much less publicly, most Holiness and Pentecostal churches and the many independent charismatic churches pray for the sick, anoint with oil, and lay on hands for healing. Sometimes healing is emphasized at a special service. More often these rituals are available in every service for anyone who presents himself or herself at the altar and requests prayers for healing. Sometimes this is during a prayer time in the midst of a service; sometimes it is during the altar call at the end of a service. In some Holiness churches, church members may request prayers for healing from the pastor before a service and the pastor will then simply announce the request and ask elders to gather at the altar around the suffering person.

More liturgical churches—Episcopal, Roman Catholic, Lutheran, for example—offer anointing, laying on of hands, and prayers for healing during one of the smaller services of Holy Communion during the week. During the service, those wishing to be anointed are requested to present themselves at the altar to receive this sacrament. Additional prayers for healing are sometimes added at this particular service. The Episcopal Church, for example, has a long tradition of healing that parallels the story told in this work and which still awaits a historian to chronicle it. Most famous within the tradition are James Moore Hickson (d. 1933), who wrote *The Revival of the Gifts of Healing* and *The Healing of Christ in His Church*,[5] and Agnes Sanford (1897–1982), author of *The Healing Light* (1947), *The Healing Gifts of the Spirit* (1966), *The Healing Power of the Bible* (1969), and her autobiography, *Sealed Orders* (1972).

Very helpful in exploring healing traditions within various Christian communions and other religious faiths is the series of books published by the Park Ridge Center for the Study of Health, Faith, and Ethics in Chicago.

## Conclusion

Divine healing has continued to be a little-known sacrament and ritual within the Christian church. Some within the Holiness and Pentecostal traditions, often unaware of their history, have drawn back from this important part of their heritage. This book may be a gift to them, a remembrance. Others have drawn back because of the "fanaticism" associated with the topic. In the twenty-first century, few would forsake doctors and drugs. Despite some questions, the routine immunization of children has spared many much suffering, long-term disability, and even death. Participating in immunization programs protects not only one's own children but also the children of others and other adults. For most adults, there is no longer a conflict between medicine and faith. Most Christians routinely consult physicians, take prescribed medicines, and submit to medical tests, procedures, and surgeries as needed.

And they also pray. But often the two realms are quite separate. What many physicians and even medical schools are now taking seriously and what many patients need to learn is that their religious faith is an important part of complementary medicine. Medical schools are adding courses on the relationships of faith to health. Physicians are learning how to ask patients about their faith and how to encourage people to make use of the resources of that faith in the healing process. In addition to drugs and therapies, physicians are beginning to prescribe prayer and meditation as part of treatment. Some physicians are asking patients if they would like to be prayed for during a consultation or before surgery or other procedures. For some time, most hospitals have had chaplains on staff to visit with patients and pray with them regularly during their stay.

In the light of the vibrant history recounted in this book, perhaps Holiness and Pentecostal people will begin to find more ways to lift up their tradition of divine healing and enter into conversation with other Christian churches and the many medical professionals who are coming to realize that religious faith is a vital component in good health and healing.

# Notes

1. Harold G. Koenig, *The Healing Power of Faith: Science Explores Medicine's Last Great Frontier* (New York: Simon and Schuster, 1999).

2. William R. Parker and Elaine St. Johns, *Prayer Can Change Your Life* (New York: Prentice Hall, 1957); see Larry Dossey, *Healing Words: The Power of Prayer and the Practice of Medicine* (San Francisco: HarperSanFrancisco, 1993), 172–75.

3. Larry Dossey, *Reinventing Medicine: Beyond Mind-Body to a new Era of Healing* (San Francisco: HarperSanFrancisco, 1999), 45–55.

4. David Edwin Harrell Jr., *Oral Roberts: An American Life* (San Francisco: Harper & Row, 1985).

5. Raymond J. Cunningham, "James Moore Hickson and Spiritual Healing in the American Episcopal Church," *Historical Magazine of the Protestant Episcopal Church* 38 (1969): 3–16.

# Bibliography

## Primary Sources

Allen, Ethan O. *Faith Healing: or, What I Have Witnessed of the Fulfillment of James V: 14, 15, 16*. Philadelphia: N.p., 1881.

Arnold, Helen. *Under Southern Skies: Reminiscenes of the Life of Mrs. Adelia Arnold*. Atlanta: Repairer Publishing Company, 1924.

Bainbridge, Harriette S. *Life for Soul and Body*. Brooklyn, N. Y.: Christian Alliance Publishing, 1906.

Baker, Elizabeth V., and co-workers. *Chronicles of a Faith Life*. 1915. Repr., New York: Garland, 1984.

Bartleman, Frank. *How Pentecost Came to Los Angeles*. Los Angeles: the author, 1925.

Boardman, [Mary]. *Life and Labors of the Rev. W. E. Boardman*. New York: D. Appleton and Company, 1887.

Boardman, William E. *Faith Work under Dr. Cullis in Boston*. Boston: Willard Tract Repository, 1874.

———. *The Great Physician (Jehovah Rophi)*. Boston: Willard Tract Repository, 1881; *The Lord That Healeth Thee*. London: Morgan and Scott, 1881.

Buckley, J. M. "Faith-Healing and Kindred Phenomena." *The Century* 27–32 (June 1886): 221–36; supplementary article, *The Century* 33–99 (1886): 781–87.

———. *Faith-Healing, Christian Science, and Kindred Phenomena*. New York: The Century Company, 1892.

Campbell, Emily Frances. *Glimpses into the Consecrated Life*. Compiled by her sister [A. H. Campbell]. Brooklyn, N. Y.: The Faith Home for Incurables, 1884.

Carter, R. Kelso. "Divine Healing." *The Century* 34 (March 1887): 777–80.

———. *Divine Healing, or The Atonement for Sin and Sickness*. New ed., rewritten and enlarged. New York: John B. Alden, 1884, 1888.

———. *"Faith Healing" Reviewed after Twenty Years*. Boston: Christian Witness, 1897.

————. *Pastor Blumhardt, A Record of the Wonderful Spiritual and Physical Manifestations of God's Power in Healing Souls and Bodies.* Boston: Willard Tract Repository, 1883.

Clark, E. C., ed. *Marvelous Healings God Wrought among Us.* Cleveland, Tenn.: The Church of God Publishing House, n.d. [c. 1944].

Cole, Mary. *Trials and Triumphs of Faith.* Anderson, Ind.: Gospel Trumpet, 1914.

Cullis, Charles. *Faith Cures; or Answers to Prayer in the Healing of the Sick.* Boston: Willard Tract Repository, 1879.

————. *Other Faith Cures, or Answers to Prayer in the Healing of the Sick.* Boston: Willard Tract Repository, 1885.

————. ed. *Work for Jesus: The Experience and Teaching of Mr. and Mrs. Boardman.* Boston: Willard Tract Repository, 1875.

Curnock, Nehemiah. *The Journal of the Rev. John Wesley, A.M.* London: Epworth Press, 1938.

Daniels, W. H., ed. *"Have Faith in God": Dr. Cullis and His Work: Twenty Years of Blessing in Answer to Prayer.* Boston: Willard Tract Repository, 1885.

Dudley, Dora G.[Griffin]. *Beulah: or Some of the Fruits of One Consecrated Life.* Rev. and enlarged ed. Grand Rapids, Mich.: published by the author, 1896.

Finney, Charles Grandison. *Lectures on Revivals of Religion.* Ed. William G. McLoughlin Jr. Cambridge, Mass.: Belknap Press, Harvard University Press, 1960.

Frodsham, Stanley H. *With Signs Following.* Springfield, Mo.: Gospel Publishing House, 1941.

Garbutt, J. William, Mrs., comp. *Rev. W. A. Dodge As We Knew Him.* Atlanta: The Franklin Printing and Publishing Company, 1906.

Gordon, A. J. *The Ministry of Healing, or Miracles of Cure in All Ages.* 3d ed. Chicago: Fleming H. Revell, 1882.

Hickson, James Moore. *The Healing of Christ in His Church.* New York: Edwin S. Gorham, 1919.

Holmes, N. J., and Lucy S. Holmes. *Life Sketches and Sermons: The Story of Pentecostal Pioneer N. J. Holmes.* Royston, Ga.: Press of the Pentecostal Holiness Church, 1920. Repr., Franklin Springs, Ga.: Advocate Press, 1973.

Ironside, H. A. *Holiness: The False and the True.* 1912. Repr., Neptune, N. J.: Loizeaux Brothers, n.d.

Judd, Carrie F. *The Prayer of Faith.* Buffalo, N. Y.: H. H. Otis, 1880, 1882.

Kiergan, A. M. *Historical Sketches of the Revival of True Holiness and Local Church Polity from 1865–1916.* N.p.: Board of Publication of the *Church Advocate* and *Good Way* at the decision of the convention of 1971 of the churches of God (commonly known as the Independent Holiness People), n.d. [1916].

Lee, Mother [Martha A.]. *Mother Lee's Experience in Fifteen Years' Rescue Work with Thrilling Incidents of Her Life.* Omaha, Neb.: N.p., 1906.

Lee, F. J., Mrs. *Life Sketch and Sermons of F. J. [Flavius Josephus] Lee*. Cleveland, Tenn.: The Church of God Publishing House, 1929.

MacArthur, William T. *Ethan O. Allen*. Philadelphia: The Parlor Evangelist, n.d. [c. 1890].

Mackenzie, Kenneth. *Our Physical Heritage in Christ*. New York: Fleming H. Revell, 1923.

Mahan, Asa. *Out of Darkness into Light; or, The Hidden Life Made Manifest*. Boston: Willard Tract Repository, 1876.

Marsh, R. L. *"Faith Healing": A Defense or, The Lord Thy Healer*. New York: n.p., 1889.

Mix, Edward, Mrs. *Faith Cures and Answers to Prayer*. Springfield, Mass.: Press of Springfield Printing Co., 1882. Repr., with critical introduction by Rosemary Gooden, Syracuse, N. Y.: Syracuse University Press, 2002.

———. *The Life of Mrs. Edward Mix, Written by Herself in 1880*. Torrington, Conn.: Press of Register Printing Co., 1884. Also appended to Rosemary Gooden edition above.

Montgomery, Carrie Judd. *"Under His Wings": The Story of My Life*. Oakland, Calif.: Office of Triumphs of Faith, 1936.

Moore, Joanna Patterson. *"In Christ's Stead": Autobiographical Sketches*. Chicago: Women's Baptist Home Mission Society, 1902.

M. [Mossman], M. [Mary]. *Steppings in God; or The Hidden Life Made Manifest*. New York: Eaton & Mains, 6th and rev. ed. with appendix, 1909.

Murray, Andrew. *Divine Healing: A Series of Addresses and a Personal Testimony*. New York: Christian Alliance Publishing, 1900. Repr., Plainfield, N. J.: Logos International, 1974.

Myland, David Wesley. *The Latter Rain Covenant and Pentecostal Power with Testimony of Healings and Baptism*. 2d ed. Chicago: Evangel Publishing House, 1910.

Palmer, Phoebe. *Faith and Its Effects; or, Fragments from My Portfolio*. New York: Published by the Author, Joseph Longkin, Printer, 1852.

———. *The Way of Holiness*. 50th American edition. New York: Foster and Palmer Jr., 1867.

Parham, Sarah T. *The Life of Charles F. Parham: Founder of the Apostolic Faith Movement*. Joplin, Mo.: Tri-State Printing Co., 1930.

Perry, Mattie E. *Christ and Answered Prayer*. Nashville: Benson Printing Company, 1939.

Platt, S. H. *My Twenty-fifth Year Jubilee; or, Cure by Faith after Twenty-five Years of Lameness*. Brooklyn, N. Y.: S. Harrison, 1875.

Prosser, Anna W. *From Death to Life*. Chicago: Evangel Publishing House, n.d.

*Record of the International Conference on Divine Healing and True Holiness*. London: J. Snow & Co., 1885.

Simpson, A. B. *The Gospel of Healing.* 1885. Repr., Camp Hill, Pa.: Christian Publications, 1994.

Smith, Amanda Berry. *An Autobiography: The Story of the Lord's Dealings with Mrs. Amanda Smith, the Colored Evangelist.* Chicago: Meyer & Brother, 1893.

Smith, Hannah Whitall. *The Christian's Secret of a Happy Life.* 1870; Old Tappan, N.J.: Fleming H. Revell, 1942.

Smith, Jennie. *From Baca to Beulah.* Philadelphia: Garrigues Brothers, 1880.

Smith, Sarah. *Life Sketches of Sarah Smith: "A Mother in Israel."* Guthrie, Okla.: Faith Publishing House, n.d. [written 1901].

Stanton, Robert L. *Gospel Parallelisms: Illustrated in the Healing of Body and Soul.* Buffalo, N. Y.: N.p., 1883.

Stockmayer, Otto. *Sickness and the Gospel.* London: Partridge and Co., n.d.

Thompson, Patrick M. *The History of Negro Baptists in Mississippi.* Jackson, Miss.: R. W. Bailey Printing, 1898.

Trudel, Dorothea. *The Prayer of Faith.* Introduction by Charles Cullis. 3d ed. Boston: Willard Tract Repository, 1872.

Warfield, B. B. *Counterfeit Miracles, or Miracles True and False.* New York: Charles Scribner's Sons, 1918.

———. *Perfectionism.* 2 vols. New York: Oxford University Press, 1931.

Wesley, John. *Primitive Physik, or an Easy and Natural Method of Curing Most Diseases.* London: N.p., 1747.

Woodworth-Etter, M. B., Mrs. *Acts of the Holy Ghost, or The Life, Work, and Experience of Mrs. M. B. Woodworth-Etter.* Dallas: John F. Worley Printing, n.d. [1912].

## Secondary Sources

Abell, Troy D. *Better Felt Than Said: The Holiness-Pentecostal Experience in Southern Appalachia.* Waco, Tex.: Markham Press, 1982.

Abram, Ruth J., ed. *"Send Us a Lady Physician": Women Doctors in America, 1835–1920.* New York: Norton, 1985.

Albrecht, Daniel F. "Carrie Judd Montgomery: Pioneering Contributor to Three Religious Movements." *Pneuma* 8 (fall 1986): 101–19.

Anderson, Robert Mapes. *Vision of the Disinherited: The Making of American Pentecostalism.* New York: Oxford University Press, 1979.

Baer, Jonathan R. "Perfectly Empowered Bodies: Divine Healing in Modernizing America." Ph.D. diss. Yale University, 2002.

———. "Playing to Mixed Reviews: Early Twentieth-Century Pentecostal Healing and the Fundamentalist Response." Paper presented at the annual meeting of the American Society of Church History, Chicago, January 2003.

———. "Redeemed Bodies: The Functions of Divine Healing in Incipient Pentecostalism." *Church History* 70:4 (December 2001): 735–71.

Bangs, Carl. *Phinias Bresee: His Life in Methodism, the Holiness Movement, and the Church of the Nazarene.* Kansas City, Mo.: Nazarene Publishing House, 1995.

Bedford, William Boyd, Jr. "'A Larger Christian Life': A. B. Simpson and the Early Years of the Christian and Missionary Alliance." Ph.D. diss., University of Virginia, 1992.

Benson, Herbert. *Timeless Healing: The Power and Biology of Belief.* New York: Scribner, 1996.

Betts, Albert Deems. *History of South Carolina Methodism.* Columbia, S. C.: The Advocate Press, 1952.

Blumhofer, Edith L. *Aimee Semple McPherson, Everybody's Sister.* Grand Rapids, Mich.: Eerdmans, 1993.

———. *"Pentecost in My Soul": Explorations in the Meaning of Pentecostal Experience in the Early Assemblies of God.* Springfield, Mo.: Gospel Publishing House, 1989.

———. *Restoring the Faith: The Assemblies of God, Pentecostalism, and American Culture.* Urbana: University of Illinois Press, 1993.

Bodamer, William G., Jr. "The Life and Work of Johann Christoph Blumhardt." Ph.D. diss., Princeton Theological Seminary, 1966.

Brasher, John Lawrence. *The Sanctified South: John Lakin Brasher and the Holiness Movement.* Urbana: University of Illinois Press, 1994.

Brown, Charles Ewing. *When the Trumpet Sounded: A History of the Church of God Reformation Movement.* Anderson, Ind.: Warner Press, 1951.

Brown, Kenneth O. *Inskip, McDonald, Fowler: "Wholly and Forever Thine." Early Leadership in the National Camp Meeting Association for the Promotion of Holiness.* Hazleton, Pa.: Holiness Archives, 1999.

———. "'The World-Wide Evangelist'—The Life and Work of Martha Inskip." *Methodist History* (July 1983): 179–91.

Burgess, Stanley M., ed. *The New International Dictionary of Pentecostal and Charismatic Movements.* Rev. and ex. edition. Grand Rapids, Mich.: Zondervan, 2002.

Burgess, Stanley M., and Gary B. McGee, eds. *Dictionary of Pentecostal and Charismatic Movements.* Grand Rapids, Mich.: Regency Reference Library, Zondervan, 1988.

Butcher, J. Kevin "The Holiness and Pentecostal Labors of David Wesley Myland: 1890–1918." Master's thesis, Dallas Theological Seminary, 1983.

Campbell, Joseph E. *The Pentecostal Holiness Church, 1898–1948: Its Background and History.* Franklin Springs, Ga.: Pentecostal Holiness Church, 1951, 1981.

Carter, R. Kelso. *Pastor Blumhardt.* Boston: Willard Tract Repository, 1883.

Chappell, Paul G. "The Divine Healing Movement in America." Ph.D. diss., Drew University, 1983.

Clark, Elmer T. *The Small Sects in America.* New York: Abingdon-Cokesbury, 1949.

Cobbins, Otho B., ed. *History of Church of Christ (Holiness), U.S.A. 1895–1965.* New York: Vantage, 1966.

Conn, Charles W. *Like a Mighty Army: A History of the Church of God 1886–1976.* Rev. ed. Cleveland, Tenn.: Pathway Press, 1977.

Cox, B. L. *History and Doctrine of the Congregational Holiness Church.* 2d ed., n.p.: 1959.

Crews, Mickey. *The Church of God: A Social History.* Knoxville: University of Tennessee Press, 1990.

Cross, James A., ed. *Healing in the Church.* Cleveland, Tenn.: Pathway Press, 1962.

Cunningham, Raymond J. "The Emmanuel Movement: A Variety of American Religious Experience," *American Quarterly* 14 (Spring 1966): 48–63.

————. "From Holiness to Healing: The Faith Cure in America, 1872–1892." *Church History* 43 (December 1974): 499–513.

————. "James Moore Hickson and Spiritual Healing in the American Episcopal Church," *Historical Magazine of the Protestant Episcopal Church* 38 (1969): 3–16.

————. "Ministry of Healing: The Origins of the Psychotherapeutic Role of the American Churches." Ph.D. diss., Johns Hopkins University, 1965.

Daniels, David Douglass, III. "The Cultural Renewal of Slave Religion: Charles Price Jones and the Emergence of the Holiness Movement in Mississippi." Ph.D. diss., Union Theological Seminary, 1992.

Dayton, Donald W. "The Rise of the Evangelical Healing Movement in Nineteenth-Century America." *Pneuma* 4 (spring 1982): 1–18.

————. *The Theological Roots of Pentecostalism.* Peabody, Mass.: Hendrickson, 1987.

Dieter, Melvin Easterday. *The Holiness Revival of the Nineteenth Century.* 1980. Rev. ed., Metuchen, N.J.: Scarecrow, 1997.

Dossey, Larry. *Healing Words: The Power of Prayer and the Practice of Medicine.* San Francisco: HarperSanFrancisco, 1993.

————. *Prayer Is Good Medicine: How to Reap the Healing Benefits of Prayer.* San Francisco: HarperSanFrancisco, 1996.

————. *Reinventing Medicine: Beyond Mind-Body to a New Era of Healing.* San Francisco: HarperSanFrancisco, 1999.

Frodsham, Stanley H. *Smith Wigglesworth, Apostle of Faith.* Springfield, Mo.: Gospel Publishing House, 1948.

Gardiner, Gordon P. *Radiant Glory: The Life of Martha Wing Robinson.* Brooklyn, N. Y.: Bread of Life, 1962.

Gevitz, Norman, ed. *Other Healers: Unorthodox Medicine in America.* Baltimore: Johns Hopkins University Press, 1988.

Goff, James R., Jr. *Fields White unto Harvest: Charles F. Parham and the Missionary Origins of Pentecostalism.* Fayetteville: University of Arkansas Press, 1988.

Goodman, Felicitas D. *Speaking in Tongues: A Cross-Cultural Study of Glossolalia.* Chicago: University of Chicago Press, 1972.

Gosling, F. G. *Before Freud: Neurasthenia and the American Medical Community 1870–1910.* Urbana: University of Illinois Press, 1988.

Gregory, Chester W. *The History of the United Holy Church of America, Inc., 1886–1986.* Baltimore: Gateway Press, 1986.

Guest, W. *Life of Blumhardt.* London: N.p., 1880.

Hamilton, Barry W. *William Baxter Godbey—Itinerant Apostle of the Holiness Movement.* Lewiston, N. Y.: Edwin Mellen, 2000.

Hardesty, Nancy A. *Women Called to Witness: Evangelical Feminism in the Nineteenth Century.* Nashville: Abingdon, 1984. 2d ed., Knoxville: University of Tennessee Press, 1999.

Harrell, David Edwin, Jr. *All Things Are Possible: The Healing and Charismatic Revival in Modern America.* Bloomington: Indiana University Press, 1975.

————. *Oral Roberts: An American Life.* San Francisco: Harper & Row, 1985.

Hartzfeld, David F., and Charles Nienkirchen. *The Birth of a Vision.* Regina, Sask.: His Dominion Supplement no. 1, 1986.

Hine, Darlene Clark. "Co-Laborers in the Work of the Lord: Nineteenth-Century Black Women Physicians." In *"Send Us a Lady Physician: Women Doctors in America, 1835–1920."* Edited by Ruth J. Abram. New York: Norton, 1985.

Ingersol, Robert Stanley. "Burden of Dissent: Mary Lee Cagle and the Southern Holiness Movement." Ph.D. diss., Duke University, 1989.

Israel, Adrienne M. *Amanda Berry Smith: From Washerwoman to Evangelist.* Studies in Evangelicalism 16. Lanham, Md.: Scarecrow, 1998.

Jones, Charles Edwin. *Perfectionist Persuasion: The Holiness Movement and American Methodism, 1867–1936.* Metuchen, N.J.: Scarecrow, 1974.

Koenig, Harold G. *The Healing Power of Faith: Science Explores Medicine's Last Great Frontier.* New York: Simon & Schuster, 1999.

————. Michael E. McCullough, and David B. Larson, eds. *Handbook of Religion and Health.* New York: Oxford University Press, 2001.

Liardon, Roberts, comp. *John G. Lake: The Complete Collection of His Life Teachings.* Tulsa, Okla.: Albury Publishers, 1999.

————. *Maria Woodworth-Etter: The Complete Collection of Her Life Teaching.* Tulsa, Okla.: Albury Publishers, 2000.

————. *Smith Wigglesworth: The Complete Collection of His Life Teaching.* Tulsa, Okla.: Albury Publishers, 1997.

Lindsay, Gordon. *The Life of John Alexander Dowie.* Dallas: The Voice of Healing Publishing, 1951.

Luchetti, Cathy. *Medicine Women: The Story of Early American Women Doctors.* New York: Crown, 1998.

MacRobert, Iain. *The Black Roots and White Racism of Early Pentecostalism in the U.S.A.* New York: St. Martin's, 1988.

Nelson, Douglas J. "For Such a Time as This: The Story of Bishop William J. Seymour and the Azusa Street Revival: A Search for Pentecostal/Charismatic Roots." Ph.D. diss., University of Birmingham, England, 1981.

Nienkirchen, Charles W. *A. B. Simpson and the Pentecostal Movement: A Study in Continuity, Crisis, and Change.* Peabody, Mass.: Hendrickson, 1992.

Niklaus, Robert L., John S. Sawin, and Samuel J. Stoesz. *All for Jesus: God at Work in the Christian and Missionary Alliance over One Hundred Years.* Camp Hill, Pa.: Christian Publications, 1986.

Numbers, Ronald L. "Do-It-Yourself the Sectarian Way." Pages 49–72 in *Medicine Without Doctors: Home Health Care in American History.* Edited by Guenter B. Risse. New York: Science History Publications, 1977.

Numbers, Ronald, and Darryl Amundsen, eds. *Caring and Curing: Health and Healing in the Faith Traditions.* New York: Macmillan, 1986. Repr., Baltimore: Johns Hopkins University Press, 1998.

Opp, James William. "Healing Hands, Healthy Bodies: Protestant Women and Faith Healing in Canada and the United States, 1880–1930." Paper presented at the Women and Twentieth-Century Protestantism Project, Chicago, April 1998.

———. "Religion, Medicine, and the Body: Protestant Faith Healing in Canada, 1880–1930." Ph.D. diss., Carleton University, 2000.

Pardington, George. *Twenty-five Wonderful Years, 1889–1914.* New York: Christian Alliance, 1914. Repr., New York: Garland, 1984.

Parker, Gail Thain. *Mind Cure in New England: From the Civil War to World War I.* Hanover, N. H.: University Press of New England, 1973.

Perkins, Eunice M. *Fred Francis Bosworth: The Joybringer.* 2d ed. N.p., 1st ed., 1921; 2d ed., 1927.

Pollack, John Charles. *The Keswick Story.* London: Hodder and Stoughton; Chicago: Moody Press, 1964.

Reid, Daniel G., et al., eds. *Dictionary of Christianity in America.* Downers Grove, Ill.: InterVarsity Press, 1990.

Risse, Guenter B., ed. *Medicine Without Doctors: Home Health Care in American History.* New York: Science History Publications, 1977.

Rothstein, William G. "The Botanical Movements and Orthodox Medicine." Pages 29–51 in *Other Healers: Unorthodox Medicine in America.* Edited by Norman Gevitz. Baltimore: Johns Hopkins University Press, 1988.

Sandeen, Ernest. *The Roots of Fundamentalism: British and American Millenarianism, 1800–1930.* Chicago: University of Chicago Press, 1970.

Schenk, Raymond Walter. "A Study of the New Testament Bases for the Teaching of Dr. Albert B. Simpson on Divine Healing." Master's thesis, Wheaton College, 1968.

Smith, Timothy. *Revivalism and Social Reform: American Protestantism on the Eve of the Civil War.* New York: Harper & Row, 1957.

Spittler, Marcus. *Pastor Blumhardt and His Work.* London: Morgan & Scott, 1880.

Stage, Sarah. *Female Complaints: Lydia Pinkham and the Business of Women's Medicine.* New York: Norton, 1979.

Stanley, Susie Cunningham. *Holy Boldness: Women Preachers' Autobiographies and the Sacred Self.* Knoxville: University of Tennessee Press, 2002.

Starr, Paul. *The Social Transformation of American Medicine.* New York: Basic Books, 1982.

Synan, Vinson. *The Holiness-Pentecostal Tradition: Charismatic Movements in the Twentieth Century.* Grand Rapids, Mich.: Eerdmans, 1971, 1997.

———. *The Old-Time Power: A History of the Pentecostal Holiness Church.* Rev. ed. Franklin Springs, Ga.: Advocate Press, 1973, 1986.

Thompson, A. E. *A. B. Simpson: His Life and Work.* Rev. ed. Camp Hill, Pa.: Christian Publications, 1960.

Turley, Briane K. *A Wheel Within a Wheel: Southern Methodism and the Georgia Holiness Association.* Macon, Ga.: Mercer University Press, 1999.

———. "A Wheel Within a Wheel: Southern Methodism and the Georgia Holiness Association." *Georgia Historical Quarterly* 75 (summer 1992): 295–320.

Turner, William Clair, Jr. "The United Holy Church of America: A Study in Black Holiness-Pentecostalism." Ph.D. diss., Duke University, 1984.

Wacker, Grant. *Heaven Below: Early Pentecostals and American Culture.* Cambridge, Mass.: Harvard University Press, 2001.

Warner, Wayne E. *The Woman Evangelist: The Life and Times of Charismatic Evangelist Maria B. Woodworth-Etter.* Metuchen, N. J.: Scarecrow, 1986.

Williams, Peter W. *Popular Religion in America: Symbolic Change and the Modernization Process in Historical Perspective.* Englewood Cliffs, N. J.: Prentice-Hall, 1980.

Williams, Ray Leonard. "William E. Boardman (1810–1886): Evangelist of the Higher Christian Life." Ph.D. diss., Calvin Theological Seminary, 1998.

Wilson, Ernest G. "The C&MA: Developments and Modification of Its Original Objectives." Ph.D. diss., New York University, 1984.

Wiseman, Nathaniel. *Elizabeth Baxter (Wife of Michael Paget Baxter): Saint, Evangelist, Preacher, Teacher, and Expositor.* 2d ed. London: The Christian Herald Co., 1928.

Wood, Dillard L., and William H. Preskitt, Jr. *Baptized with Fire: A History of the Pentecostal Fire-Baptized Holiness Church.* Franklin Springs, Ga.: Advocate Press, 1982.

Young, James Harvey. "Patent Medicines and the Self-Help Syndrome." Pages 95–116 in *Medicine Without Doctors: Home Health Care in American History.* Edited by Guenter B. Risse. New York: Science History Publications, 1977.

# Index